Cybercrime in Canadian Criminal Law

Sara M. Smyth, LL.M., Ph. D.

Member of the Law Society of British Columbia

CARSWELL®

A cataloguing record for this publication is available from Library and Archives Canada.

ISBN: 978-0-7798-2889-0

Composition: Computer Composition of Canada Inc.

Printed in Canada by Thomson Reuters

 THOMSON REUTERS

CARSWELL, A DIVISION OF THOMSON REUTERS CANADA LIMITED

One Corporate Plaza
2075 Kennedy Road
Toronto, Ontario
M1T 3V4

Customer Relations
Toronto 1-416-609-3800
Elsewhere in Canada/U.S. 1-800-387-5164
Fax: 1-416-298-5082
www.carswell.com
E-mail www.carswell.com/email

For Margaret Ann Smyth and David L. Greenbank, with love and gratitude.

Preface

This book was specifically written for undergraduate and graduate criminology students, as well as university students in the fields of law, policing and computing science in Canada. It attempts to provide an overview and detailed understanding of some of the most complex and sophisticated crimes to emerge in the past 20 years or so. This book examines how the nature of crime has radically changed with the advent of digital communication technologies. We have come to rely heavily on the Internet as an essential tool for education, recreation and commerce. The Net also facilitates rapid communication between anyone, anywhere around the world. However, the central reason for the rapid increase in criminal activity on the Internet is what Cooper has referred to as the Internet's "triple-A engine" of accessibility, affordability and anonymity.[1] The Internet poses unique challenges for law enforcement officials because it transcends jurisdictional boundaries, as well as the many legal and normative constraints that regulate behaviour in the real world.

As this book will illustrate, cyberspace has become a perfect venue for a new kind of sophisticated criminal who continues to evade detection by law enforcement officials around the world. Long before the Internet, criminals used a variety of "low-tech" methods to commit their crimes. Traditional offline methods are still used, of course, but the Internet has given criminals free access to a wealth of information and resources to facilitate harmful and illicit activities. However, just as with traditional kinds of criminal activity, crime on the Internet ranges from the highly sophisticated to the mundane.

In the chapters that follow, you will learn about the various kinds of cyber-attacks being perpetrated throughout the globe, including the dissemination of malware, hacking, denial of service attacks and so on. You will also learn about Internet crimes committed against children, including child pornography and child luring. Many individuals who would never have sought child pornography out in the real world are now accessing these materials online because they are so freely and widely available in cyberspace. The same rationale applies to the disturbing crime of child luring: the anonymity and accessibility of the Internet now makes it easy for those with a sexual interest in children to seek out children online, with little risk of personal exposure. For these same reasons, the Internet has also facilitated the traditional crime of stalking and harassment, and further given rise

---

[1] A. Cooper and E. Griffin-Shelley, "Introduction: The Internet: The Next Sexual Revolution," in A. Cooper (Ed.), *Sex and the Internet: A Guidebook for Clinicians* (New York: Brunner & Routledge, 2002) at 1-15.

to the new problem of cyber-bullying. This book devotes significant consideration to each of these important problems, and it also addresses the substantive laws that can be used to prosecute offenders in Canada as well as abroad.

This book is divided into four major sections. Part One is titled "Introduction to Cybercrime and the Regulation of Cyberspace." Chapter 1 explains the history behind the creation of the Internet. There is no question that the Internet is a one-of-a-kind communications medium, which has evolved more rapidly and changed the way people live and work more significantly than any other innovation that preceded it. Yet the Internet and computers, in general, were not always viewed as important instruments of social change. In fact, in 1943, Thomas Watson, the founder of IBM, famously remarked that the world had room for only about five computers.[2] This comment provides a somewhat humorous example of how many influential scholars and policy-makers, as well as key industry players, failed to grasp the astounding potential, both positive and negative, that information technology would offer to the world.

Watson's view turned out to be erroneous, of course, and during the next several decades, the computer became the fastest-growing medium of international communication. The Internet was highly instrumental in facilitating this revolutionary trend. The Internet was born in the late 1960s as an American military tool, funded by the United States Department of Defense, as part of an experiment to connect computers across the United States.[3] This project led to the establishment of a national computer network that was originally confined to use for academics and government research.

Since that time, the Internet has vastly expanded its reach and is now used to promote social, economic, educational, recreational, military, commercial and other policy-driven priorities, including the provision of numerous public and private goods and services. The entire purpose and function of cyberspace, at least insofar as the Western world is concerned, is directly related to these goals, in addition to being a tool that facilitates social networking, cultural pursuits, and the promotion of advertising. In spite of that, the Internet remains an open system and no single individual or entity truly can or will ever have total control over the many uses and aspects of it.

One could also argue that the inherent openness of the Web, or more precisely the fact that it is a global system that is always "open" and available for use at any given time by millions of people from all corners of the world, both enables and subverts a form of mutual trust and reliance among its users. The interconnectivity and openness that characterizes the inherent structure of the Internet, which facilitates anonymous interaction between people from many different countries, who would otherwise never likely "meet" in real space, and who have vastly different cultural, moral, religious and political beliefs, has also led to very significant security threats, which might be said to be inevitable given its global scale and reach.

---

[2] Frances Cairncross, *The Death of Distance* (Boston: Harvard Business School Press, 1997) at 9.
[3] *Ibid* at 10.

This global reach, which is neither entirely unique nor independent of the "real world," has enormous relevance to the regulation of cyberspace because the globalization of online communications has made it more difficult to control crime and raised new concerns about the protection of individual privacy. Chapter 2 explains the difficulties with attempting to regulate behaviour in this unique space. Of course, while we can describe the Internet using "spatial" metaphors, it is nothing more than a medium for the transfer of data. In reality, cyberspace is no more of a unique "space" than that which exists between two individuals who are speaking with each other on the phone, or communicating over a shortwave radio. However, the Internet is far more extraordinary than those other mediums of communication because of its vast reach and the fact that it facilitates anonymous interaction between individuals from distinct geographic spheres in a way that completely transcends the spatial and temporal restrictions that characterize real space. Data is transmitted easily between geographically remote places in cyberspace and can work its way through multiple sites in many jurisdictions before reaching its intended target.

This is perhaps why the virtual world has been characterized as a unique "place," that exists outside the boundaries of any single legal jurisdiction. This suggestion might sound quirky, or even absurd, but many of the most influential pioneers in the field of cyber-law popularized the idea of cyberspace as a utopian "frontier," similar to the Wild West. One gets the sense of cyberspace as being a boundless, lawless environment that any person can discover, take up residence in and generally do as he or she pleases. Cyberspace was also said to promote the formation of interpersonal relationships that are exclusively conducted in virtual, or computer-generated, environments. These ideas were enormously important to the work of early cyber-law scholars, as I describe in Chapter 2, who envisioned the emergence of an innovative social network, without boundaries or borders, where any person could freely express whatever he or she wished without recourse from any earthly power or being.

Yet experience has demonstrated that there is no perfect society or utopia in cyberspace, even on a small scale, just as there is no such environment in the real world. The central shortcoming of the early musings and declarations about cyberspace was that they failed to recognize the Internet's vast potential for facilitating criminal activity. In doing so, they ignored the critical importance of government institutions, commercial enterprises and ordinary individuals, operating together to both enable and restrict speech and a wide range of other activities on the Web.

Part Two is titled "Traditional Crime in Cyberspace," and this section introduces readers to crimes that have been committed for decades, which are now being facilitated by the Internet. Some of the topics explored here include fraudulent online auctions, securities scams and consumer credit card fraud. For example, in Chapter 3, readers will learn about identity theft and phishing, which is a new type of online scam. Chapter 4 focuses on what many would consider to be the most disturbing and monstrous kind of cybercrime: child sexual exploitation. As we will learn from that chapter, cyberspace makes it possible for individuals to trade child sex abuse images and to interact directly with potential child victims by engaging in online chats that can lead to a real-space meetings where actual abuse can occur. Similarly, in Chapter 5, readers will learn about how the Internet facilitates another age-old phenomenon: stalking and bullying.

Part Three is titled "Computer Misuse Crimes" and it aims to provide readers with an overview of the technical and legal issues surrounding new electronic crimes. The various crimes explored in this section did not exist prior to the Internet, unlike those explained in the previous section. However, we can trace the history and evolution of these new cyber-attacks and observe that they have become more technically sophisticated and innovative as technology has progressed. Previously, large-scale events, such as network worms were about technical superiority. Today, adversaries are primarily motivated by economic incentives and attack to seize control of compromised systems and to turn their assets into revenue.

The bulk of this section is devoted to explaining the various ways that computers and computer networks can be attacked or otherwise used to commit crimes. You will learn about a wide range of cybercrimes, from malware to hacking and denial of service attacks. As you read, try to think about how cybercrime incidents can be committed in a number of different ways, ranging from the relatively simple to the highly complex. In addition, keep in mind that many cybercrimes overlap.

It is also critical to note that today's attacks are highly sophisticated and they often take advantage of social engineering techniques, through trickery and deceit, and they may also employ data mining techniques to gather sensitive information. Clearly, cyber-attacks are no longer being perpetrated by curious pranksters in college dorm rooms. Instead, they are now the trusted tools of organized criminals who are preying on the fact that our society increasingly depends upon the networked environment for a wide range of critical functions and services, from banking to e-commerce.

Chapter 6 introduces readers to the distribution of malware and the new kinds of highly sophisticated attacks that are now being perpetrated on the Web. Similarly, in Chapter 7, you will learn about the phenomenon of hacking and denial of service attacks. In this chapter, you will read about the motivations of hackers, as well as their unique subculture, and the kinds of activities that are being perpetrated on the Net. You will also learn about the new underground economy that provides hackers and others with an interest in perpetrating malicious attacks with products and services to facilitate their harmful conduct.

The final chapter in this section, Chapter 8, introduces readers to the important problem of spam. Many people think that spam emails are simply an annoying nuisance; however, this chapter also provides important information about how this popular form of electronic communication is being used to perpetrate very harmful and malicious attacks. Throughout the discussion of the various types of crime being committed on the Net is an overview of the legal framework for dealing with these problems. You will learn that Canada has fallen behind other Western industrialized nations in enacting legislation to combat these threats. You will also learn about the obstacles associated with investigating and prosecuting online offenders, including the need for international cooperation and user education.

Part Four is titled "Specific Problems with the Regulation and Prosecution of Cybercriminals." Chapter 9 explains the specific problems associated with the inter-jurisdictional nature of cybercrime and provides a detailed overview of some of the important mechanisms used to facilitate international cooperation in cyberspace. The transnational nature of cybercrime is an issue that features prominently throughout this book. It makes the investigation and prosecution of computer crime especially problematic. For example, how are we to determine which country's laws will govern the investigation and prosecution of a cybercriminal who has perpetrated his or her crime throughout the world?

This begs the question of whether the inherent openness and global reach of the Internet has led to new security threats by facilitating the exchange of information.[4] I believe that it does and that this is an unfortunate inevitability. The Internet has opened up new communications channels and created exciting new learning opportunities for those who have access to it. Yet it has also enabled individuals to perpetrate crimes on an unprecedented scale, with vast distances between themselves and their victims. The entry costs are now far lower than those required to commit crime in the real world (for example, child pornography was previously only available to individuals who were able to penetrate highly secretive networks whereas now it can be easily accessed by a person sitting alone in his or her living room) and one of the biggest advantages claimed by those committing digital crimes is the relative anonymity they are granted in cyberspace.

Chapter 10 discusses the importance of privacy and *Charter* principles in the investigation of cybercrime cases. It also provides an overview of the process of digital forensics, including the various types of electronic evidence and the methods of obtaining and analyzing it. Of particular importance is the difficulty of adapting our traditional rules of evidence to the unique features of digital evidence.

The approaches to Internet regulation discussed in this section are complimentary and must be implemented on a local, national and international scale to achieve effective Internet regulation. While each of these measures is important, an effective global solution to the problem of cybercrime can only be achieved when all stakeholders are brought together. In other words, not only does Canada need to focus on achieving effective regulatory control, there is also a need for self-regulation, as well as industry regulation and international harmonization and cooperation.

---

[4] This not only includes online child pornography but can include: communications between an adult and child, for the purpose of child luring; information that is related to the planning or commission of an offence, such as terrorism or drug dealing; malicious code that is intended to disrupt or shut down a network or harm a computer or computer system; fraudulent requests for information to facilitate or carry out theft; and so on.

Table of Contents

PART THREE
Computer Misuse Crimes

Table of Cases

PART ONE

INTRODUCTION TO CYBERCRIME AND THE REGULATION OF CYBERSPACE

1

Introduction to Cyberspace and Cybercrime

KEY TERMS AND CONCEPTS

- American Standard Code for Information Interchange (ASCII)
- Architecture
- ARPANet
- Binary digits
- Bus
- Central processing unit
- Client-server
- Clock
- Content layer
- Donald Davies
- End-to-end
- File Allocation Table
- File system

- Hypertext Transfer Protocol (HTTP)
- Interface Message Processors (IMPs)
- Internet Protocol (IP) addresses
- Internet Service Provider (ISP)
- Interrupt message
- John Postel
- Motherboard
- Operating system
- Packets
- Packet-switching
- Paul Baran

- Peer to Peer (P2P)
- Physical layer
- Platters
- Port
- Root Server System (RSS)
- Slack space
- TCP/IP
- The Internet/The Net
- Underground economy
- USB
- World Wide Web

CYBERCRIME AND THE INTERNET

The Internet is a term for the computer networks that link users around the globe. The revolutionary idea for this interlocking network was pioneered by two researchers, Paul Baran and Donald Davies who were unknown to each other at the time.[1] Baran joined the mathematics division of the RAND Corporation in

---

[1] Katie Hafner and Matthew Lyon, *Where Wizards Stay Up Late: The Origins of the Internet* (New York: Simon and Schuster, 1996) at 53.

1959 and developed an interest in how to build a communications network as a defence mechanism.[2] By 1960, the escalating arms race between the United States and the Soviet Union heightened the risk of a nuclear ballistic missile attack against the United States. Baran came up with the idea that it was possible to create an electronic communication system that would survive and continue to function even if large portions of it were wiped out.[3]

During that time period, American telephone networks were dominated by AT&T. There were a number of limitations associated with that network, including the fact that no more than five links could be connected in tandem without diminishing signal quality. The fact that telephone networks were connected to one or more centralized sources also rendered them vulnerable to attack. Furthermore, telephone switches took 20 to 30 seconds to establish a long-distance connection over a phone line.[4] And since all telephone communications were circuit-switched, a single communications line was reserved for one call at a time.[5] This meant that during idle periods in a conversation, the line would remain occupied and continue to consume valuable resources.

According to Baran, it was possible to create a network built of many nodes, each connected to other nodes, so that even after a nuclear war, it would be possible to locate and use routes through the network without any degradation in the efficiency and quality of the transmission. In addition, Baran realized that the network would be far more efficient if messages could be broken down into small segments and transmitted separately.[6] This revolutionary idea would come to be known as **packet-switching**.

In Baran's mind, the "message blocks" could follow different paths to their destination and the recipient computer could reassemble them into a complete message. He foresaw that this model would be dramatically more cost-effective and efficient than the telephone lines because multiple messages could share the same line. The fragments of communication could also be transmitted out of sequence, as long as they could be reassembled into a complete package upon receipt. Hence, what Baran also envisioned was that each switching node would contain a routing table that could determine the best route for each unit of data to take. As soon as a message block was received at a node, it could be passed on to the next node using the best available route. If a particular route was inaccessible or busy, it would simply follow the next best available path.

During the same time period, another man by the name of Donald Davies, a physicist with the British National Physical Laboratory, wrote a series of notes in which he set out his ideas for a new computer network that was much like the one envisioned by Baran.[7] He subsequently delivered a public lecture in London describing the idea of transmitting small blocks of data, which he called **packets**,

---

[2] *Ibid* at 53-56.
[3] Marjie T. Britz, *Computer Forensics and Cyber Crime – An Introduction*, 2nd ed. (New Jersey: Prentice Hall, 2009) at 35.
[4] Hafner and Lyon, *supra*, note 1 at 58.
[5] *Ibid*.
[6] *Ibid* at 60.
[7] *Ibid* at 64-65.

through a digital network. After the lecture, he was approached by a stranger who told him that Baran had been circulating the very same idea within the United States Department of Defense community.[8] As noted, Davies and Baran did not know each other and they would not meet until several years later.

Advanced Reserach Project Agency (ARPA)

Established by President Eisenhower in the late 1950s, the Advanced Research Project Agency (ARPA) was created in response to the diminishing relationship between the Soviet Union and the United States and the race for outer space.[9] Its mission initially focused on space defense, global surveillance satellites, and space stations; however, when the National Aeronautics and Space Administration (NASA) was created in 1958, ARPA's mandate was broadened to research and development (R&D), which encompassed ballistic missile defense, nuclear testing and military command and control issues. Cyberspace was first conceived by a small group of men who worked for this agency during the 1960s, led by Professor JCR Licklider, the first director of Information Processing Techniques Office (IPTO), a section of ARPA charged with supporting the country's most advanced computer R&D projects.

By late 1966, a man named Bob Taylor had become the director of IPTO.[10] Taylor envisioned creating a computer network to link together researchers across the country so they could share information and ideas. Taylor recruited computer scientist Larry Roberts to work with him on the project. Roberts mapped out his plan to connect computers to one another over dial-up telephone lines, which he would call ARPANet.[11] The computers that would control the network were to be called **interface message processors** or **IMPs**, which would interconnect the network, send and receive data, check for errors, and route the data to its intended destination.

When he presented this data at a prestigious computer conference, he learned about the ideas developed earlier by Davies and Baran.[12] In fact, Baran became a consultant to the group Roberts put together to design the network, which was formally known as the Advanced Research Project Agency Network (ARPANet). Roberts thought the network should begin with four major sites, and eventually expand to about nineteen. The initial network consisted of four sites, where the IMPs were located, that linked four universities (UCLA, Stanford, UC Santa Barbra and the University of Utah) as part of an experiment to connect computers across the United States.[13] The function of the IMPs was to rapidly transfer bits from a source location to another specified destination. They were built as sophisticated messengers with the ability to disassemble messages, store packets of data, check for errors, and route the packets to their destination points.

---

[8] *Ibid.*
[9] *Ibid* at 12-20.
[10] *Ibid* at 12.
[11] *Ibid* at 76.
[12] Ibid at 77.
[13] Cairncross, *The Death of Distance* (Boston: Harvard Business School Press, 1997) at 10.

The IMPs could only move data packets back and forth and ensure that they were correctly transmitted to their destination. It was up to the host computer to figure out what to do with the messages when it received them and how to communicate with another host computer. Thus, a common protocol was needed that could be used by the host machines; this was called the host-to-host protocol.[14] The protocol had to be able to move packets between computers, regardless of whether they contained graphic images, files, or email communications. By 1970, a small group of graduate students from the four host site universities came up with a host-to-host protocol that facilitated communications between hosts.[15] Similarly, the first file transfer protocol (FTP) was created and made it possible to share files between machines.[16]

By 1971, researchers had figured out how to allow many different users to access the network. Initially, users of the ARPANet had to connect to the IMPs through a host computer. Each IMP was incapable of supporting more than four host interfaces at a time and none could handle a terminal connection.[17] There needed to be a way for multiple users to connect with a single IMP through a terminal device in order to open the network up to a wide range of people. This led to the construction of a multi-line IMP, which was capable of handling the traffic of up to 63 terminals at once. Furthermore, although the ARPANet was not designed as a message system, by the end of the 1970s its creators had discovered how to email each other.[18] Message traffic was what spurred the network's rapid growth as a communications tool.

It wasn't until the early 1970s that computer scientists Bob Kahn and Vint Cerf came up with a common standard, or language, to enable individual computer users to communicate on the Internet by enabling two computers to send and receive information over the network.[19] This is what led to the development of **Transmission Control Protocol (TCP)**, which facilitates computers to "speak" to each other.[20] Recall that within ARPANet, the destination IMP was charged with the task of reassembling packets into a single message. However, TCP shifted reliability away from the network itself to the destination hosts. Within the TCP framework, the network's only function is to deliver packets. As long as the network has a gateway that can route packets to their intended destinations, the receiving hosts can manage the rest.

The Net Expands

From 1973 to 1975, the Net expanded rapidly at a rate of about one node per month.[21] To serve the growing user community, large databases scattered

---

[14] Hafner and Lyon, *supra*, note 1 at 146.
[15] *Ibid* at 156.
[16] *Ibid* at 174.
[17] *Ibid* at 171.
[18] *Ibid* at 187-189.
[19] Cairncross, *supra*, note 13 at 11.
[20] Craig McTaggart, "A Layered Approach to Internet Analysis" (2003), 48 McGill Law Journal 571 at 573.
[21] Hafner and Lyon, *supra*, note 1 at 228.

across the Net began growing in popularity. Then, in 1978, computer scientists came up with the idea of separating the portion of the TCP that deals with routing packets of data and creating a distinct **Internet Protocol (IP)**. Thus, TCP became responsible for breaking up messages into packets, detecting errors, resending lost packets and reassembling the packets in the correct order. The IP was only responsible for routing individual data packets. The **TCP/IP** protocol remains the backbone of the Internet that we commonly know and use today.[22] This allows various computers all over the world, each with unique IP addresses using TCP/IP standards or protocols, to send and receive information by establishing a connection over which various packets of information can be transmitted back and forth according to a common language and set of rules.

By the mid-1980s, many different networks had emerged, all using TCP/IP protocols. This collection of linked networks eventually came to be called the **Internet**. The gateways, which were the successors of IMPs, were soon replaced by routers. Networks also began springing up in other countries throughout the world, each connected to the United States. This is how the Internet became a global phenomenon and, indeed, it is now a loosely connected network of TCP/IP networks spanning the entire globe. Computer scientists also created the **World Wide Web**, a multimedia branch of the Internet, using hypetext transfer protocol.[23]

Another important innovation that was created in the mid-1980s was the graphical user interface. Until this time, anyone who used a computer needed to learn special commands since the computer presented only a prompt (c:>) on the screen.[24] Xerox engineers designed the first graphical user interface that used a mouse as well as a keyboard to interact with the computer's operating system using small graphic images, known as icons, rather than typing commands.[25] Following this, in 1984, Apple introduced the first graphical user interface for the Macintosh line of computers and Microsoft followed the next year with the introduction of Windows.[26]

This fascinating story helps us to understand that the Internet was designed according to the **end-to-end** principle, along the **client-server** model, which means that it consists largely of computers at the "end" of a network, which are the machines we use to access the network and computers within the network that link other computers, such as the machines, or "servers," run by an **Internet Service Provider (ISP)**.[27] In order for an individual to connect to the Internet, he or she needs to use a service provider, which can range in size from a small, local provider of Internet dial-up services to a university or a large telecommunications carrier that conducts business in multiple jurisdictions throughout the world.

---

[22] Jack Goldsmith and Tim Wu, *Who Controls the Internet?* (Oxford: Oxford University Press, 2006) at 23.

[23] Hafner and Lyon, *supra*, note 1 at 258.

[24] Jim Keogh, *The Essential Guide to Computer Hardware* (Upper Saddle River, NJ: Prentice Hall, 2002) at 27.

[25] *Ibid.*

[26] *Ibid.* at 27.

[27] Lawrence Lessig, *The Future of Ideas* (New York: Vintage Books, 2004) at 34.

ISPs use unique **Internet Protocol (IP) addresses**, which they assign, to route data on their networks. The IP address is simply an addressing apparatus (such as 137.142.12.1), similar to a postal address or a telephone number in real space. As with those tools, the IP address must be unique to allow communication between stationary mainframe computers with different IP addresses. According to this model, every Internet user is both a client and server, capable of both requesting and supplying data. For example, IP addresses are used to enable the transmission of communication between a user's Web browser and a particular website when he or she is surfing the Web. Further, when an email is transmitted between users, IP addresses are used in the header of the email message to ensure that the communication is delivered to the correct recipient.

Historically the job of assigning IP addresses belonged to one man. In 1969, **Jon Postel** joined the Network Management Centre at UCLA, which played a major role in the development of ARPANet. Back in the early days of ARPANet, there seemed to be an almost limitless supply of unique IP addresses that could be assigned. From the late 1960s to the early 1980s, Postel assigned and kept track of all the identifiers, networks and addresses on the system. By the early 1980s, however, Postel could no longer keep up with the mounting requests for new IP addresses. The exponential growth of the Internet meant that engineers would have run out of IP addresses had they not come up with a system that quickly generates an IP address for a computer when it logs in![28]

Fortunately, the staff behind the ARPANet Network Information Center at the Stanford Research Institute came up with the Domain Name Server (DNS). A complex system of servers located around the world, known as the Root Server System (RSS), links domain names to IP addresses so that the routers know where to send information when a user requests a Web page associated with a particular Uniform Resource Locator (URL) or attempts to send an email to another individual. The ISP manages the distribution and reconfiguration of packets of information that are sent along various interconnected ISP networks, from one computer to another.[29]

For example, when you log onto the network through your ISP, the ISP uses the DNS to match the domain name (e.g., www.sfu.ca) with the IP address you're searching for. The RSS knows the IP address of the name server that manages .com top-level domains and transmits it to your ISP. The ISP then sends a query to that name server asking for the IP address of sfu.ca. Your browser then connects to this server and asks it for the IP address for www.sfu.ca and then contacts the server and requests the Web page. The process is managed by the TCP/IP language or protocol that provides the standards for how computers can seamlessly communicate with each other by sending and receiving information. The DNS and RSS are now managed by the **Internet Corporation for Assigned Names and Numbers (ICANN)**.

The part of the Internet most people are familiar with is the World Wide Web. The Web contains a collection of hyperlinked pages of information that are

---

[28] Siva Vaidhyanathan, *The Anarchist in the Library* (New York: Basic Books, 2004) at 15-16.
[29] *Ibid* at 32.

distributed using a network protocol called **Hypertext Transfer Protocol (HTTP)**. This interface opened the Internet up to ordinary users and, in 1993, the use of the Web proliferated as individuals were able to use dial-up modems to connect with an ISP and gain access to this vast communications medium.[30] Since that time, Internet use has exploded and it is now possible to connect using wireless connectivity, as well as **Peer to Peer (P2P)** networks.

Typically, a pure P2P network architecture involves a number of participants who make the files stored on their hard-drives directly available to other users. This type of network arrangement differs from the client-server model where communication is usually to and from a central server. The distributed nature of P2P networks makes them a highly robust and efficient means to share content because there is no single point of failure in the network. For criminals, these networks are particularly useful because there is no data stored on a central server that could be accessed by law enforcement. P2P networks will be further discussed throughout this book.

THE INTERNET'S UNIQUE LAYERED ARCHITECTURE

Internet regulation and governance consists of far more than simply the technical issue of routing communications and assigning Internet addresses. It also includes broader issues such as the safety and security of networks, as well as public policy making and implementation at both national and international levels. The starting point for thinking about policy development and regulation in cyberspace, which will be discussed in detail in Chapter 2, is to conceive of the Internet as consisting of a number of unique layers.[31] The reason this is important is that it is possible to implement regulatory changes in cyberspace through design or architectural controls. While this will be explained in much greater detail later on, it is important to note at this point that we have the power to leverage or compel regulatory changes through code-based solutions, in addition to other regulatory tools.

The **physical layer** of the Internet consists of the computer equipment and telecommunications networks through which the Internet functions.[32] The **operational layer** of the Internet consists of standards and protocols, as well as ISP functions essential to the operation of the Internet. These layers are controlled by private entities, including telecommunications carriers, who carefully manage and oversee the delivery of Internet data. These carriers are also highly regulated by the Canadian government.

At the **application layer**, software applications make Internet content available and facilitate Internet transactions.[33] It is important to note that at this layer, the Internet is partly free and partly controlled – that is, there is free software or open source software and closed source software. At the **content layer**, which

---

[30] Britz, *supra*, note 3 at 36.
[31] McTaggart, *supra*, note 20 at 573.
[32] *Ibid.*
[33] *Ibid.*

includes the data available through the Internet, as well as the transactions facilitated by the Internet, much is controlled. For example, not everything online is free; much of it is protected by copyright and intellectual property laws. What is unique about the Internet is the way it mixes freedom and control at each of these different layers. This means that each layer of the Internet is subject to varying patterns of control by a variety of different parties.

From a technical standpoint, the Internet is an open network, which means that the TCP/IP protocols are publicly accessible and non-proprietary. It is easy to join and no central server needs to be informed of a new participant. In order to communicate with others, one only needs to obtain the necessary software and a connection. TCP/IP networks have no central server responsible for managing the network. No single entity administers the Internet. It exists and functions because hundreds of thousands of separate operators of computers and networks use common data transfer protocols to exchange information. Messages can travel a variety of alternate paths (i.e., from the United States to France to Canada to Sweden to reach China).

The Internet is also a packet-switching network, which means that before being transmitted over the Internet, a message is broken up into small, fixed-length blocks, or **packets**, and each packet is routed independently of the others to the recipient machine. The recipient machine is responsible for reassembling all of the packets back into a single message. This makes it more difficult to intercept a message travelling over the network. The packets are distributed using **routers**, which manage the connection between two or more networks. Routers assess the address of the packets and decide how to route them to their final destination.

Also, the network only transmits information in digital form, in pulses of electrical energy representing binary digits "1" and "0." These digits are known as **bits** and a **byte** is a sequence of eight bits (e.g. 00110010). A programming word is a sequence of eight bytes. Programming words are combined into sentences and paragraphs that make up code, which are instructions telling computers how to operate. Physical distance is rendered irrelevant to online communications and digital information can move quickly across the globe with no degradation in quality. The reason is that there are no real "things" (i.e., physical/tangible property) distributed, only strings of 1s and 0s.

Furthermore, the Internet is built around an end-to-end design. This means that rather than locating intelligence within the network, intelligence is placed at the ends. In other words, complexity and intelligence is located in the software running at the applications layer. This means that the network only performs simple functions (i.e., data transport). It delivers packets, but what happens to them after that is of no concern to the network itself but is controlled by the applications running on the user's machine.

THE ANATOMY OF A COMPUTER

The essential function of a computer is to process and store information. Knowledge about the operation of a computer hard drive is valuable for two central reasons: it is necessary to understand how some forms of computer crimes are carried out, such as the launch of a computer virus; and, more importantly, it is critical to comprehend computer forensics and the retrieval of electronic evidence. Thus, this section provides a general overview of how a computer works.

The binary number system is used to represent information inside a computer. Binary math might seem confusing at first; however, it's best understood if you first think about the decimal system, which is used for everyday math.[34] The decimal system contains ten digits, zero through nine. When we express a number such as 7,431 we know that the seven is in the thousands position, the four is in the hundreds, the three is in the tens, and so on. We could also express this number as $(7 \times 1000) + (4 \times 100) + (3 \times 10) + (1 \times 1)$ or, alternatively, as $(7 \times 10^3) + (4 \times 10^2) + (3 \times 10^1) + (1 \times 10^0)$.[35]

The same is true in the binary system, whereby each number, letter or symbol is recognized by the computer as a string of eight zeroes and ones. The key thing to remember is that in the binary number system there are only two digits: zero and one. Each digit has the value of increasing powers of two.[36] This means that if we start at zero and work our way through to 21, the decimal and binary numbers look like the chart in Figure 1.1.

Figure 1.1: Decimal and Binary Numbers

0 = 0	11 = 1011
1 = 1	12 = 1100
2 = 10	13 = 1101
3 = 11	14 = 1110
4 = 100	15 = 1111
5 = 101	16 = 1000
6 = 110	17 = 10001
7 = 111	18 = 100010
8 = 1000	19 = 10011
9 = 1001	20 = 10100
10 = 1010	21 = 10101

How do you figure out the binary number of 10011? You calculate the following: $(1 \times 2^4) + (0 \times 2^3) + (0 \times 2^2) + (1 \times 2^1) + (1 \times 2^0)$. Thus: $16 + 0 + 0 + 2 + 1 = 19$. Of course, computers need to be able to work with letters of the alphabet as well as numbers. This is why engineers developed the **American Standard Code for Information Interchange (ASCII)** and other standards to

---

[34] Keogh, *supra*, note 24 at 14.
[35] Craig Ball, "Computer Forensics for Lawyers Who Cant Set the Clock on Their VCR," (2005) at 13, available online at: http://www.craigball.com/cf_ccr.pdf.
[36] *Ibid.*

assign values to letters and symbols. These standards use a similar set of numbers to represent upper and lower case letters, as well as punctuation marks, and so forth. For example, the upper-case letter "M" is stored in the computers memory as "01001101."[37] Each number is a bit. The word bit, in fact, is a short version of the words "Binary digIT."[38] Each string is known as a byte of data. A program, such as a word processor, is used to convert letters and symbols into binary numbers.

A computer hard drive is a sealed aluminum box that is often mounted above or below the floppy disk or CD-ROM drives.[39] The photo in Figure 1.2 shows the inside of a hard drive.

Figure 1.2: A Hard Drive's Interior

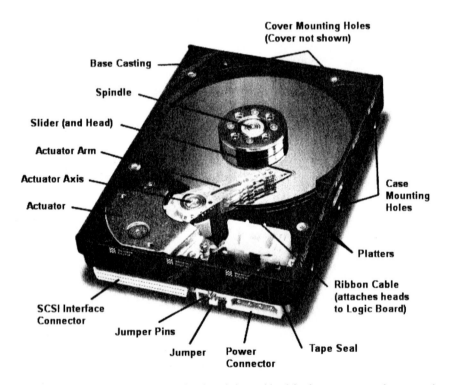

The **motherboard** is the main circuit board inside the computer that contains the central processing unit, the **clock** (which sends information, in electronic pulses, between the processor and other components including memory and ports)

---

[37] Orin Kerr, "Searches and Seizures in a Digital World" (2005), 119 Harvard Law Review 531 at 538-539.

[38] Ball, *supra*, note 35 at 13-14.

[39] Ball, *supra*, note 35 at 19.

and the computer memory.[40] It contains various chips connected together by etched wires, called a **bus**, attached to the motherboard. The integrated circuit on the motherboard also enables external devices to connect directly with it. Electricity flows from the power cord at 120 volts of current, which is too strong to safely operate the computer.[41] Thus, the computer's power supply converts 120 volts AC to less than 15 volts of direct current. The DC voltage is used to distribute information throughout the computer.[42] Electricity flows inside the computer and generates heat; however, the heat is removed from around the motherboard by a fan used to increase airflow and cool the various components.

The most important part of the motherboard is the central processor; indeed, this is where the brains of the computer are located. The central processor, also known as a processor, is the integrated circuit that carries out instructions written by programmers. There are three kinds of information received by the processor: interrupt messages, instructions and data.[43]

Instructions are programs that tell the computer to perform a specific task, such as running a particular program. Data is information the computer uses to perform the task.[44] An **interrupt message** is a signal to the central processor to stop what it is doing and do something else. When a device wants the processor to do something, such as restart the computer, the device sends the processor an interrupt message.[45] There are several interrupt request lines within the motherboard and each device that can make an interrupt request is allocated a line. The interrupt vector table, which is loaded into memory at startup, stores information about the types of interrupts that can be processed by the central processing unit.[46] The register, which is a small amount of memory contained in the processor, temporarily stores data and instructions.

The motherboard also contains memory chips, including ROM (read-only memory chips) and RAM (random access memory).[47] The processor can read information from the ROM, such as how to load programs, but cannot change any of the information. In contrast, RAM can be updated by the processor to store instructions (a program) or information (data). Other components on the motherboard are used for external features, such as sound cards, modems, keyboards and external ports.

---

[40] Keogh, *supra*, note 24 at 42.
[41] *Ibid* at 56.
[42] *Ibid*.
[43] Keogh, *supra*, note 24 at 60.
[44] *Ibid*.
[45] *Ibid* at 61.
[46] *Ibid* at 52.
[47] *Ibid* at 50.

Figure 1.3: Measuring the Real Quantity of Memory

Expression	Quantity	Real Quantity
Byte	1 byte	1 byte
Kilobyte (KB)	A thousand bytes	1,024 bytes
Megabyte (MB)	A thousand kilobytes	1,048,576 bytes
Gigabyte (GB)	A thousand megabytes	1,073,741,824 bytes
Terabyte (TB)	A thousand gigabytes	1,099,511,627,776 bytes

Information is transported as a binary value that is encoded as a voltage inside the computer. The height of the wave indicates the voltage. This means that high voltages represent a binary number of one and low voltages represent a binary number of zero.[48] The clock provides the pulse necessary to vary the DC voltage, so the appropriate information will flow over the etched wires on the motherboard, which transport information inside the computer. The more clock cycles that occur per second, the more quickly information will flow inside the computer. The processing speed, which is the internal clock speed, is measured in megahertz (MHz).[49]

The way that data is stored on the hard drive is related to the operating system running on the computer. The **operating system** is a set of programs that operate the computer hardware and interface between the hardware and the user. It is responsible for the management of activities and the sharing of resources of the computer, including reading and writing information onto disks. The most popular operating system is Microsoft Windows. The program within the operating system that interfaces with the disk drive is the file system. The **file system** is the name for the structure in which files are named, stored and organized on the hard drive. The file system also reads and writes data to the hard disk drive.

The hard disk drive sits inside the computer in a sealed metal box that prevents air and dust from getting in.[50] It is made up of magnetized metal **platters** that contain millions of magnetized metal points, which are all contained inside a box in the computer. The platters rotate at an extremely high speed (up to 10,000 revolutions per minute). Each platter contains tens of thousands of rings, which are called tracks, resembling the growth rings visible on the inside of a tree. The tracks are evenly divided into sectors. The sector is the physical space on the platter where data is stored. If many sectors are contained on a platter, it has a higher capacity to store data. The space on the platters is divided into discrete subparts known as **clusters** or allocation units.

A cluster is a group of sectors where data is stored. Each cluster has a fixed number of bytes, regardless of the size of the data being written to the disk. This means that if a small file is written to a large cluster, a portion of the cluster will

---

[48] *Ibid* at 56.
[49] *Ibid* at 51.
[50] *Ibid* at 152.

remain empty. The empty portion of the cluster is called **slack space,** but it is unavailable for use by another file until the existing file is deleted and written over by a larger file. A photo of the hard disk drive's interior is found in Figure 1.2.[51]

The heads that read and write data are mounted onto **sliders**, which are attached to arms. This is similar to a record player's arm and needle that moves over the bumps and grooves on the vinyl to produce sound vibrations. Retrieving data from a computer involves entering commands that obtain data from the magnetic platters, process it and provide it to the user. Whenever a user enters a command, the platters spin and the magnetic heads (on the sliders) are directed over certain areas of the platters. As the magnetic heads pass over the platters, an electrical current is generated, which is how the zeros and ones are stored and retrieved. When a user requests a particular file, the computer must also be able to retrieve it quickly, on command.

The operating system also keeps a list of where the files are located on the hard drive, which is known as the **File Allocation Table**. When a user requests a file, the computer consults the table and then directs the magnetic heads to the location of the appropriate cluster of information stored on the platters. Understanding the file system and operating system are essential to understanding why deleted data can often still be recovered by forensic examiners. These issues will be explored in Chapter 10.

A **port** is a circuit on the motherboard that is used to connect external devices to the computer. There are a number of different kinds of external devices that plug directly into a bus on the circuit board, including the monitor, mouse, keyboard, speakers and printer. Some ports are dedicated for particular devices, such as the keyboard and mouse. The **Universal Serial Bus (USB)** is another critical port found on a motherboard, which can be used to connect electronic storage devices. Computer storage devices also come in many shapes and sizes. They include hard drives, floppy disks and thumb drives. All of these devices store zeroes and ones, which can be converted into letters, symbols and numbers.

CYBERSPACE AND CRIMINAL ACTIVITY

The Internet is an open system and no single individual or entity can or will ever have total control over the many uses and aspects of it. The interconnectivity and "openness" that characterizes the inherent structure of the Internet, which facilitates anonymous interaction between people from many different countries who would otherwise never likely "meet" in real space, has enormous relevance to the regulation of cyberspace because the globalization of online communications has made it more difficult to control crime and raised new concerns.

History teaches us that criminals can find a way to use just about any new technology to benefit themselves and harm others, and clearly computer

---

[51] Ball, *supra*, note 35 at 18.

technology is no different.[52] It is important to be mindful of the fact that computer crimes come in a variety of forms and there is no standard way of categorizing them. Even the term used to describe crimes involving the innovative use of technology can be inter-changed with a variety of other definitions: computer-related crime; high-tech crime; cybercrime; electronic crime; digital crime; Internet crime; and computer-assisted crime.[53] The origins of computer crime lie in science fiction forums, especially science fiction novels, such as Orwell's *Nineteen Eighty Four* and cyberpunk cult classics, such as Gibson's *Neuromancer* and Stephenson's *Snow Crash*. Later, a number of popular movies adopted the same sci-fi cyberpunk ideas, including *War Games*, *Hackers*, and *The Matrix*.

Generally speaking, computer crime refers to the use of a computer to facilitate or carry out a criminal offence.[54] It also consists of using electronic gadgets to access, control, manipulate, or use data for illegal purposes. It can describe the harms or crimes that result from opportunities created by networked technologies. The tools of cyber-criminals include cell phones, fax machines, digital cameras, voice recorders, scanners, copiers, laptop computers and more. Computer crimes continue to pose enormous challenges for individuals, businesses and societies.

One approach to understanding computer crime is to differentiate those crimes in which the computer is the instrument used to commit the offence; the target of the offence; or incidental to the offence.[55] While these categories often overlap, they are helpful to understand the different forms of computer crime.

In cases where the computer is the instrument, it is the means to a criminal end. For example, the computer can be used to steal information (e.g., banking, credit card or health care information) or to create, store and distribute child pornography. Alternatively, the computer can be the target of the offence when a criminal targets the computer network itself. These attacks tend to involve unauthorized access to and interference with information systems. For example, denial-of-service attacks and the dissemination of malicious code can cause system damage and/or cause the network to crash. Lastly, the computer can be merely incidental to the offence.

It should be kept in mind that digital technology can be used to facilitate almost any type of crime. Thus, computers can be significant to law enforcement because they contain evidence of a crime. For example, a cell phone can contain evidence about the location of a suspect in a murder case. Or a narcotics dealer might use a computer to store records relating to drug trafficking. From this perspective, the terms cybercrime and computer crime can be used to describe

---

[52] Scott Charney and Kent Alexander, "Computer Crime" (1996), 45 Emory Law Journal 934 at 934.

[53] Samuel C. McQuade, *Understanding and Managing Cybercrime* (New York: Pearson, 2006) at 15.

[54] Michael ONeill, "Old Crimes New Bottles: Sanctioning Cybercrime" (2000), 9 George Mason Law Review 237 at 241.

[55] Peter Grabosky, *Electronic Crime* (Upper Saddle River, NJ: Pearson, 2007) at 11.

many different forms of IT-enabled crimes, whether they violate existing criminal laws or not.[56]

We can also differentiate between "old" or conventional crimes and "new" crimes committed with new technology.[57] Traditional crimes include identity theft, fraud, child pornography, luring and stalking. If we take away the Internet, the behaviour continues because offenders revert to using other forms of communication and information-gathering. New crimes include viruses, worms, hacking and denial of service attacks. These crimes are *true* forms of computer crime (i.e., informational, globalized and networked). They often use malicious software to automate victimization. Finally, **quasi-traditional crimes** consist of phishing and spam (i.e., traditional crimes perpetrated by entirely new means). These are existing crimes for which network technology has created entirely new global opportunities. If you take away the Internet, the behaviour can continue by other means, but not on such a large volume or global scale.

It is trite to say that technological innovation has led to the emergence of increasingly complex types of crime. It also goes without saying that the number of computer crime incidents have increased along with the number of computer users. In fact, cybercrime is likely to become one of the most significant threats facing law enforcement and its potential to cause harm might be far greater than with respect to real-world crime.[58] The reason is that the shift from a tangible environment to an intangible one means that many of the spatial and temporal constraints that apply to criminal activity in the real world are no longer relevant.

For example, a bank robbery is high risk with a relatively low return on investment when compared with computer crime. A burglar can only steal so much property from so many victims at a time. As well, real-space perpetrators tend to live or work in the same jurisdiction as their victims. Naturally, this is not true of online perpetrators, who can reside anywhere in the world and typically never meet their victims face-to-face.

Consider all of the planning and organization that must go into a complex criminal scheme like a bank robbery in the real world. The perpetrator would need to purchase supplies, like guns, masks and a vehicle. He or she would need to visit the bank and determine where the vaults are located. Also, the perpetrator would need to figure out when money is taken in and out of the bank, where the security guards and cameras are located, as well as the times that the bank is open. When carrying out the crime, he or she would need to get in and out quickly, and secure the loot without being apprehended or injured. In the virtual realm, a bank robber can carry out the crime quickly, without leaving the comfort and safety of his or her living room. Also more people can be victimized and a larger financial return is available by doing far less work than in the real world. The amount of money that can be stolen is limited only by technological tools. Moreover, the anonymous nature of online communications enables the perpetrator to avoid detection and arrest.

---

[56] McQuade, *supra*, note 53 at 17.
[57] *Ibid.*
[58] ONeill, *supra*, note 54 at 238.

WHAT CHALLENGES DOES COMPUTERCRIME POSE FOR CRIMINAL JUSTICE?

Under-reporting by victims continues to be a major concern. The reasons for not reporting computer crime vary considerably; however, the end result is that it is extremely difficult to precisely determine the amount of damage caused by cybercriminals.[59] Individuals might not realize they've been victimized until long after the fact (this is particularly common in cases of identity theft) or the damage might be too minimal to justify the hassle of reporting. In such cases, the incident might be reported only to the bank and might not appear as an Internet-related crime.

When it comes to reporting, private corporations are often more concerned with civil liability and protecting their assets, as well as ensuring that their systems are working properly, than with pursuing criminal prosecutions. Corporate entities might be afraid to report, especially given the risks of negative publicity and copycat crimes. The impact on the company's stock value and the loss of existing and future customers might be too significant to warrant reporting. The company might simply decide to handle the matter internally rather than pursuing legal remedies. This is particularly true if the intrusion is caused by a disgruntled employee of the company. Even if such intrusions are reported, law enforcement officials often cannot assist because it is difficult to prove that the "access" to the computer system was not authorized by the company.

It is important to be aware of the fact that IT security professionals can now use a variety of sophisticated software tools to provide them with visibility into user-controlled areas of company networks to see if there are any risks to the data. For instance, EnCase Enterprise allows visibility into laptops, desktops, file servers and email servers to determine the cause of suspicious network activity. From a central location, network administrators can quickly determine exactly how and when an internal or external security breach took place. In addition, the software enables them to quickly respond to threats, such as fraud, malicious code or other harmful processes running on the affected computers. This can help to lessen the risk of public exposure and damaging lawsuits while, at the same time, avoiding disruption to business and network operations.

In the case of law enforcement, there are a number of obstacles that prevent police from effectively targetting fraud, malicious software and other online threats. Foremost is the fact that most cybercrimes are small in impact and fall outside routine police duties. Traditionally, police tend to give priority to cases in which the suspects and victims are local. Cybercrime offences tend to occur in the networked, globalized environment, which falls far outside the localized sphere of most law enforcement activities.[60]

The fact is that outside of the realm of child exploitation, there is little incentive for law enforcement agents to investigate harms that occur across

---

[59] Charney and Alexander, *supra*, note 52 at 938.
[60] David S. Wall, "Cybercrime, Media and Insecurity: The Shaping of Public Perceptions of Cybercrime" 22 International Review of Law, Computers and Technology (2008) 45 at 56.

international boundaries. For practical purposes, it is extremely difficult to gather evidence in cases where the perpetrator is located in another country than the victim.[61] In addition, many police lack the technological sophistication and resources to pursue Internet criminals. While many local police units in major Canadian cities, as well as the RCMP, now have specialized units that deal with computer forensics and Internet-related investigations, the Internet poses a forensic problem for units in rural areas. In addition, even in cases where there are specialized forensic investigators to deal with Internet-related cases, the necessity of getting evidence and information from overseas, using Mutual Legal Assistance Treaties (MLAT) or diplomatic channels poses a major obstacle and frequently leads to significant time delays. These issues are further explored in Chapter 9.

How Serious Is the Cybercrime Problem?

News articles about cybercrime are abundant and the media seems to have an insatiable appetite for stories about this new phenomenon. Despite the prevalence of cybercrime stories in the media and the claim that hundreds of thousands of Internet users are victimized by computer criminals each year, there has been a surprising lack of legal (more specifically, prosecutorial) response,[62] especially in Canada. In truth, cybercrime incidents are down, but attacks are now more targetted and complex, better funded and severe.

In April 2009, the cyber-security group Symantec published their *Global Internet Security Threat Report,* which reports threats and vulnerabilities that Symantec observed for 2008. Symantec reports that Web-based attacks are now the primary means of malicious activity carried out online and most of these attacks are carried out against users who visit legitimate websites that have been rendered vulnerable by attackers.[63] The proliferation of the Internet and the increasing use of the Web for everyday activities presents attackers with a growing number of targets as well as new means to launch harmful attacks. In addition, many attacks are now automated,[64] which means they can be carried out extremely quickly against a large pool of potential targets.

Some of the most common techniques used by attackers include exploiting a vulnerable Web application running on a server (e.g., to modify the pages available to users visiting the site to post malicious content or otherwise deface the site) or attacking the host operating system.[65] If the attacker embeds a malicious iframe that can redirect a user's browser to another Web server under the attackers control, attacks can be launched against individual visitors to the site.[66] In 2007, Symantec reported 712,000 site-specific vulnerabilities identified. In 2008, there

---

[61] Peter Swire, "No Cop on the Beat: Underenforcement in E-Commerce and Cybercrime" (2008) 7 J. on Telecomm. and High Tech. L. 107 at 108.

[62] Wall, *supra*, note 60 at 45.

[63] Symantec, *Global Internet Security Threat Report, 2009* at 5.

[64] *Ibid.*

[65] *Ibid* at 5-6.

[66] *Ibid.*

were 12,885 site-specific vulnerabilities, which is roughly a 27% decline from the previous year.

Symantec found that the United States was the top country of origin for attacks, accounting for 25% of all worldwide activity. However, while the United States remains the top country for malicious activity, Symantec also reported that there has been a steady increase in malicious activity in countries that do not have such a robust Internet infrastructure.[67] The reason is that attackers can move their servers to these safe haven countries, and disseminate harmful and malicious content from there, knowing that the states lack the legal and technical resources to deal with these threats. For example, countries that have a rapidly expanding network of ISPs might have difficulty monitoring and filtering the expanding volume of traffic on their networks. The graph in Figure 1.4 illustrates the malicious activity that has occurred in the past two years or so by country.

Figure 1.4: Malicious Activity by Country

2008 Rank	2007 Rank	Country	2008 Overall Precentage	2007 Overall Precentage	Malicious Code Rank	Spam Zombies Rank	Phishing Websites Host Rank	Bot Rank	Attack Origin Rank
1	1	United States	23%	26%	1	3	1	2	1
2	2	China	9%	11%	2	4	6	1	2
3	3	Germany	6%	7%	12	2	2	4	4
4	4	United Kingdom	5%	4%	4	10	5	9	3
5	8	Brazil	4%	3%	16	1	16	5	9
6	6	Spain	4%	3%	10	8	13	3	6
7	7	Italy	3%	3%	11	6	14	6	8
8	5	France	3%	4%	8	14	9	10	5
9	15	Turkey	3%	2%	15	5	24	8	12
10	12	Poland	3%	2%	23	9	8	7	17

Source: Symantec

One of the most worrisome cybercrime trends in 2008 was the emergence of a full-blown **underground economy** in which credit-card information, identity theft information, and spam and phishing software are available for low cost. Symantec reports that roughly $276 million worth of goods and information is available on online black markets.[68] Figure 1.5 shows the kinds of goods and services currently being offered through the underground economy in cyberspace.

In addition, the production and distribution of items, such as customized malicious code and phishing kits available for download on the Internet, has led to the widespread proliferation of harmful code. According to Symantec, this represents over 60% of the approximately 2.6 million malicious code threats that the company has detected in total. In 2008, there were 1,656,227 malicious code threats, up from only 624,267 in 2007. As malicious software, or malware, becomes ever more sophisticated, its reach throughout the Internet will likely increase. This problem is explained in greater detail in Chapter 6.

---

[67] *Ibid* at 8.
[68] *Ibid*.

Figure 1.5: Goods and Services Available on Underground Economy Servers

2008 Rank	2007 Rank	Item	2008 Percentage	2007 Percentage	Range of Prices
1	1	Credit card information	32%	21%	$0.06 – $30
2	2	Bank account credentials	19%	17%	$10 – $1000
3	9	Email accounts	5%	4%	$0.10 – $100
4	3	Email addresses	5%	6%	$0.33/MB – $100/MB
5	12	Proxies	4%	3%	$0.16 – $20
6	4	Full identities	4%	6%	$0.70 – $60
7	6	Mailers	3%	5%	$2 – $40
8	5	Cash out services	3%	5%	8% – 50% or flat rate of $200 – $2000 per item
9	17	Shell scripts	3%	2%	$2 – $20
10	8	Scams	3%	5%	$3 – $40/week for hosting $2 – $20 design

Source: Symantec

Why Should We be Concerned about Computercrime?

Given the number of individuals and businesses that rely on the Internet, the threat of cybercrime is an important concern for everyone. As a society, there are a number of reasons we need to be concerned about computer crime and it is clear that the harm suffered as a result of cyber-attacks cannot be measured in terms of dollars alone.[69] Every person and organization relying on computers has data that is vulnerable to attack and, thus, in need of protection. Cybercrime incidents and the number of individuals and businesses that rely on computers are on the rise. Society depends on networked information for many critical functions (e.g., social networking and communication, banking, health care, taxation, education, commerce). Indeed, computer criminals have even threatened the public's health and safety as is clear from attacks against medical data,[70] including patient files, as well as an air traffic control tower. We have a societal obligation to prevent crime and reduce the harm to victims.

CONCLUSION

Advances in computer technology have rapidly increased in the last ten years or so. Clearly, technical innovation has created astounding opportunities for education, research and public discourse. At the same time, the Internet has led to a noticeable increase in socially undesirable behaviour and it is currently being used to commit a wide range of criminal activities. As discussed earlier, computers can be the target or the means for criminal attacks. They can be targetted to obtain

---

[69] McQuade *supra*, note 53 at 18.

[70] In one virus incident, a British health authority lost vital information from its hematology department and an Italian university lost almost a years worth of AIDS research information. Alexander and Charney, *supra*, note 52 at 937. See also Paul Festa, "DOJ Charges Youth in Hack Attacks" CNET, March 18, 1998, available online at: http://news.cnet.com/2100-1023-209260.html#ixzz11PloAvLu.

information or to cause damage or disruption to the network. Or they can simply be the instrument of the crime. Alternatively, computers can be used to store evidence of the crime, such as when a drug-dealer keeps records of customer accounts. As such, it is important for law enforcement officials and members of the general public to understand that there are a wide variety of criminal activities involving computers.

Our increasing dependence on networked technologies makes us highly vulnerable to those who use these platforms for harmful means. While law enforcement officials have made great strides in their ability to deal with computer-related crimes, they continue to be outmatched by their lack of technical sophistication and resources. Similarly, individual users are largely unaware of the fact that criminals are continually finding new vulnerabilities and methods by which to victimize consumers. These realities have frustrated law enforcement officials around the world as they struggle to overcome the inter-jurisdictional nature of cybercrime, while criminals continue to operate on the Net with near impunity.

QUESTIONS FOR FURTHER THINKING AND DISCUSSION

1. Have you experienced a cybercrime threat or attack? If so, what happened?
2. Briefly discuss the history of the Internet, then consider its most recent advances.
3. Are virtual communities just like real-life communities? How are they similar or different?
4. Do most cybercrime offences consist of traditional crimes perpetrated by new means or are they new crimes altogether?
5. Why are some individuals and companies reluctant to report cybercrime victimization?
6. What are some of the common myths about computer crime?
7. What do you think society's perception of cybercriminals is? Do you think the media stereotypes all or certain kinds of cybercriminals?
8. In what ways do cybercrime offences differ from real-space crimes?
9. What are some of the difficulties associated with estimating the true social and financial impact of cybercrime on the Canadian economy?
10. What kinds of goods and services are offered for sale in the underground economy? Why are they useful to cybercriminals?
11. Why do we need to be concerned about computer crime as individuals and as a society?
12. The Internet was designed to be open with distributed control and mutual trust among users. Some believe this design has led to new security threats. In what ways is this true or not true?

2

Introduction to the Regulation of Cyberspace

KEY TERMS AND CONCEPTS		
• Bits and bytes	• Cybertip.ca	• MUD
• Code is Law	• EFF	• *Neuromancer*
• COE Convention on Cybercrime	• John Perry Barlow	• Second Life
• Cyberspace	• Julian Dibbell	• Social contract
	• Lawrence Lessig	• Social norms

INTRODUCTION

This chapter provides an introduction to the regulation of cyberspace. I will examine some of the stumbling blocks that early cyberlaw theorists encountered when trying to comprehend how this unique environment could be controlled. As we saw in the last chapter, cyberspace is an open and highly robust network that developed slowly over time. It evolved from academic institutions, largely as a result of sophisticated research undertaken by the United States government, to become the most pervasive system of communication ever imagined. Over the past 40 years or so, the Internet has become an ideal venue for both recreation and commerce. Beginning in the 1990s, for example, unique online businesses emerged, such as Amazon and eBay, facilitated by unlimited growth potential and the promise of minimal government intervention.

The open and widely distributed nature of the Internet suggested that it would be difficult to create a regulatory structure to govern it. This is not difficult to understand; especially, given that cyberspace was designed to be a network of networks, without any single point of control at the operations level. Moreover, as the Internet evolved over time, it connected an increasing number of users throughout the world. Yet many of the features that make the Internet an important vehicle for legitimate endeavors also make it an ideal instrument for crime. The anonymity and relative ease of access provided by the Internet, in addition to a general trust among users, create an incentive for savvy criminals to victimize a wide range of unsuspecting individuals and institutions.

CYBERSPACE AS A UNIQUE PLACE

Cyberspace, which was originally a term from William Gibson's science-fiction novel *Neuromancer*, is used to describe the conceptual space where words, data, human relationships, wealth and power are experienced by people in a virtual environment.[1] Unlike physical frontiers, cyberspace is a human construct. This means that we formulate the rules and design of the Internet entirely on our own. However, the metaphor of cyberspace as a unique "place" or "frontier" has been used in a variety of academic circles, including architecture and urban planning, to describe the spatial composition of virtual space and the electronic communities formed on it.

Many scholars described the Internet as a unique "place" where participants, who had never met in real life, could connect in a vibrant community where physical identity and geographic location no longer mattered. Later on, as scholars turned their minds to the legal and political ramifications of these new social spaces, they expanded upon the vision of cyberspace as a unique environment to incorporate the idea that a new kind of utopian society could be established with control emanating from the bottom up, by users themselves, rather than directed downwards by the state. The central theme behind the early debates about the sovereignty of cyberspace is that because of its distinct social and physical makeup, cyberspace was not amenable to the application of existing laws established with regard to the real physical world.

In order to describe the physical and social dimensions of cyberspace, a number of early writers provided first-hand accounts of their experiences in online communities, identifying the unique spatial characteristics of the virtual world. For example, in his highly influential book, *City of Bits*,[2] William Mitchell, of MIT's School of Architecture and Planning, described the Internet as anti-spatial and distinct from the real world in that it is "nowhere in particular but everywhere at once."[3] He observed that you cannot tell someone where it is, or describe its shape and proportions, or tell a person how to get there because it is not like meeting places in real space.[4] Other scholars rejected the rampant use of this metaphor and pointed out that no one is in cyberspace or actually lives there; and, of course, it is data, not people, who travel in the virtual realm.[5] In addition, while

---

[1] Howard Rheingold, *The Virtual Community: Homesteading on the Electronic Frontier* (Cambridge, Mass: MIT Press, 2000) at xx.

[2] (Cambridge, Mass: MIT Press, 1995).

[3] *Ibid* at 8.

[4] *Ibid*.

[5] Mark A. Lemley, "Place and Cyberspace" (2003), 91 California Law Review 521.

it is true that people talk of visiting a website; what they're *really* talking about is sitting down in front of a computer and sending a request for information to the provider of the website, which responds by sending back data. While this remains true, technological innovation has enabled users to *immerse* themselves in simulated environments instead of just observing them on a computer screen. As such, many of us actually *do* inhabit virtual worlds instead of merely participating in them from a distance. Of course, the "places" that currently exist in cyberspace are software programs running on the Internet, such as **Second Life**, which is an elaborate virtual world that millions of people now inhabit regularly. The principle of end-to-end design, discussed in Chapter 1, which locates intelligence in the software programs running at the application layer, is actually what facilitates the creation of multi-dimensional virtual places that many of us now frequent.

Just like in the real world, many of these cyberspace places are public – like the streets and squares in Second Life – but others are highly private, which means that you need a special password or other means to authenticate that you belong. At the same time, though, many of these private spaces in cyberspace can be broken into, as with homes and businesses in real space, and we have witnessed over the past two decades the emergence of hackers and other miscreants committing all sorts of transgressions in virtual worlds.

In the early to mid-1990s, John Perry Barlow wrote a number of columns in *Wired* magazine in which he argued that cyberspace would be self-governed by participants, beyond incursion from territorial governments in the real world.[6] Barlow was by no means your stereotypical computer geek. In fact, he worked as a cattle rancher in Wyoming and also wrote lyrics for the Grateful Dead. However, in the early 1990s Barlow began to think and write about the new social network known as the Internet. He was also the first person to use William Gibson's science fiction term cyberspace to describe this revolutionary new social space.[7]

Together with his friend Mitch Kapor, the founder of Lotus 1-2-3, Barlow created the **Electronic Frontier Foundation (EFF)**. The founders of the EFF wanted to protect individual freedom against government intervention in cyberspace. The central premise behind Barlow's work, which served as the founding principle for the EFF, was that the inherent design of the Internet made it resistant to externally imposed regulation. In other words, cyberspace would remain free from real-world regulation because it could not be governed by territorially defined rules.

Barlow maintained that cyberspace is an independent frontier with its own rules and normative standards and that it would be impossible for government to regulate it.[8] After the United States government attempted to pass legislation

---

[6] Jack Goldsmith and Tim Wu, *Who Controls the Internet?* (Oxford: Oxford University Press, 2006) at 17.

[7] As I mentioned earlier, cyberspace is the term first used by William Gibson in his 1984 novel *Neuromancer*.

[8] Goldsmith and Wu, *supra,* note 6 at 17.

regulating speech on the Internet, Barlow wrote his famous "Declaration of Cyberspace Independence,"[9] in which he declared: "I come from Cyberspace, the new home of the Mind. On behalf of the future, I ask you of the past to leave us alone. You are not welcome among us. You have no sovereignty where we gather." He went on to proclaim that "cyberspace does not lie within your borders" and that participants would form their own "social contract" within the virtual world "that is both everywhere and nowhere" at once.

Social Contracts in Cyberspace

What exactly does Barlow mean when he states that Internet users would form their own **social contract**? Social contract theory is almost as old as philosophy itself and rests at the heart of works by Thomas Hobbes and John Locke. In his famous text, *Leviathan*, Hobbes wrote that without government, men would be forced to live in the state of nature in which life would be ". . .solitary, poor, nasty, brutish and short." For Hobbes, in the state of nature there are three constants:

1.　individuals will violently compete to secure the basic necessities of life;
2.　they will challenge others and fight out of fear for their personal safety; and
3.　they will seek reputational glory.

In other words, those forced to live in the state of nature would constantly fear for their lives and struggle to survive. The solution that Hobbes proposed was for individuals to enter into a social contract through which they would be bound with their fellow man to be governed by a single authority. By subjecting themselves to an institution of orderly government to make decisions on their behalf and manage the relations between its subjects, individuals would secure the benefits of living in a secure society.

John Locke also believed that each person should forsake his or her liberty in return for being allowed to enjoy the safety and comfort of citizenship. However, the central difference between Hobbes and Locke is that Hobbes saw the state of nature as necessarily violent and unsafe whereas Locke viewed natural law as a state of equality and freedom. According to Locke, natural law is a state in which individuals can live together as part of a community. For Locke, it was necessary for individuals to form a government and enter into a civil society so that the standards and values of the community could flourish pursuant to natural law. He also believed it necessary for individuals to consent to be governed; in other words, he introduced an element of democracy into social contract theory. These ideas were picked up by Barlow, who argued that the participants of cyberspace would form their own social contract and agree to be bound by a more just and fair system of rules.

According to Barlow, the new virtual environment would be more open and tolerant than the real world, and it would be "a world that all may enter without privilege or prejudice accorded by race, economic power, military force, or station

---

[9] John P. Barlow, "A Declaration of Cyberspace Independence" available online at: http://homes.eff.org/~barlow/Declaration-Final.html.

of birth."[10] In another of his well-known essays, entitled "Selling Wine Without Bottles: The Economy of Mind on the Global Net," Barlow asserted that "digital technology is also erasing the legal jurisdictions of the physical world, and replacing them with the unbounded and perhaps permanently lawless seas of Cyberspace."[11] According to Barlow, cyberspace is a new world where "information wants to be free," and is, by its very essence, resistant to externally imposed regulation.[12] In his view, given the difficulty of regulating bits, traditional notions of property, expression, identity and legal regulation simply could not apply.

But what would happen in elaborately detailed role-playing environments, where users could create their characters and enter a virtual community populated with other virtual characters and things? As the electronic world was constructed over time, many people began to wonder what kind of space it would be. Would a framework be constructed to mimic real space, complete with social norms, laws, locked buildings, fences, public squares and parks? What kinds of freedoms would be restricted or enabled there? Would our property, privacy and freedoms be protected or diminished? Would it allow us to say whatever we wanted and do whatever we pleased?

One of the earliest and most famous cybercrime incidents was the rape in cyberspace documented by technology journalist Julian Dibbell. In a brilliant memoir entitled *My Tiny Life*, Dibbell provides readers with an intimate account of his own experiences in the social networks of LambdaMOO, a type of **MUD** (a multi-user dungeon or multi-user domain) where thousands of people logged on to create fictional identities and engage with one another inside an illusory kingdom.[13] An important part of the story focuses on how one character named "Mr. Bungle" was able to "rape" other users inside LamdaMOO. His tool was a tiny voodoo-doll that allowed him to take control of people and make them do disgusting things. Mr. Bungle's acts, which were clearly not physical rapes, were painful experiences for the participants nonetheless.

Due to the antics and abuses of Mr. Bungle, the participants realized that their virtual world had been irrevocably changed from an open and playful environment into one that could be devastated by real-world concerns, including violence and hatred, and required the imposition of some form of social order or control. The members of the community struggled to come up with a solution and eventually one member, a wizard named JoeFeedback, took initiative and eliminated Mr. Bungle from the online world by destroying or "toading" him.[14] Following this, the participants realized that they needed rules to govern their

---

[10] *Ibid.*

[11] John P. Barlow, "Selling Wine Without Bottles: The Economy of the Mind on the Global Net," published in *Wired*, February 1993 at 86, available online at: http://homes.eff.org/~barlow/EconomyOfIdeas.html.

[12] *Ibid.*

[13] Julian Dibbell, *My Tiny Life: Crime and Passion in a Virtual World* (New York: Henry Holt, 1998).

[14] *Ibid* at 484.

virtual world and a mediation system to resolve disputes. However, they were ultimately unsuccessful at keeping Mr. Bungle at bay.

Although Mr. Bungle was, in effect, banned from LambdaMOO, he returned days later, as Dr. Jest, under a different user account (it is no great leap of logic to assume that the person who was in control of Mr. Bungle saw the incident as little more than a game). The ease by which he was able to circumvent the virtual punishment underscores the fact that virtual mischief can be perpetrated with little or no real consequence in cyberspace. In the eyes of the real world legal system, the event was only an episode in a game and there was no real-life legal basis for recourse against Mr. Bungle. Nonetheless, the moral of the MOO story is that, as Lessig puts it, "cyberspace will not take care of itself,"[15] and some form of regulation is needed to prevent technology-generated environments from being exploited by antisocial characters and criminals.

The Bungle incident also suggests that the need for regulation is even more important in cyberspace because individuals can hide behind their virtual identities and engage in harmful behaviours that they might not even consider acting out in the real world. Yet efforts to regulate are problematic due to the plasticity of cyberspace; if wrongdoers are unable to attain their goals, they can simply change their location or identity. From this point forward, it became apparent that cyberspace could not function without some kind of regulation. But the problem of who or what was going to govern cyberspace, and by what means, had yet to be resolved.

The Regulation Debate

The radical side of this debate can be seen in claims that real world governments have no place in cyberspace and that users will resolve their problems on their own. David Johnson and David Post are the most influential writers to address the question of whether cyberspace should be characterized as a distinct legal entity. They argued, in articles written together, as well as independently by Post, that cyberspace is "borderless" and beyond the limited physical boundaries of the territorial sovereign.[16] They focused on illustrating how interactions between cyberspace participants transcend physical locations, making it impossible to pinpoint where a transaction takes place, and they maintained that distinct rules and dispute resolution mechanisms would emerge on the Net that would have "no clear parallel" in the real world.[17]

Johnson and Post argued that due to these unique characteristics, cyberspace subverts the power of local governments to assert control over individuals or things because it fundamentally challenges the idea that regulation must be based on borders between physical spaces and territorially defined rules.[18] Like Barlow, who maintained that real-space governments could not regulate the bits of

---

[15] Lawrence Lessig, *Code and Other Laws of Cyberspace* (New York: Basic Books, 1999) at 61.

[16] David R. Johnson and David Post, "Law and Borders – The Rise of Law in Cyberspace" (1995), 48 Stanford Law Review 1367 at 1392.

[17] *Ibid.*

[18] *Ibid* at 1370.

cyberspace, Johnson and Post argued that traditional laws, which are firmly rooted in the concept of territoriality, would be rendered ineffective in cyberspace due to the absence of physical boundaries and borders. They regarded the ability to control behaviour in cyberspace as having only a tenuous connection to physical space, making it very difficult, if not impossible, for governments to regulate information on the virtual network because real-world laws are based on the idea of territorial sovereignty.[19] Furthermore, even if a territorial government could apply its laws to the Internet, online activity would be subject to the simultaneous application of the laws of all territorial sovereigns at once and this would lead to the ineffective application of too many sources and types of law.[20]

The community of cyberspace participants and network service providers were said to be ideally suited to developing standards and rules that could apply to the global virtual network.[21] Thus, the "law of the Internet" would emerge not from a single authority and be externally imposed, but from the networks themselves. Network operators would determine what rules to impose through service agreements with their users or implement them into the architecture of their networks and users would decide which online communities to join.[22]

Johnson and Post were correct in maintaining that network service providers and users have a key role to play in establishing rules for the Internet. We have witnessed many examples of user democracy in practice in cyberspace, as well as the ability of administrators to regulate conduct on their networks through the use of contract and code. The failure to respect these rules can result in the individual's expulsion from an online community. While Johnson and Post were right to suggest that individuals have a role to play in establishing rules to govern online interactions, the law of the Internet cannot be constructed by participants and administrators alone.

In an article in which he responds to the arguments put forward by Johnson and Post, Lawrence Lessig tells readers that "Johnson and Post want to argue for a separation between real space law and cyberspace law that I don't believe can be sustained, nor do I believe that it should."[23] Rather than approaching the problem by focusing on the separateness of cyberspace and assuming that government regulation of the Net is "an illegitimate extra-territorial power grab,"[24] Lessig maintains that Johnson and Post failed to show how cyberspace will be "in any special way immune from real space regulations"[25] and suggests that government regulation in cyberspace is not only possible, but potentially more effective at ensuring compliance than when applied in the real world.[26] In other words, cyberspace can be regulated through the formation of contractual

---

[19] *Ibid* at 1371.

[20] *Ibid* at 1374.

[21] *Ibid* at 1388.

[22] David G. Post, "The Unsettled Paradox: The Internet, the State and the Consent of the Governed" (1997), 5 Independent Journal of Global Legal Studies 521.

[23] Lawrence Lessig, "The Zones of Cyberspace" (1996), 48 Stanford Law Review 1403 at 1403.

[24] *Ibid* at 1404.

[25] *Ibid* at 1406.

[26] *Ibid* at 1408.

agreements between ISPs and their customers and, for example, by real-world governments requiring ISPs to modify the technical architecture of their networks so as to facilitate user control.

In his subsequent book, *Code and Other Laws of Cyberspace*, Lessig defends his ground-breaking theory of cyberspace regulation and resolves the problems of sovereignty and jurisdiction that stymied earlier cyberlaw theorists. Lessig challenges the notion that cyberspace cannot be regulated by pointing out that in the electronic realm, "Code is Law."[27] By this, he means that the Internet is not inherently uncontrollable; rather, its essential elements, or its hardware and software, can be used to both enable and restrict cyberspace use and behaviour. Lessig tells readers in his article, "The Zones of Cyberspace," that in order to enforce law in cyberspace, the regulator need not "threaten or cajole;" it only needs to change the code, such as by implementing a system of passwords, and determine how the user will access the system.[28] The user will be forced to obey these "laws as code" not because he or she necessarily wants to, but simply because one has to comply in order to use the system.[29] The coded rules are clearly not optional because they are embedded within the structure of the virtual world.

However, Lessig goes beyond merely introducing the concept of code is law to readers; in fact, he explains how a variety of different incentives and restraints can be used to achieve the desired outcome in cyberspace regulation. In his book *The Future of Ideas*,[30] Lessig points out that the Internet has a number of different layers – which he terms the physical layer, the code layer and the content layer – that can be used to regulate cyberspace use and behaviour. For example, the physical layer, which comprises the physical content of the Internet, including the cables, switches, routers, and so on, can be controlled in much the same way that the government regulates the telephone networks in real space.

As such, we can see how the government might control this layer by requiring ISPs to configure their networks to make them intercept-capable, in the same way as telephone lines are subject to interception by law enforcement, which is otherwise known as wiretapping, in real space. At the code level, software manufacturers can design their products so as to both enable and restrict certain kinds of behaviour, just as Web page designers can create password-protected spaces that are off-limits to some people but not to others. Note that in cyberspace, technical decisions made by ISPs and businesses in designing and implementing their communication networks, including the implementation of filtering and blocking software, firewalls, encryption and authentication, determines what activities, and also what crimes, can occur and how these acts can be detected.[31]

---

[27] Lessig, *supra*, note 15 at 35. It is noteworthy that the phrase "code is law" is often attributed to Lawrence Lessig; however, this work expands upon that of William Mitchell who first wrote that ". . .on the electronic frontier, code is law."

[28] Lessig, *supra*, note 23 at 1408.

[29] *Ibid*.

[30] (New York: Vintage Books, 2001).

[31] K. A. Taipale, "Internet and Computer Crime: System Architecture as Crime Control" Center for Advanced Studies in Science and Technology Policy Working Paper No. 03-2003, February 2003 at 5.

Finally, at the content layer, the government can enact real-space laws that regulate the kinds of materials that individuals can access and distribute online. For example, child pornography laws prohibit the creation, possession and dissemination of these materials in cyberspace as well as real space.

REGULATION IN CYBERSPACE

It should now be apparent that regulation in cyberspace can occur at multiple levels and can emanate from many different sources, including state and non-state actors. Contrary to what the cyber-libertarians believed, multiple systems of regulation do exist in cyberspace and are highly effective at achieving control and regulating content on the Net. In other words, cyberspace is a highly complex and sophisticated environment; however, it is also remarkably amenable to regulation by real-world governments.

The Role of Government

When a government decides that it wants to curtail illicit information on its ISP networks, it has a variety of approaches to choose from.[32] One is to require ISPs to block or filter out objectionable content and prevent its citizens from viewing it. China and some other tightly controlled regimes, such as Saudi Arabia and Singapore, use this option.[33] Since 1995, when Chinese authorities began permitting commercial Internet accounts, at least 60 sets of regulations have been issued with the objective of controlling Internet content, using individual citizens and ISPs as essential tools in their crackdown on Internet communications. The lesson provided by the Great Firewall of China is that virtually any powerful government has the capacity to achieve enormous control over Internet activity within its borders.[34]

All Internet traffic into China passes through state-controlled portals and the authorities tightly control which sites can be accessed and keep records of who accesses which sites.[35] The Chinese government also blocks certain websites outside its borders that it deems a threat to the Chinese nation.[36] It does this by requiring all Chinese ISPs to implement filtering technology that screens out all sites and information deemed banned by the Chinese government, according to their URLs or IP addresses.[37]

---

[32] Frances Cairncross, *The Death of Distance* (Boston: Harvard Business School Press, 1997) at 187.

[33] *Ibid.*

[34] Goldsmith and Wu, *supra*, note 6, at 89.

[35] Cairncross, *supra*, note 32, at 186.

[36] Goldsmith and Wu, *supra*, note 6 at 92.

[37] *Ibid* at 93. Goldsmith and Wu also note at 95 that the Chinese government has been assisted by large American corporations, such as Cisco and Microsoft, which have developed technology enabling China to censor information within its borders. For example, the authors note that Microsoft MSN Spaces service, which allows Chinese citizens to set up their own blogs, blocks titles like "freedom" and "democracy" and generates an error message stating that the message "includes forbidden language" and must be deleted.

The system also automatically blocks or deletes all messages containing forbidden words from websites, ensuring that they are never viewed by anyone or are quickly erased.[38] By using technology to filter out or censor a broad range of information, including independence groups, human rights organizations and religious or spiritual sites and information related to Western lifestyles, politics and values, China operates the most sophisticated and wide-reaching system of Internet filtering in the world.[39]

It goes without saying that implementing these measures in Canada would significantly curtail our democratic rights and freedoms, particularly freedom of expression, which also protects our right to access information. While the Chinese example illustrates that it would be technically possible for us to create closed national Internet networks, we clearly do not want to take such extreme measures because the benefits that might be achieved in terms of crime reduction would not likely outweigh the negative impact that this would have on our privacy and liberty guarantees. Implementing these measures would also be far too expensive, even if Parliament were somehow able to justify overriding fundamental rights to this extent. Not only would there be an enormous financial burden placed upon the Canadian taxpayer, businesses might decide to stop operating or investing in Canada if we were to adopt such a drastic approach to Internet regulation. Yet this case illustrates that virtually any powerful nation, even a democratic one such as ours, can implement sweeping censorship measures, limiting what information its citizens can access and express online with the appropriate technical tools at its disposal.

The Role of the Third Party

As we have seen, third parties also have an essential role to play in law enforcement on the Internet. ISPs are the most obvious targets for government regulation because they maintain primary, if not exclusive, control over their networks, including the cables, wires, routers and switches that transmit information in cyberspace. More importantly, these networks are frequently owned by cable and telephone companies that are already subject to a high degree of government regulation in North America.[40] This places them in an ideal position to assist with monitoring conduct on their networks, removing harmful content and whistle-blowing.[41]

Building on these requirements, the government can require ISPs to assist with architectural control and investigative support. In this sense, ISPs can be required by law to modify their networks to assist law enforcement officials with the collection, retention and provision of valuable evidence in cybercrime cases and they can also be called upon to assist with the interception of communications over their networks for law enforcement purposes. One can therefore see that

---

[38] *Ibid* at 96.
[39] *Ibid* at 94.
[40] *Ibid* at 73.
[41] Taipel, *supra*, note 31 at 7.

there is a need for a high degree of cooperation between the government and third parties in the regulation of cyberspace.

Further, every ISP has the contractual right to demand, collect and retain a wide range of personal information about its customers as a condition of service. Thus, ISPs are the gatekeepers of highly secretive information, including client identification details, essential to providing law enforcement officials with the tools they need to investigate and prosecute serious crimes. This places ISPs in an ideal position to assist law enforcement agents with establishing the identity and location of cybercriminals in the real world.

Similarly, for some kinds of criminal activity on the Net, victim identification and reporting is a highly effective strategy. For example, cyber-reporting initiatives have already been implemented successfully throughout North America, including Canada which has its own **Cybertip.ca**. Increasing public education and awareness about the risks of online victimization, in addition to providing the public with information about how to make a report and what to expect when a report is made, are also helpful strategies to control crime on the Internet.

However, Johnson and Post weren't wrong to be concerned about the fact that cyberspace has no territorially-defined jurisdictional boundaries. As you learned in Chapter 1, messages in cyberspace can be transmitted from any physical location to any other without any physical impediment or delay. Location remains extremely important to regulation; however, cyberspace undermines this concept altogether.

The difficulty in locating and apprehending perpetrators long after they have committed their offences, and the lack of technical expertise among law enforcement officials, magnified by the expansiveness of the Internet, pose significant challenges for law enforcement officials. What can Canadian police do, for example, if a criminal disseminates an extremely harmful virus from a small Eastern European country that causes millions of dollars worth of damage to the Canadian Internet community?

Government Cooperation

Clearly, cybercrime is an innovative form of criminal activity that requires a unique approach to address the fact that emerging technologies are being used to perpetrate crime on a global scale. You will find that these themes are discussed throughout this book and play an important role in understanding how cybercrime is currently being combatted in Canada and abroad. At the top, or tertiary, level, it is significant that Internet crime cuts across international boundaries. Further, the problem is simply too big for any single nation to tackle alone. There has been increased media and law enforcement attention given to the problem of cybercrime. In recent years we have also witnessed an international push for increased cooperation, as well as efforts to harmonize laws dealing with computer crime and to criminalize the many different aspects of these offences. Virtually every country is threatened by cybercriminals and it will require a collaborative effort on the part of law enforcement and industry players from around the world to attack this problem on a global scale. The failure of even a single nation to enact effective regulations can hamper law enforcement efforts because cybercriminals can move their illicit operations to less strict countries, creating safe havens for misconduct and abuse.

National governments must work together to identify regulatory priorities within their own countries and harmonize their regulatory standards with those of other nations. It is significant that Canada has signed, but not ratified, the Council of Europe's Convention on Cybercrime,[42] the first multilateral agreement aimed at harmonizing computer crime statutes throughout the world and enabling states to cooperate with each other in the investigation and prosecution of digital crimes. Currently, this treaty provides the best means by which to effectively combat Internet-related crime on a global scale.

It enables many countries to work together by pursuing a common criminal policy based on international cooperation and the harmonization of domestic legislation. The Convention also requires signatory states to update their technological capabilities for combatting digital crime by implementing sophisticated evidence gathering techniques to lawfully intercept online communications, share resources and obtain information about those who use the Internet for criminal purposes. Parliament must take these steps, which are necessary for Canada to ratify the Convention, and encourage other nations to do the same. These issues will be explored in further detail in Chapter 9.

At the secondary level, there are architectural constraints that can be implemented by ISPs, which provide connectivity to the Internet, to facilitate the detection of Internet-related crimes. Since ISPs maintain primary, if not exclusive, control over their networks, including the cables and routers that convey information, as well as the data transmitted by their users, they are in an ideal position to assist law enforcement agents with the regulation of digital information. This regulatory approach, which is Lessig's Code is Law theory in practice, is vital because the investigation and prosecution of cybercrime offenders heavily depends on the collection of evidence maintained exclusively by ISPs. It is also critical to keep in mind that the government can require third parties to implement architectural measures that either enable or restrict user behaviour. This is essential to controlling crime on the Net.

For example, existing wiretapping laws can be updated so they can be used to enable law enforcement agents to achieve the goals of suspect identification and evidence gathering online. To make these new laws effective, ISPs can be required to modify the structural elements of their networks to permit law enforcement agents to intercept online communications with judicial authorization. The reason this regulatory approach is so important is that Internet-related investigations often take time to develop and critical information may be lost if the ISP does not have adequate data retention policies. Compelling ISPs to cooperate with police and disclose information when necessary is one of the few tools that we have to target online offenders and obtain valuable evidence in a timely manner. These issues will be explored further in Chapter 9.

---

[42] The Council of Europes *Convention on Cybercrime*, Budapest, 23.XI.2001, available online at: http://conventions. Coe.int/Treaty.en.Treaties/HTM/185.htm.

At the primary, or most basic, level are "self-help" measures that the individual can take to protect herself or himself against victimization. Regulatory measures that can be put into practice at this level include cyber-reporting and the implementation of filtering and blocking technologies on one's own computer. This level of regulation is particularly important to our ability to combat cybercrime given the structural nature of the Internet. It is also highly significant that network communities can directly regulate their own members through the use of social norms. A community is, after all, simply a group of people with a common interest or understanding. Once a community of individuals is identified and formed, it can adopt a set of standards or norms (i.e., the normative conduct that will be acceptable to members of the community).

If these standards or expectations are not adhered to, the members of the community can express their displeasure by shaming or rebuking the non-abiding member. The important thing to keep in mind about these social norms is that they differ from legally enforceable rules. Social norms are not binding upon community members – individuals can choose to take them or leave them – and the only form of punishment that one might face for refusing to follow them is to be singled out as some sort of failure for not living up to the expectation of one's peers. Laws, on the other hand, are not optional; we must follow them or face the threat of punishment by the state. More will be said about the influence of community norms and legal standards upon user behaviour in cyberspace later on in this book.

In Chapter 1, I discussed the fact that the Internet was designed to accommodate a variety of networks without a centralized management source. In other words, intelligence and complexity is placed at the ends of the network rather than in the centre, as was traditionally the case with respect to telephone communications. This gives Internet users and ISPs a great deal of power and control and necessitates a high level of responsibility from them. Given the importance of shifting accountability closer to the source of the problem, public education is another important aspect of combatting computer crime. Naturally, if we are going to shift a high level of accountability onto users, they must be educated about what the risks are and how to deal with them.

It is important to keep in mind that the layers of regulation are complimentary and must be realized together. Indeed, a multi-faceted solution is the only one likely to be effective at combatting any form of computer crime. While it is unlikely that this problem will ever completely disappear, all members of the Internet community must do their part to deal with computer crime. These issues will be further explored in subsequent chapters.

CONCLUSION

Time has proven that cyberspace is highly amenable to regulation. However, there is no perfect solution to regulation within this complex and multi-layered global information system. In the next part, you will be introduced to how the nature of crime has radically changed with the advent of digital technologies.

Indeed, the fact that cyberspace facilitates the rapid, anonymous communication between anyone, anywhere in the world has meant that a variety of traditional crimes can now be perpetrated far more easily in cyberspace. As you explore these issues in the next few chapters, keep in mind the complex stories behind the design and regulation of cyberspace learned in this section. This will help you to think about how these problems can best be dealt with.

QUESTIONS FOR FURTHER THINKING AND DISCUSSION

1. Do you agree with Barlow's vision for the Internet? In what ways was he right or wrong? Does his vision still have relevance today?
2. How does the complex history of the Internet make it more difficult to design a regulatory structure for cyberspace?
3. What are some of the unique ways that crime can be controlled in cyberspace?
4. Why do you think that major corporations such as Microsoft would be interested in supporting a cyber-libertarian organization such as the EFF?
5. Given the cultural, moral, religious and legal variations around the world, do you think it's possible to regulate cyberspace through content-based restrictions alone or do you think that the inherent structure of cyberspace demands that architectural solutions be implemented as well?

PART TWO

TRADITIONAL CRIME IN CYBERSPACE

3

Identity Theft and Cyber Fraud

KEY TERMS AND CONCEPTS

- Autorooters
- Bill S-4
- Botnets
- Browser hijacking
- Business opportunity fraud
- Cash out
- Consumer sentinel
- Counterfieitlibrary
- DNS records
- Email spoofing
- Federal Trade Commission

- Identity theft
- IRC servers
- Keylogging software
- Mass scanning
- Nigerian fraud
- Operation firewall
- Pharming
- Phishing
- Phishing scam
- Phone Busters
- PIPEDA
- Pump and dump
- Pyramid schemes

- ShadowCrew
- Social engineering
- Spyware
- The catch
- The hook
- The lure
- URL Hiding/ Encoding
- Web-based Forums
- Work at home schemes

INTRODUCTION

Over the past few years, identity theft has skyrocketed in North America. What used to be a relatively time-consuming enterprise has become relatively easy and commonplace with the help of the Internet and related technologies. Not long ago, stealing another person's identity was a complicated and difficult task that required a great deal of time and effort to carry out. Today, however, given the proliferation of computer technologies, individuals can gain ready access to their victims and access large amounts of personal information about their intended targets with relative ease. This may be due to a global shift toward online banking and consumer purchases. Indeed, in Canada, as many as 67% of Internet users currently bank online.[1] Bank account credentials are especially attractive to cybercriminals because they can be used to withdraw hard currency.

Cyber-threats are becoming more complex and one of the recent and concerning trends is away from the curious hacker who uses his or her skill for fun and toward greater sophistication. People with technical skills who produce malicious software programs are joining forces with financially motivated criminals who want to steal personal information and financial assets. The underground market in stolen information creates an additional incentive for criminals to perpetrate crimes. The nature and scope of the problem, combined with the fact that victimization tends to be under-reported in this area, have made it difficult to define the extent of the problem. Identity theft techniques range from relatively simple methods, including dumpster-diving and mail theft, to highly complex attacks involving sophisticated software programs. Moreover, given the rapidly evolving nature of technology, identity thieves are constantly developing new tools and techniques to assist them in carrying out their attacks.

WHAT IS FRAUD?

From the outset, it is important to understand that there is a difference between identity theft and identity fraud. **Fraud** is a traditional non-computer crime that has existed for centuries. It involves the use of tools and techniques to defraud people out of their money or property, as well as the fraudulent use of personal information. Identity theft, on the other hand, pertains to the unauthorized collection of personal information.

The *Criminal Code* has long contained a provision targetting fraud, which reads as follows:[2]

380. (1) Every one who, by deceit, falsehood or other fraudulent means, whether or not it is a false pretence within the meaning of this Act, defrauds the public or any person, whether ascertained or not, of any property, money or valuable security or any service,

    (a) is guilty of an indictable offence and liable to a term of imprisonment not exceeding fourteen years, where the subject-matter of the offence is a testamentary instrument or the value of the subject-matter of the offence exceeds five thousand dollars; or

    (b) is guilty

        (i) of an indictable offence and is liable to imprisonment for a term not exceeding two years, or

        (ii) of an offence punishable on summary conviction,

where the value of the subject-matter of the offence does not exceed five thousand dollars.

The explosion of the Internet has given rise to a vast array of illegal activities involving fraud. What began with relatively simple scams has grown exponentially into highly sophisticated and complex activities involving professional software tools and legitimate businesses. The substantial global

---

[1] Symantec, *Report on the Underground Economy*.
[2] R.S.C. 1985, c. C-46.

increase in fraudulent activity may be attributable to significant increases in worldwide Internet access as well as the widespread use and proliferation of the online economy.

One popular category of fraud is in the online retail sale of goods and services, which is commonly known as Internet auction fraud. Many of us are familiar with and have used online commercial auction sites, such as eBay. In recent years, the popularity of these websites has skyrocketed and it is now possible to find an auction site for just about any type of good or service that one could want, from vacations to watches, computers and even luxury automobiles. Given this staggering growth, it is not surprising that there has been an increase in the number of so-called "non-deliverables;" in other words, fraudsters are purporting to offer popular goods and services for sale through online auction sites, allowing bidders to drive up the price by bidding on the items and then failing to deliver the goods. Typically, victims are informed that they are successful bidders, and send their money to the seller, but never receive the promised merchandise. In a variation of this approach, the criminals send counterfeit merchandise in place of the promised goods.

Consumers interested in a particular auction often want to know if other buyers have had negative experiences with the seller. Criminals, however, sometimes use fake favourable information about themselves to make it appear that there are other satisfied customers out there and to give a false sense of security about their products and services. In addition, the winning bidders often provide their personal information and credit card numbers as part of the auction process and this information is sometimes used to commit additional fraud (such as purchasing items over the phone or online) or to commit identity theft (such as selling the information on the online black market).

A more sophisticated version of this scam involves placing banner advertisements on an auction site that offers the same types of goods being auctioned. Prospective buyers who click on the banner advertisement are taken to a different website that is not part of the auction site, and offers none of the protections that leading auction websites provide for their members. Another approach involves using unsolicited commercial email (spam) to lure prospective victims to a website that purports to offer items of the same type that are available through well-known online auction sites.

In retail sales, some criminals have tried to mislead consumers into visiting their websites by making their products or services confusingly similar to those offered by a legitimate company. In doing so, the criminal also hopes to trick customers in order to cash in on the legitimate company's reputation and goodwill. For example, in *United States v. Lee*,[3] the Hawaii Marathon Association operated a website with the URL "www.hawaiimarathon.org" to enable runners to register online. The defendant copied the authorized Marathon website, and created his own site with the confusingly similar name, "www.hawaiimarathon.com." Runners who came to his website thinking that it was the real Hawaii Marathon

---

[3] No. 99-00560 SOM (D. Haw., Dec. 9, 1999).

site were charged a $165 registration fee, which was $100 more than the real site charged for entry.[4]

Pyramid schemes are another example of online fraud that have become prevalent on the Internet. Pyramid scheme operators typically offer enormous earnings or investment returns based on commissions for recruiting new members into the pyramid. Recruitment commissions are based on the continuous supply of new members because those who are recruited to join the bottom of the pyramid must pay a fee, which is then used to pay out those who have reached the top. Inevitably, though, when no more new recruits can be found to join the pyramid, these schemes fall apart and the remaining participants lose the money they invested. Business opportunity **fraud** or "work at home" schemes are also rampant on the Internet. As part of these schemes, con artists offer unsuspecting victims the opportunity to work at home, for a fantastic salary, in exchange for a small processing fee. In many of these cases, victims send money to what they believe to be legitimate businesses, which are actually postal mailboxes operated by scam artists who simply collect the money and disappear!

Another major category of fraud is online investment fraud. The most widely publicized form of online market manipulation is the pump and dump scheme. In a nutshell, these are spam campaigns that attempt to boost the value of a worthless stock by encouraging gullible investors to purchase it. In a typical pump and dump scheme, criminals identify one or more companies, then purchase a large amount of stock with low value. The scammer then sends out spam emails that contain the ticker symbol of the stock, advising recipients to purchase it. The gullible victims purchase the stock in large quantities, causing the price to rise dramatically. The scammer then sells his shares and realizes a quick profit. Subsequently, the stock plummets in value, leaving legitimate investors with substantial financial losses.

Clearly, for a scam of this kind to work, victims must be persuaded to purchase a large amount of stock in a short amount of time. Thus, another notable feature of online market manipulation schemes is the speed with which the scheme's participants can induce dramatic, though short-term, fluctuations in stock prices, and can realize substantial profits by correctly timing their purchases and sales. The typical means used to carry out this scam include posting favourable (but false and misleading) representations on financial message boards or websites, and making undisclosed payments to people who are ostensibly independent but who will recommend the targetted stock.

Lastly, advance fee fraud, which is also called 419 fraud or Nigerian fraud, has grown considerably in recent years.[5] Originally, fraud artists in Nigeria would send unsolicited but official-looking letters to the postal mailboxes of unsuspecting Americans. With the help of the Internet, advance fee fraud

---

[4] The defendant also operated another website where he sold Viagra over the Internet without a prescription. (The defendant later pleaded guilty to wire fraud and unlawful sale of Viagra, and in February 2001 was given a split sentence of ten months imprisonment.)

[5] United States Department of State, "International Financial Scams" Febrary 2007, available online at: http://travel.state.gov/pdf/international_financial_scams_brochure.pdf.

scenarios are constantly evolving, and no longer originate just from Nigeria, but from countries around the globe. However, all of these scams have one thing in common – the victim is led to believe that he or she has a chance to attain something of very great personal value (e.g., financial reward, a romantic relationship, etc.) in return for a small financial payment.

For example, in a common scenario, the scammer and the victim meet online – often through an Internet dating site. The scammer has already set up a fake profile, using pictures from modelling sites. Scammers frequently spend hours and sometimes months chatting with their victims. Thus, as far as the victim is concerned, the scammer really cares about him or her. Once a relationship is established, in a long string of unfortunate events, the fictional boyfriend, girlfriend and/or fiancée claims to be in America and goes to Nigeria on business. The scammer has incredibly bad luck – often getting into car crashes, arrested, mugged, beaten, or hospitalized – usually all within the course of a couple of months. Then, someone needs an operation or hotel owners hold the scammer hostage, and hundreds of dollars are needed to pay the bill. Of course, these bills and bribes need to be paid before the fictional boyfriend or girlfriend can return home and meet the victim in real space.

There are many different versions of this scam, including the next-of-kin scam, tempting you to claim an inheritance of millions of dollars belonging to a long-lost relative, and then asking you for money for various bank and transfer fees. It might surprise you that a large number of vulnerable and naïve people are actually taken in by these scams each year. In fact, the United States Secret Service says it gets 13,000 complaints a month from people who have received these solicitations and it estimates that these schemes have cost Internet users hundreds of millions of dollars annually, with many victims too afraid or embarassed to report their losses.[6]

WHAT IS IDENTITY THEFT?

There is no universally accepted definition of identity theft and the term describes a variety of illegal acts involving the theft or misuse of personal information. Generally speaking, **identity theft** is the illegal use or transfer of a third party's personal information with unlawful intent. It is a traditional crime that existed long before the advent of the Internet; however, identity theft has increased exponentially in recent years and shows no signs of abating. Identity theft is often committed to facilitate other crimes including credit card fraud, computer fraud, mail fraud and fraud targetted at financial institutions.

Online identity theft, in which confidential information is obtained through a computer network and used for profit, is a rapidly growing enterprise. Note that prior to the Internet, a typical case of identity theft involved one person stealing information and then using it for personal gain. Today, technology has facilitated

---

[6] Allan Lengel, "E-Mail Opens New Door for Familiar Scam Tactic" *Washington Post*, April 29, 2002, B01.

the involvement of many people along a chain or continuum of criminal activity. In addition, the expansion and popularity of conducting commercial transactions on the Internet has vastly increased the opportunity to commit crimes involving identity theft. The trend of posting personal information over the Internet has also increased opportunities to obtain private information for illegal means.

A Curious Tale of Mistaken Identity

This case of mistaken identity involves a 72-year-old man named Derek Lloyd Sykes who the FBI was investigating in conjunction with an alleged telemarketing fraud involving millions of dollars in Texas. Since 1989, Sykes had been using the name of a 72-year-old retired engineer named Derek Bond from Bristol England who had never met Sykes and had no connection with him or his crimes. The FBI issued a warrant for the arrest of Sykes, mistakenly using the name of Derek Bond. At the time, the Englishman, Derek Bond, was on a wine tasting holiday in South Africa and he was arrested at gunpoint by South African police, pursuant to the FBI warrant. The police relied on the warrant issued in the name of Derek Bond (the identity Sykes was using) and the two men were the same age and looked similar. The innocent Mr. Bond spent 20 traumatic days in a South African prison before his ordeal ended! It turned out that Mr. Bond was a victim of identity theft. Sykes was soon arrested in Las Vegas in connection with the multi-million dollar fraud.

Figure 3.1: Identity Theft Complaints in Canada (2006)

JURISDICTION	VICTIMS	LOSSES IN $
AB	612	$1,439,474.29
BC	1,190	$2,035,365.27
MB	249	$151,860.16
NB	67	$92,396.07
NL	29	$30,107.04
NU	1	$0
NWT	7	$3,102.62
ON	3,353	$7,584,188.86
PEI	11	$17,059.00
QC	2,040	$4,674,504.44
SK	94	$61,192.28
YK	7	$2,379.23
UNKNOWN	12	$3,102.62
TOTALS	**7,778**	**$16,283,776.91**

Identity Theft Facts and Figures

In 2008, Phone Busters reported 12,142 identity-theft complaints in Canada and losses amounting to $9,590,385 (see Figure 3.1 for a breakdown by Province in 2006). In 2008, identity theft attempts increased by 9.9 million, or 22%, over the previous year in the United States. The Canadian Council of Better Business Bureaus states that identity theft is the fastest growing type of fraud in North America with losses in the billions of dollars each year. It also estimates that identity theft may cost Canadian consumers, banks and credit card companies, stores and other businesses more than $2 billion annually.

How Does Identity Theft Happen?

As discussed earlier, identity theft techniques include relatively unsophisticated methods, such as dumpster-diving or searching through garbage, to shoulder-surfing, which involves the careless sharing of personal information or listening-in on a person's phone calls or peering over a person's shoulder when they type sensitive information into their laptop. It also includes the theft of:

- personal information by employees (also known as insider threats),

- portable computers or laptops,

- pre-approved credit solicitations and cheques from an individual's mail box or garbage and

- skimming and ATM manipulation, which involves reading and recording personal information encoded on the magnetic strip of credit or ATM cards.

It is noteworthy that as USB memory keys, portable hard drives, laptops and cell phones have become smaller and less expensive, their compact size and vast storage capacity has increased the risk of loss and theft. A single device can contain personal information about millions of people, which makes them highly susceptible targets for identity theft.

More elaborate identity theft techniques include the use of keyloggers, phishing and pharming, which are discussed in detail later in this chapter. In addition, **bots**, which are programs that are covertly installed on a user's machine to allow an attacker to remotely control it, are also being used to distribute phishing attacks and spyware, and to harvest confidential information from victims. Unfortunately, these techniques are inexpensive and easy to implement, particularly given the wealth of information and resources provided about such schemes in the underground economy. Each of these techniques is explained in further detail. Note, as well, that the underground economy also specializes in the sale of stolen personal information. As such, identity theft can include the theft of an individual's password or credit card information to the trafficking in whole identities.

Costs of Identity Theft

Identity theft continues to be a very significant security issue, particularly for organizations that store large amounts of personal information. Based on data available for 2007, approximately 8.4 million American residents were victims of identity theft, which is roughly 3% of the total population.[7] Victims of identity theft may suffer significant financial loss as well as damage to their reputation or credit rating. There may be losses associated with the time, expense and emotional stress incurred to recover losses. These problems are compounded by the fact that it can take months or even years for individuals to discover that they have been targetted and victimized by identity thieves.

Almost a third of households that have experienced identity theft discovered it by missing money or noticing unfamiliar charges on an account. In fact, the most common problem encountered by victims of identity theft is being contacted by a debt collector or creditor about banking problems or issues with credit card accounts. The delayed notification or awareness of victimization necessarily means that many cases of identity theft are unreported, as victims may believe that there is little, if anything, that can be done to catch an online identity thief once he or she has gotten away and vanished into the ether, so to speak.

Similar concerns arise for government and business, which can suffer financial loss and damaged reputations as a result of identity theft. There may be significant losses in terms of the cost of lost merchandise and time and money spent trying to prevent and then investigate and respond to identity thefts. A business can suffer a loss of customers as well as damage to its reputation and decline in its share price. Consumer confidence may be shaken and consumers might be wary of engaging in similar kinds of online transactions again.

For small companies that do the majority of their business online, these negative effects can be devastating. The need to deal with the security breach can also be costly for a company, which may need to notify customers and set up a call centre to field angry calls from irate customers. Given their limited resources and small number of employees, small businesses often have an especially difficult time dealing with the financial costs of identity theft and working with law enforcement officials to investigate the crimes. Company executives and managers might also fear the emergence of copycat attacks if news of the attack becomes public. As such, company officials might decide to handle the matter internally and not involve the police.

However, the lack of reporting has an effect upon our ability to understand the nature of this crime and develop best practices methods. This makes it difficult for policy-makers to get a sense of how significant the problem is and how to best address it. It also might be why Canada has been so slow to enact legislation to specifically target identity theft. In fact, until late in 2009, there were no *Criminal Code* offences targeting the preparatory stages of identity theft. This is discussed in further detail later in this chapter.

---

[7] Symantec, *Global Internet Security Threat Report, 2009* at 19.

THE UNDERGROUND ECONOMY

As mentioned earlier in this chapter, the widespread proliferation of identity theft has led to the creation of a robust underground economy for the trading of stolen information, as well as the purchase and sale of rogue software programs. Indeed, the primary focus of the underground economy is to inflict damage on or steal money from the general population of Internet users.[8] Two of the most common platforms available to participants in the online underground economy are channels on **Internet Relay Chat servers** and Web-based forums.[9] Both feature discussion groups that participants use to buy and sell goods and services – sometimes fraudulently.

Potential buyers for advertised goods and services will privately contact the sellers to negotiate the deal and finalize payment. The seller will usually arrange to forward the goods to the buyer upon payment, options for which include using online currency exchange services or the exchange of goods. Many purchasers also use the services of experienced cashiers, who convert the stolen goods into real currency, either through money transfers or online currency exchange. This is commonly known as the **cash out**.

It is noteworthy that there are a number of prominent groups and organizations that have been active in the trade of fraudulent goods and services in the underground economy. The Internet enables these individuals to connect with each other and trade their knowledge and expertise, as well as to buy and sell fraudulent and stolen goods and services. These networks are powerful and extend across jurisdictional boundaries. Note that these networks function in a similar way to the forums established by pedophiles to trade child pornography, as I will discuss in Chapter 4.

In the case of fraud and identity theft, it is also important to observe that the members of these underground networks are frequent participants in sophisticated organized crime operations. For example, one of the first groups to gain significant attention as a Web forum for online fraud was **ShadowCrew**. The members of ShadowCrew spanned many countries, including the United States, Bulgaria, Canada, Sweden and Poland.[10] This international gang with thousands of members focused on online identity theft and ran a website known as Counterfeitlibrary, which offered information and discussions about forgery, identity theft and credit card fraud.[11] They also offered advice and tutorials on a wide range of fraud-related topics including how to obscure the source of an attack using proxies and how to spam. The group was active until 2004, when its key members were arrested as part of an 18-month international sting operation known as Operation Firewall. In total, there were 28 members arrested in eight American states and

---

[8] James Graham, Rick Howard, Ralph Thomas and Steve Winterfeld, *Cyberfraud: Tactics, Techniques and Procedures* (Boca Raton: CRC Press/Taylor & Francis, 2009) at 11.

[9] Symantec, *supra*, note 1.

[10] David Cole and Sourabh Satish, "Crimeware Business Models" in *Crimeware*, Markus Jakobsson and Zulfikar Ramzan (eds.) (Upper Saddle River, NJ: Addison-Wesley, 2008) at 356.

[11] Symantec, *supra*, note 1 at 9.

six countries, and 1.7 million stolen credit cards were also recovered, along with log-in information for more than 18 million email accounts.[12]

ShadowCrew had administrators and contacts who operated throughout the United States and Eastern Europe and the content on their website was available in both English and Russian. Many of the participants in these forums also use nicknames, which is similar to the hacking subculture discussed in Chapter 7, and may give them a sense of security in that they believe they are less likely to be apprehended. It may also help them to feel as though they are the privileged members of a private club. Many arrests and indictments of participants in the underground economy suggest that they are scattered throughout Eastern Europe and North America. The fact that Internet attacks are becoming increasingly sophisticated, as well as located within both developed and developing countries, suggests that there is a growing need for international cooperation to address the organization of rogue groups on the Internet.

Stolen personal information sold through the underground economy includes credit card data, bank account information, email accounts and other information that can be exploited for profit. The forums also provide a means for users to buy, sell and trade stolen information and fraud-related services. Services can include cashiers who transfer funds from stolen accounts into true currency, phishing and scam page hosting, and job advertisements for roles such as scam developers or phishing partners. It is also important to keep in mind that there are a number of malicious tools being sold in the online underground economy that provide access to identities, credentials, hacked hosts and other exploits. Individuals can be hired to find vulnerabilities in a specific target, which could include, for example, a particular software application, operating system or piece of hardware. If the vulnerability is found in a wide-reaching system, it can be used to deliver spam, spyware or adware, which can be used for both malicious purposes and monetary gain.

Attack kits include tools that automatically scan and exploit Web vulnerabilities to sophisticated botnets. They can be used to perpetrate denial of service (DoS) attacks, spam and phishing campaigns and finding vulnerabilities in Web servers and websites. There are a number of Russian-made hacking toolkits available that exploit Web browser vulnerabilities and install malware. In addition, there are other toolkits that are popular for setting up fraudulent schemes, such as phishing attacks.

A botnet can be especially valuable because it can enable an attacker to control a network of exploited computers, launch a DoS attack, harvest information or conduct spam or phishing campaigns. It can also generate revenue for the cybercriminal, since it can be rented out for a specific attack or on a periodic basis. SQL injection attack tools are also popular with the underground economy because it can enable attackers to steal sensitive information stored within the databases behind websites, and can also let attackers bypass log-in or other authentication requirements and manipulate website content. As I discuss in Chapter 6, this can enable the attacker to launch other attacks from the

---

[12] Cole and Satish, *supra*, note 10 at 356.

compromised site. Other popular products offered for sale in the underground economy include spam and phishing kits, as well as banking Trojans, backdoors, keystroke loggers and password stealers, all of which can generate significant income for the attackers.

Given that all of these activities are highly illegal, both the seller and purchaser of these goods must ensure that they will not be detected and apprehended by law enforcement. Therefore, much of the activity on the underground economy appears to originate in countries without robust cyber-security laws, such as Russia and the Ukraine rather than in North America or the European Union.[13] The fact that there are so many underground websites and IRC rooms created for putting the sellers and purchasers of malicious and fraudulent goods together makes it easier for these individuals to network with each other away from the purview of law enforcement.

Information Targets

Credit cards advertised for sale on the underground economy include the credit card number and expiry date, and may also include the name on the card, the billing address, phone number and PIN. One of the reasons that credit cards are among the most popular goods advertised for sale on the underground economy is that there are many ways that credit card information can be obtained and used for fraud. These include phishing schemes, monitoring merchant card authorizations, the use of magnetic stripe skimmers or breaking into databases and other data breaches that expose sensitive information. Credit cards are also used very frequently in North America and are the most popular payment method. For example, there were 22 billion credit card transactions in the United States in 2006.[14] Making online purchases is also relatively easy. Online shopping can be simple and fast, and a final sale often requires just credit card information.

Financial accounts, the second most popular target for sale on the underground economy, includes bank account credentials, online currency accounts, online payment services and online stock trading accounts. These accounts are popular with fraud artists because currency can be directly withdrawn from them. Spam and phishing information is the third ranked category of advertised goods and services for sale because they are very effective toward surreptitiously gathering credit card information and access to financial accounts. This information can be sold on the black market for financial gain, thus helping the underground economy, and it can also be used to victimize ordinary users, or traded with other criminals for new malicious software programs or phishing toolkits.

It is noteworthy that while the online credit card fraud market has evolved significantly in the last several years, a number of high-profile law enforcement investigations have caused many of the once notorious actors in this business to go underground. As such, much of the communication about credit card fraud is now conducted on more secretive and obscure underground channels, such as

---

[13] Graham, et al., *supra*, note 8 at 12.

[14] Symantec, *supra*, note 1 at 17.

instant messaging services and secure email; however, these forums continue to serve important networking and business-related functions, such as providing information about how to commit credit card fraud and connecting those in the illicit credit card fraud world with one another. It is also important to keep in mind that rogue groups are also producing and distributing customized malicious code and phishing kits, as well as hosting malicious websites, which has led to a substantial increase in the proliferation of malicious code during the past couple of years.

PHISHING

The word **phishing** comes from the analogy that Internet scammers are using email lures to "fish" for passwords and financial data from the sea of Internet users. Phishing is primarily carried out for financial gain. It is one of the most popular cyber-attacks committed today.

Phishing is a form of identity theft that occurs on the Internet that originated in the early 1990s. It is a well-known technique that involves setting up a fraudulent website that is designed to look like it is the website of a trusted financial institution or some other legitimate entity. Phishers have become increasingly adept at luring end users to their phishing sites.

During a phishing scam, an attacker attempts to retrieve a user's confidential information by mimicking communications from a trustworthy organization. The email sent to the user urges him or her to click on a link to the fraudulent site (for example, by threatening account closure). The fraudulent website records the information entered by the victim (such as the log-in and password or credit card information and bank account credentials) and then transmits it back to the attacker, who either uses it to steal money from the victim or sell the information to other like-minded criminals using the underground economy. This method of attack has been made easier by the relatively recent proliferation of online banking. In other words, users who are accustomed to conducting their banking online may be more easily fooled into entering their personal information into fraudulent websites that mimic the look and feel of trusted financial services providers.

The increase in phishing websites is also motivated by the continued popularity of phishing toolkits. These kits, which are offered for sale on the underground economy, enable phishers to carry out their attacks much more easily by automatically creating websites that mimic those of trusted financial institutions. In fact, a phishing toolkit is simply a set of scripts that allow an attacker to automatically create websites with the look and feel of legitimate brands, including the images and logos associated with them. These kits are developed by individuals or groups of individuals who sell them in the underground economy. Attackers are therefore able to perpetrate these scams with minimal effort and technical sophistication.

How Is Phishing Carried Out?

There are three basic phases in the phishing process.

1. *The Lure*: A phisher typically spams a large number of users with an email message. The email is designed to con or scare the user into following a URL hyperlink embedded in the email to a website controlled by the phisher. Keep in mind, though, that email is not the only kind of lure used – it's just the easiest!
2. *The Hook*: A website mimics the look and feel of a genuine institution (designed to convince the user of its legitimacy). Victims are tricked into entering passwords or account information to avoid disruption or cancellation of service.
3. *The Catch*: The phisher makes use of the collected information for some harmful purpose, such as fraud or identity theft.

Making the Lure Convincing

Social engineering is a well-known term for the art of conning someone into doing something they wouldn't ordinarily do (e.g., revealing passwords or PIN). This is a favourite tool of those who seek to target innocent victims through online phishing campaigns. The phisher provides a plausible reason or incentive for the user to click on the hyperlink provided in the spam email. Examples include network or account security upgrades (e.g., "If you don't update your account information for our network security upgrade, your account will be terminated."); financial incentives/rewards (e.g., "We will give $50 to the first lucky participants in our online survey"); and the threat of account closure.

It is interesting to note that phishers and other online fraud artists frequently use current events to help them swindle unsuspecting consumers. For example, in financially-troubled times, phishers often prey upon the public's vulnerability and desperation, such as by spoofing well-known financial institutions and offering low interest loans. In fact, the majority of phishing attacks in 2008 pretended to be from legitimate businesses operating in the financial services sector, hoping to gather information for financially motivated attacks or for sale on the underground economy.[15]

In another recent example, a group of Latvian criminals scammed the Vancouver Olympic Organizing Committee (VANOC) and ticket sellers on the fan-to-fan Olympics website for close to $2 million at the end of the 2010 Winter Games.[16] The group used fake credit cards to purchase tickets from Olympic fans online, just as hordes of people were scrambling to get tickets to the hockey finals, as well as other high-profile events. Two Latvian nationals with links to organized crime pleaded guilty in a Vancouver court to fraud over $5,000 in connection with the bogus transactions.

---

[15] Symantec, *Global Internet Security Threat Report, 2008* at 74.
[16] Sarah Boesveld, "Latvian Criminals Scammed VANOC Ticket System for $2-million," *Globe and Mail*, May 19, 2010, available online at: http://www.theglobeandmail.com.

Technical Tricks

Phishing employs a large number of specialized techniques to appear legitimate or to take advantage of victims.

- *Email spoofing*: Attackers make the sender of the email appear to be different from the actual sender's identity. Note that a large percentage of spam today is sent by phishers and uses email spoofing.

- *Mass Scanning*: Systems are now being compromised by automated tools referred to as autorooters. Autorooters scan Internet Protocol (IP) address ranges searching for vulnerable systems to exploit.[17]

- *URL Hiding/Encoding*: Phishers make the URL look official and legitimate (e.g., www.citibank.com is spoofed as citibank.mycitibank.com to appear to be a URL from a trusted source). It is also possible for the phisher to spoof URLs. One such technique involves using JavaScript that hides the URL window at the top of the browser with a graphic or text that resembles the URL for the website being spoofed.

- *Domain Name Server (DNS) Hijacking*: The attacker can gain access to the Domain Name System records on a server and modify them so requests for the real Web page are redirected to a fake page the attacker created. Or, the attacker can register a similarly confusing name.

- *Browser Hijacking*: The attacker changes Web browser settings to switch home pages or hijack search functions.

- *Browser Hijacker*: This type of malware program is used to alter your computer's browser settings so you are redirected to the attacker's websites.

- *Redirection*: A technique of moving visitors to a different site when its address has been changed – often used with browser hijacking.

- *Spyware*: Hidden programs that can record your keystrokes and obtain log-in ID/financial information. For example, one of the most sophisticated types of spyware is keylogging software that automatically installs itself in the victim's computer and records keystrokes.

- *Botnets*: Networks of computers that have been infected by malicious code can be used to distribute phishing emails.

PHARMING

Pharming is an advanced form of phishing that redirects the connection between an IP address (the consumer seeking a legitimate site) and its target (the legitimate site). This can be accomplished with malicious programs (e.g., hijackers and redirectors) that redirect users' network traffic to other sites. The

---

17 David Watson, Thorsten Holz and Sven Mueller, "Know Your Enemy: Phishing," available online at: http://www.honeynet.org/papers/phishing/.

link is altered so consumers are unwittingly redirected to another site. This is similar to a phishing attack because it is designed to extract confidential data from victims by pretending to be from a trusted source.

The difference between pharming and phishing, however, is that pharming attacks redirect the victim's DNS to a malicious server when attempting to visit a legitimate website, whereas phishing attacks trick users to visit malicious websites through the use of social engineering techniques. Pharming can also involve DNS cache poisoning in which an attacker modifies the DNS server's cache so that it will point to the malicious address rather than the legitimate one.

SPYWARE

Spyware is any technology that aids in gathering information about a person or organization without knowledge or consent. It operates secretly, hoping not to be noticed by the user whose machine has been invaded. The most common use for these programs is to steal confidential information, by recording keystrokes (i.e., keylogging), as well as websites visited by the user. Spyware is commonly sold commercially as it has the potential for non-criminal use.[18] It can be lawfully used by an employer to conduct surveillance of employees, particularly where harmful or malicious activity is suspected. For example, Hewlett-Packard (HP) used spyware to help it investigate a leak from its corporate employees to CNet reporters.[19] Spyware and trojan horse programs were used to infiltrate the reporters' computers to figure out who was the source of the leak.[20] It can also be used by law enforcement officials as part of their investigations. Thus, we can understand spyware as technology that is not inherently bad but that contains the potential for misuse by those who intend to cause harm.[21]

KEYSTROKE LOGGING SOFTWARE

Keystroke loggers, or key-loggers, are software programs (a form of spyware, as discussed above) that record each key typed on the victim's keyboard. With keylogging software installed on the victim's machine (often delivered as executable (.exe) files attached to emails or installed as hardware), the phisher can wait for the user to visit a website (e.g., a legitimate banking or e-commerce site) and steal the username and password. After keystrokes are logged, they can be hidden in the machine for later retrieval or periodically transmitted to the attacker via the Internet.

In its 2008 *Global Internet Security Report*, Symantec observed that more often now than in the past, attackers are focusing on stealing information and compromising users for financial gain. For example, in 2008, 78% of confidential

---

[18] Cole and Satish, *supra*, note 10 at 367.
[19] *Ibid* at 371.
[20] *Ibid*.
[21] *Ibid* at 367.

information threats exported user data and 76% used a keystroke-logging program to steal personal information from the victim, such as online banking credentials. Keep in mind that once attackers obtain financial data or other personal information, they frequently sell it on the underground economy.

POLICY APPROACHES TO IDENTITY THEFT

It should be apparent that while effective laws to combat cybercrime are essential, they are only part of the solution. Their effectiveness is directly related to how they are interpreted and enforced. In addition, legal measures must also be supported by adequate resources and effective education. Of course, governments and businesses are the most important actors in the battle against identity theft. Both governments and businesses can develop effective internal policies and procedures to protect their assets and keep their employees safe from victimization.

In addition, the government can respond by developing effective identity theft policies. It is particularly important that the Canadian government recently enacted the first national identity theft statute. In addition, consumer education, victim assistance and research are critical to combatting identity theft. Companies that issue debit and credit cards, as well as Canadian banks, ISPs, retailers and consumer reporting agencies can also have a major impact upon fraud and identity theft prevention by fostering effective consumer education and awareness practices.

One of the major challenges faced by law enforcement agencies in their effort to combat identity theft is the fact that there is often a large geographic gap between the victim and the identity thief. This problem is highlighted by the fact that there is now a robust underground economy in stolen identity information, which connects like-minded individuals from around the world. Tracking down those responsible for the crime and prosecuting the offender is particularly challenging when the victim and the attacker are in completely different countries on opposite sides of the world!

In these cases, law enforcement officials must deal with multiple jurisdictions that may have completely different laws or legal systems. Some businesses or law enforcement agencies might refuse to cooperate or provide valuable evidence unless they are required to do so by their local laws, through the use of search warrants and the like. This means that Canadian law enforcement officials are routinely faced with the added challenge of seeking information-sharing and cooperation with other agencies and organizations outside of Canada.

Another problem with our ability to combat identity theft is the fact that criminals are using increasingly sophisticated technological tools to perpetrate their crimes and hide from the authorities. Identity thieves now use the Internet for a wide range of sophisticated activities, including trafficking in personal information and credit card data. The robust underground economy in fraud-related information and activities provides criminals with an additional layer of protection and anonymity, especially for those who take advantage of highly sophisticated technological tools offered for sale, such as keystroke loggers and botnets.

The result is that many identity theft cases are unsolved because it is simply too difficult to catch all of the sophisticated and well-organized criminals in the inter-jurisdictional realm of cyberspace. These problems are further compounded by the fact that many police officers do not have the technical knowledge and expertise, as part of their training, to deal with these kinds of cases. And even where police officers do receive the necessary training, they often lack the technological resources, time and manpower needed to deal with these highly sophisticated cybercriminals operating from within multiple jurisdictions through the Internet. Key challenges include the difficulty in gathering evidence and networking with law enforcement officials in other jurisdictions to share information and resources.

One of the most significant initiatives launched in Canada to counter identity theft is PhoneBusters, which was launched in 1993 by the Ontario Provincial Police to counter telemarketing fraud. Since then, the RCMP and the federal Competition Bureau have become partners in this initiative. PhoneBusters is the central agency in Canada for the collection of information about telemarketing, fraud and identity theft. It also educates consumers and tracks consumer complaints about mass marketing, telemarketing and identity theft scams.

LEGISLATION

Prior to the enactment of the new identity theft legislation, which is discussed later in this section, the *Criminal Code* did not contain any specific identity theft offence. The only provision that could be used to counter this type of crime was the fraud provision, which is set out below. With the exception of the offences dealing with computers (s. 342.1) and devices to obtain computer service (s. 342.2), the *Code* offences relating to property and theft predate computer technology and the Internet. The relevant provisions read as follows:

Unauthorized use of computer
342.1 (1) Every one who, fraudulently and without colour of right,
        (a) obtains, directly or indirectly, any computer service,
        (b) by means of an electro-magnetic, acoustic, mechanical or other device, intercepts or causes to be intercepted, directly or indirectly, any function of a computer system,
        (c) uses or causes to be used, directly or indirectly, a computer system with intent to commit an offence under paragraph (a) or (b) or an offence under section 430 in relation to data or a computer system, or
        (d) uses, possesses, traffics in or permits another person to have access to a computer password that would enable a person to commit an offence under paragraph (a), (b) or (c)
is guilty of an indictable offence and liable to imprisonment for a term not exceeding ten years, or is guilty of an offence punishable on summary conviction.

Possession of device to obtain computer service
342.2 (1) Every person who, without lawful justification or excuse, makes, possesses, sells, offers for sale or distributes any instrument or device or any

component thereof, the design of which renders it primarily useful for committing an offence under section 342.1, under circumstances that give rise to a reasonable inference that the instrument, device or component has been used or is or was intended to be used to commit an offence contrary to that section,

> (a) is guilty of an indictable offence and liable to imprisonment for a term not exceeding two years; or
>
> (b) is guilty of an offence punishable on summary conviction.

Forfeiture

(2) Where a person is convicted of an offence under subsection (1), any instrument or device, in relation to which the offence was committed or the possession of which constituted the offence, may, in addition to any other punishment that may be imposed, be ordered forfeited to Her Majesty, whereupon it may be disposed of as the Attorney General directs.

There have been few prosecutions under s. 342.1 or 342.2 in the context of identity theft. In *R. v. Singh*,[22] the accused pled guilty to three offences related to capturing debit card information and associated personal identification numbers under s. 342.2 of the *Code*. He had installed a digital video recorder hard drive, debit card reader (or skimmer, which is used to capture and store the electronic account data encoded on the magnetic strip of a bank card) and cameras in three gas stations to duplicate the debit card information and videotape customers as they entered their PINs. The information was then misused and financial institutions were defrauded for more than $92,000. The court found that the circumstances of the crimes were serious and warranted incarceration. As such, Singh was sentenced to 20 months imprisonment.

In *R. v. Huynen*,[23] the accused police officer accessed the Canadian Police Information Centre system several times for his own personal use to check on individuals at the request of a friend. An individual named Sokalski, who was allegedly involved in the drug trade, had lost money and wanted to recover it by locating the individuals responsible. He got his friend, McPake, to use his connections, including Huynen, to attempt to locate them. The Crown alleged the accused knew or ought to have known about Sokalski's activities, and despite that fact used his position as a police officer to check information for McPake, some of which he knew or ought to have known would or could go back to Sokalsksi.

Huynen was convicted of illegal use of a computer and fined $1,000. The court found that he knew or ought to have known the potentially devastating impact that this information might have had in the wrong hands for the wrong purpose. Aggravating circumstances included the number of searches and the length of time over which they were conducted. Although Huynen had no prior record and had already lost his job and his chosen profession, there were aspects of denunciation and deterrence that were to be reflected in the sentence.

This case can be contrasted with *U.S. v. Czubinski*.[24] In that case, the accused was an employee of the Internal Revenue Service (IRS). In order to perform his

---

[22] (2006), 2006 CarswellAlta 746, [2006] A.J. No. 686 (Alta. Prov. Ct.).

[23] (December 12, 2006), [2006] M.J. No. 475, Wyant C.J. (Man. Prov. Ct.).

[24] 106 F.3d 1069 (C.A.1 (Mass.), 1997).

duties, which mainly involved answering questions from taxpayers regarding their returns, Czubinski routinely accessed income tax return information about taxpayers from one of the IRS's computer systems. In 1992, he carried out a number of unauthorized searches of these files, looking at income tax information relating to various friends, acquaintances and political rivals. He was later convicted of nine counts of wire fraud and four counts of computer fraud for accessing and reading this confidential information.[25] The Appeals Court overturned the convictions on the basis that Czubinski merely satisfied his curiosity by viewing the income tax records and there was no evidence that he actually printed out, recorded or used the information he browsed. In other words, the mere browsing of the records of people about whom he had a personal interest was not reprehensible enough to sustain a conviction for computer or wire fraud.

There is also an offence in the *Code* that deals with mischief in relation to data, which reads as follows:

Mischief in relation to data
430 (1.1) Every one commits mischief who willfully
    (a) destroys or alters data;
    (b) renders data meaningless, useless or ineffective;
    (c) obstructs, interrupts or interferes with the lawful use of data; or
    (d) obstructs, interrupts or interferes with any person in the lawful use of data or denies access to data to any person who is entitled to access thereto.

. . .

(8) In this section, "data" has the same meaning as in section 342.1.

However, this provision has not been used to prosecute anyone in Canada for committing fraud or identity theft.

As we have seen, the Internet has facilitated the unauthorized collection, possession and trafficking of personal information for the purpose of both current and future criminal activity. There has been an increasing need for Parliament to address these problems. *Bill S-4, An Act to Amend the Criminal Code (Identity Theft and Related Misconduct)* received Royal Assent on October 22, 2009.[26] It creates several new *Criminal Code* offences targetting those aspects of identity theft not already covered. Note that there was no identity theft offence prior to this. More specifically, it focuses on the preparatory stages of identity theft by making it an offence to obtain, possess, transfer or sell the identity documents of another person. The key provisions of this legislation are as follows:

- *Clause 1*: Adds section 56.1(1) to (4) of the *Code* – making, possessing, transferring, offering or selling "identity documents" of another person (up to 5 years in jail).

- *Clause 10*: Identity Information – for someone to be found guilty of identity theft, the prosecution must prove that he or she knowingly obtained or possessed another person's "identity information." The bill defines identity

---

[25] Under 18 U.S.C. 1030 (a)(4).
[26] S.C. 2009, c. 28.

information as "any information – including biological or physiological information – of a type that is commonly used, alone or in combination with other information, to identify or purport to identify an individual." The new s. 402.1 of the *Code* gives examples of identity information: name; address; date of birth; written, electronic or digital signature; social insurance number, health insurance or driver's licence number; credit or debit card number; number of an account at a financial institution; passport number; user code; password; fingerprint or voice print; retina or iris image; and DNA profile.

- *Clause 10*: Adds s. 402.2(2) of the *Code* – transmitting, making available, distributing, selling, offering for sale or possessing another person's "identity information" (up to 5 years in jail).

- *Clauses 4 and 5*: Add ss. 342(3) and 342.01(1) of the *Code* – fraudulent use or possession or trafficking of credit card data and knowingly possessing, importing or exporting devices that can be used to fraudulently copy credit card data (up to 10 years in jail).

- *Clause 8*: Adds ss. 368(1)(c) and (d) of the *Code* – using forged documents as if they were genuine, selling/making available forged documents, possessing forged documents with the intent to use them (up to 10 years in jail).

- *Clause 9*: Adds s. 368.1 of the *Code* – dealing in devices used to create forged documents (up to 14 years in jail).

Privacy Legislation

Although Canada only recently enacted legislation to deal with the problem of identity theft, privacy legislation already existed with respect to private sector organizations that collect, use or disclose personal information in the course of commercial activities. There are, in fact, a number of provisions in the Personal Information Protection and Electronic Documents Act (PIPEDA)[27] that can significantly reduce the risk of identity theft by placing limits on the collection, use and disclosure of personal information.

PIPEDA requires organizations engaged in commercial activities to adopt a number of safeguards with respect to the personal information they collect. Personal information is defined in the Act as "information about an identifiable individual, but does not include the name, title, or business address or telephone number of an employee of an organization."

Specifically, it requires organizations to comply with ten principles set out in the Model Code (Schedule 1), which include:

1. collection limitation (the parties should limit how information is collected and collection must be with consent and knowledge that the information is being collected);
2. data quality (the data must be accurate and relevant);

---

[27] S.C. 2000, c. 5.

3. purpose specification (the party must specify the purpose for which the information will be collected);
4. use limitation (once information is collected for one purpose it cannot be used for another purpose, unless the individual consents or this is authorized by law);
5. security safeguards (the information must be secured from risk, e.g., from attacks by hackers);
6. openness (transparency, i.e., the individual should know what is being done with his or her information);
7. individual participation (the individual should have access to his or her information and be able to look at it and correct inaccuracies); and
8. accountability (there must be an oversight mechanism).

Note also that PIPEDA imposes limits upon how long an organization can retain personal information. This means that even if personal information is collected with the consent of the individual, it cannot be stored in perpetuity. This helps to reduce the risk of identity theft by making it clear that organizations should get rid of information that they no longer need.

DATA BREACH NOTIFICATION LEGISLATION

In mid-July 2010, the British Columbia Lottery Corporation's online casino, PlayNow.com, was shut down hours after it was launched. The reason was that the personal information of more than 130 people was inadvertently shared with other customers on the website. The problem was apparently caused by a data crossover that made the names, contact information and, in some cases, credit card and banking information visible to other gamblers.

This incident should be the tipping point in the discussion of notification and data breach, not because it was so damaging, but because our governments hold a wide variety of data about us of enormous scope and scale. Currently, there is no unified mandatory reporting system at the federal and provincial levels for private or public sector data breaches. As a result, estimates about the magnitude and frequency of data breaches are based largely on speculation; and, more importantly, individuals are not always told about compromises in the confidentiality or integrity of data containing their sensitive personal information, which can cause substantial harm, embarrassment and expense in the long term.

On May 1, 2010, Alberta became the first province to implement new mandatory breach notification requirements. The *Personal Information Protection Act* (PIPA)[28] requires organizations to notify the Alberta Privacy Commissioner of a loss, theft or unauthorized disclosure of personal information, outlining the circumstances of the breach and the personal information that was lost, along with an assessment of the risk of harm to individuals, and how many people are likely to be affected. Organizations must also state what they have done to reduce the risk of harm and notify victims.

---

[28] S.A. 2003, c. P-6.5.

Unfortunately, PIPA has some teeth, but not many, when applied to private sector data breaches, and it has no application to government organizations whatsoever. In fact, the legislation only requires organizations to report a breach where "a reasonable person would consider that there exists a real risk of significant harm to an individual as a result of the loss or unauthorized access or disclosure." Where this real risk threshold lies is anybody's guess.

While, of course, nothing prevents an organization from notifying third parties directly when there has been a loss or theft of their personal information, private organizations in Alberta can establish the legal definition of a real risk of significant harm based on what they consider to be important, or merely business as usual. Since these decisions are made in secret, and given that there are few reasons why an organization would want to come forward and subject itself to onerous duties and penalties, not to mention the fact that notifications might drain profits and generate bad publicity, we may find that they are not self-triggering their notification requirements. This is concerning because there are valid public policy reasons why accountability and transparency are needed: we want to know that breaches are occurring so policy-makers aren't forced to rely on anecdote alone; and we also want to provide incentives for organizations to be proactive about preventing security breaches.

As discussed, the Canadian government has done little to mandate data breach notification at the federal level. As noted, while PIPEDA requires businesses to notify consumers when their personal information is breached, it adopts the same approach taken in Alberta, allowing a private organization to determine whether or not to even disclose a breach, depending on whether there's a real risk of significant harm.

PIPA and PIPEDA are on the right track toward implementing a long-overdue notification regime. However, Parliament needs to implement a broader regulatory initiative with the right carrots and sticks in mind. For example, organizations should be encouraged to implement effective access controls and security programs, ensuring that risks are understood and managed. Since both public and private organizations are concerned about negative publicity, a notification regime is likely to be effective at securing cooperation in this respect. And, of course, Parliament should give far less discretion to these entities in determining whether disclosure should occur at all.

IDENTITY THEFT POLICIES AND LEGISLATION IN THE UNITED STATES

Since 1998, the **Federal Trade Commission (FTC)** has been the lead federal agency for combatting identity theft. It is responsible for gathering information about identity theft and for tracking identity theft complaints. Victims of identity theft and fraud can also contact a nationwide hotline to report their problems and receive information. Complaints are entered into the Data Clearinghouse, which is shared electronically with law enforcement agencies nationwide through the **Consumer Sentinel** project. Canada's PhoneBusters is a key partner of this initiative and some other Canadian law enforcement agencies also have access to the Consumer Sentinel. The FTC also provides resources to identity theft victims in the United States and conducts training sessions for law enforcement.

The United States also has a powerful legislative framework for dealing with the problem of identity theft. The *Identity Theft and Assumption Deterrence Act of 1998,*[29] which was enacted in 1998, criminalizes the unauthorized use of another person's identity and provides for penalties of up to 15 years imprisonment and a maximum fine of $250,000 (USD). In 2004, President Bush signed the *Identity Theft Penalty Enhancement Act*[30] that prescribes prison sentences for those who use identity theft to commit other serious crimes, such as terrorism. The law establishes the offence of aggravated identity theft. Those convicted of aggravated identity theft must serve an additional mandatory 2-year prison term. For example, if someone is convicted of mail fraud in a case involving stolen personal information, judges now impose two sentences, one for mail fraud and one for aggravated identity theft. Judges are also not allowed to let those convicted of aggravated identity theft serve their sentence on probation.

Note also that *The Fair and Accurate Credit Transactions Act*[31] requires consumer reporting agencies to comply with the demands of a consumer to place a fraud alert on his or her file when the consumer believes he or she is about to become the victim of identity theft. When a fraud alert is placed on the victim's file, the consumer reporting agency must provide two copies of the consumer's credit report free of charge. The Act also prohibits consumer reporting agencies from reporting negative information about the consumer resulting from identity theft. It is also noteworthy that California has gone farther than other states to combat identity theft and help victims.[32] The state passed a law that obligates businesses to protect confidential information, confirm the identity of those to whom they extend credit, and notify customers of breaches in security affecting personal information. To date, as many as 44 states have implemented data breach notification laws.

A number of cases have come before the United States courts involving identity theft; however, no court has considered the increased risk of identity theft to constitute harm or injury. In other words, plaintiffs must show evidence of actual injury. For example, in the case of *Bell v. Acxiom Corp.,*[33] the defendant was a company that stored personal, financial or other company information for their corporate clients. In 2003, its computer bank was hacked by Scott Levine, a client. Levine downloaded personal information concerning other Acxiom clients, including April Bell. Bell then sued Acxiom, on behalf of herself and other clients, alleging that Acxiom had failed to protect its clients' data and that she was at a higher risk of receiving junk mail and becoming an identity theft victim. The court found that Bell had no standing to sue because she had not

---

[29] Title 18 United States Code, section 1028.
[30] Pub. L. No. 108-275 (2004).
[31] Cal. Civ. Code 1798.29(a) (2005).
[32] California Security Breach Information Act, SB 1386, Senate Bill 1386.
[33] No. 4:06CV00485-WRW (E.D. Ark., October 3, 2006).

suffered actual harm. The judge noted that Bell had not asserted that she had actually received a single marketing mailer nor had her identity stolen.

Similarly, in *Walters v. DHL Express*,[34] the plaintiff shipped five boxes of personal effects; however, the boxes arrived damaged and the plaintiff's birth certificate and tax returns were missing. Walters sued DHL for increased risk of identity theft, but the court dismissed his claim for damages against the carrier on the basis that the damages were founded on speculation rather than actual loss. In addition, in *Guin v. Brazos Higher Education Service Corp. Inc.*,[35] Brazos was a non-profit corporation that serviced student loans. Wright was an employee of Brazos who worked from home. Wright's home was burglarized and items were stolen, including the laptop issued to him by Brazos. The plaintiff, Stacy Guin, acquired student loans through Brazos and alleged that Brazos owed him a duty of care to secure his private information and not put it at risk of loss, theft or tampering. The court rejected the argument that an increased risk of identity theft constituted damages where there was no evidence that any party whose information could have been on the laptop had actually experienced identity theft.

CONCLUSION

This chapter explored the many aspects of computer fraud and identity theft. It is clear that the growth of the Internet and e-commerce has opened up new avenues for fraud and identity theft to be committed against individuals and organizations. The Internet enables con artists to hide behind a cloak of anonymity, which makes it necessary for law enforcement officials and policy-makers to act quickly to stop newly emerging deceptive schemes before they can become widespread. Moreover, given that the Internet transcends national boundaries, law enforcement officials must be more creative and cooperative to successfully combat online fraud and identity theft.

There are a number of relatively simple things that individuals can do to protect themselves from online victimization. People should be encouraged to only share personal information when absolutely necessary and to be wary of providing their phone numbers and email addresses to others, even when purchasing goods in major retail stores. Individuals also must be in the habit of carefully reviewing their banking and other financial statements and be careful of sharing identity information in public, including when using a portable computer in public. People should also be encouraged to never carry unnecessary information with them, like their social insurance number. These details should be memorized and never disclosed to anyone unless absolutely necessary.

Individuals and organizations also need to keep home and office computers secure, which means ensuring that up-to-date anti-virus software and firewalls are installed. Individuals should never open emails from unknown or untrusted sources, especially not attachments. Finally, individuals should also periodically

---

[34] May 12, 2006 (Ill. District Court).
[35] Feb.7, 2006 (Minn. District Court).

request to see their own credit reports in order to make sure that there have been no surprise charges or loans taken out in their name.

QUESTIONS FOR FURTHER THINKING AND DISCUSSION

1. What is the difference between identity theft and fraud?
2. What is the primary reason that phishing scams are perpetrated?
3. What are the essential elements of a phishing scam?
4. Why do you think phishing is unlikely to disappear any time soon?
5. What affect does the delay in the victim's awareness of victimization have on our ability to deal with the problem of identity theft?
6. Why do you think the Canadian government waited so long to deal with the problem of identity theft through the enactment of specific legislation?
7. Do you think the fraud provisions in the *Criminal Code* are sufficient to deal with the various forms of Internet fraud discussed in this chapter?
8. What are the implications of identity theft for individuals and companies?
9. Are there any differences between the cases of *R. v. Huynen* and *U.S. v. Czubinski*? To the extent there is a difference, which is the better approach? Do you agree or disagree with the results?
10. Do you agree with the court that the sentence of incarceration was appropriate in the case of *R. v. Singh*, given the serious nature of the crime and the need for deterrence and denunciation?
11. What are some of the difficulties associated with estimating the true social and financial impact of identity theft on the Canadian economy?
12. How might Canada improve its response to fraud and identity theft in the future?

4

Child Sexual Abuse and the Internet

KEY TERMS AND CONCEPTS

- A "child"
- *Act to Amend the Child and Family Services Act to Protect Ontario's Children*
- Anonymizers
- Anonymous remailers
- *Ashcroft v. Free Speech Coalition*
- Attitudinal harm
- Border searches
- Bruce Ryder
- *Charter*, s. 1
- *Charter*, s. 2(b)
- *Child and Family Services Act*
- Child Exploitation Tracking System (CETS)
- Child pornography
- *Child Pornography Prevention Act* (CPPA)
- *Child Pornography Reporting Act*

- Child sexual abuse material
- *Criminal Code*, s. 163.1
- *Criminal Code*, s. 172.1
- Cognitive distortions
- *Constitution Act*, 1867
- *Constitution*, s. 52
- Cybertip.ca
- Freedom of expression
- Fuelling fantasies and inciting offences
- Grooming and seduction
- Inchoate offence
- Indirect harms
- International Criminal Police Organization (Interpol)
- Morphed images
- Online child luring
- Online networks
- Operation Cleanfeed
- Pith and substance
- Pressing and substantial
- Proportionality test
- *Protect Act of 2003*

- *Protection of Children Against Sexual Exploitation Act*
- *R. v. Alicandro*
- *R. v. Legare*
- *R. v. Oakes*
- *R. v. Sharpe*
- Reasonable and demonstrably justifiable
- Reasonable limit
- Reasonable suspicion
- Reasoned apprehension of overbreadth
- The Council of Europe's Convention on Cybercrime
- The Fourth Amendment

• The *Harm Principle*	• *U.S. v. Arnold*	• Virtual Global
• The *Oakes* Test	• *U.S. v. Ickes*	Taskforce (VGT)
• Uniform Crime	• *U.S. v. Romm*	• Wonderland Club
Reporting Survey	• USENET newsgroups	
(UCR)	• Virtual communities	

INTRODUCTION

Child sexual abuse on the Internet includes the creation and distribution of **child pornography** (also known as child sexual abuse material), online child luring, as well as child exploitation through prostitution, child trafficking and child sex tourism. The creation, possession and distribution of child pornography are not new crimes. However, these materials were historically only available to a small group of individuals through highly secretive networks, given the significant social and legal stigma associated with them. While the Internet did not create the problem of child pornography or child victimization, it has facilitated the international exchange of these images quickly and anonymously. It has provided an ideal forum for child sexual abuse enthusiasts to connect with each other and share images and stories about child victimization and abuse. These images are now easy to create, store, disseminate and copy witl. very little financial cost or risk of exposure to the police.

The Internet now enables child sexual abuse images to be distributed widely throughout the world and accessed privately and anonymously by those who have not necessarily committed **contact sexual offences** against children themselves. These images can also be stored and transported easily with the help of laptops, cell phones, USB devices and other small electronic storage devices. With sophisticated and up-to-date technologies, the images can be encrypted or otherwise hidden from detection by law enforcement. They can also be reproduced endlessly and altered simply with digital editing programs. Child sexual abuse images can also be captured and disseminated live, in real time, as the abuse is taking place.

WHAT IS CHILD PORNOGRAPHY?

There is no objective standard for determining what constitutes a child pornography image. Those who have studied these images have identified a variety of materials from pictures of fully-clothed children taken from catalogues, advertisements and other perfectly legal sources, to pictures of nude and semi-nude children, to more explicit images featuring their genitalia and, in some cases, depicting explicit sexual abuse.[1] In the most egregious cases, child pornography depicts infants and young children who are forced or coerced to commit heinous sexual acts with adults, other children, or animals. These children are victimized

---

[1] Max Taylor, Gemma Holland and Ethel Quayle, "Typology of Pedophile Picture Collections" (2001) 74(2) The Police Journal 97 at 98, available online at: http://www.ipce.info/library.3/files/nat_dims_kp.htm.

when the child pornography is created and they are re-victimized whenever someone views these images for sexual gratification. The images are evidence of child sexual abuse and thereby constitute a digital crime scene.

The Internet now offers a wide variety of child pornography materials, including erotic images and stories, video clips and live sex images and discussions, ranging from the relatively harmless to the exceptionally hard core. Child pornography makes up only a fraction of the total number of pornography images available on the Internet; however, research studies indicate that hundreds of thousands of child pornography images and video clips are currently available online.[2] While the Internet appears to be the principal medium for the distribution of child pornography throughout the world, it is difficult to determine precisely how much child pornography is Internet based because its production and collection are highly secretive and the available material is constantly changing.[3] Law enforcement agencies can only estimate the increase in production and distribution and most of the figures come from public hotlines where people can report sites with child sex abuse images as well as official government statistics about charges and conviction rates. These sources reveal that the growth of the Internet child pornography trade occurred slowly over time in North America.

Prior to the Internet, individuals who were interested in acquiring child pornography had to directly contact others who could supply them with pictures, films or magazines, or produce their own materials. This meant that child pornography enthusiasts had to place themselves in positions of significant personal risk.[4] Those who sought to purchase or trade child pornography images were primarily restricted to small, highly secretive networks through advertisements in magazines, newspapers or mail solicitations. Much of this distribution was informal and fragmented, including a network of private production mainly designed to serve the sexual interests of those producing it.[5]

Due to various law reform initiatives and the mobilization of police resources to combat the problem, by 1986 law enforcement officials were able to significantly reduce the distribution of child pornography through the mail and other commercial avenues.[6] Those with an interest in child pornography needed to find a more secretive means to distribute and acquire these materials. This is how the Internet became essential to the child pornography trade, surprisingly early, in the mid-1980s.[7]

---

[2] Michael C. Seto, "Pedophilia and Sexual Offences Against Children" (2004) 15 *Annual Review of Sex Research* 321 at 70.

[3] Taylor, Holland and Quayle, *supra*, note 1 at 97; Ethel Quayle and Max Taylor, "Paedophiles, Pornography and the Internet: Assessment Issues" (2002) 32 British Journal of Social Work 863 at 865.

[4] Seto, *supra*, note 2 at 54.

[5] D. MacDonald, "Sexual Offences Against Children: The Bagdley Report" Ottawa, Canada: Library of Parliament, Research Branch, 1987 at 14.

[6] Philip Jenkins, *Moral Panic: Changing Concepts of the Child Molester in Modern America* (New Haven: Yale University Press, 1998) at 40-41.

[7] Yaman Akdeniz, *Sex on the Net* (Reading, UK: South Street Press, 1999) at 49.

Expansion with the Internet

The invention of the computer modem made it possible for users to access bulletin board systems, which allowed them to form discussion groups and share information confidentially.[8] Computer bulletin boards were sometimes used to pass on mailing lists of collectors and other paper-based sources of child pornography, such as magazines and books that the individual could obtain through mail or courier services.[9] While running a bulletin board service was time-consuming and expensive, it offered child pornographers an anonymous and speedy means to exchange images, as well as a means to communicate and connect with one another.

During this period, law enforcement agents were not aware that child pornographers were using computers to facilitate the buying, selling and trading of images. As a result, digital technologies provided an obscure and highly secretive means to share illicit materials out of sight from law enforcement officials.[10] By the late 1980s, producers and consumers of child pornography were among the most sophisticated users of computer technology and their accumulated technical skills and expertise enabled them to master many useful innovations.[11] Before long, it became possible for child pornographers to access materials from a wide range of sources online and to create, store and disseminate large files containing both pictures and movies. With each technological innovation, the child pornography trade continued to thrive and flourish, and the law enforcement officials who pursued the perpetrators were left further behind.

Since then, the child pornography market has developed rapidly from a small, underground, highly secretive "cottage" industry into one in which very large volumes of pornographic images of children, some of which are extremely violent and sadistic, are available on the Internet at little or no cost. A central reason for the rapid increase in the number of individuals involved in this trade is the fact that the perceived risk of being caught is fairly low.[12] Law enforcement agents from around the world have had some recent success in shutting down the large-scale commercial child pornography websites that used to operate quite freely and openly in cyberspace.

However, the Internet remains the most popular medium for the distribution of child pornography because it provides offenders with an unparalleled degree of anonymity and convenience. In 2003, the National Criminal Intelligence Service in the United Kingdom estimated that the number of child pornography websites had doubled worldwide.[13] Since 1997, the number of child pornography images on the Internet is estimated to have increased by 1,500%. The Internet

---

[8] Jenkins, *supra*, note 6 at 41.

[9] Sharon Moyer, "A Preliminary Investigation Into Child Pornography in Canada" a working document of the Department of Justice Canada, May 1992 at 5.

[10] Jenkins, *supra*, note 6 at 43.

[11] *Ibid* at 47.

[12] Seto, *supra*, note 2 at 55.

[13] National Centre for Missing and Exploited Children, 2005.

Filter Learning Centre has suggested that there are 116,000 daily Gnutella[14] child pornography requests and that teen porn is in the top 20 of all adult search requests.[15] Currently, Interpol has amassed a database of more than 520,000 illegal child sexual abuse images. These figures speak to the volume of child pornography images currently circulating on the Internet.

The computer and the Internet now facilitate the child pornography industry in numerous ways. An individual can copy traditional paper-based images using a scanner and store them electronically, on the hard disk, floppy disk or CD-ROM, where they can be disseminated to others at virtually no cost. Many pictures from 30 or 40 years ago, or even longer, which were once distributed privately or commercially through sex shops and mail order, have been digitized and are currently circulating on the Internet.[16] High-quality pictures and film clips can be downloaded within seconds and will not deteriorate over time in the same way as magazine images or photographs do.[17]

Encryption software is also used to increase anonymity and reduce the chance of detection by scrambling data so that it cannot easily be read by others. Individuals who download images can also use **anonymizers**, or **anonymous remailers**, which makes it difficult to locate them, much less prove that they possessed or downloaded the images. As a result of these developments, individuals are now acquiring extremely large collections of child pornography from the Internet on an unprecedented scale.[18]

In addition to the World Wide Web, which permits individuals to set up websites containing child pornography, another major source for online child pornography text and images are **USENET newsgroups**, which are the offspring of the electronic bulletin boards that were popular in the 1980s.[19] USENET is an electronic news bulletin board service that allows users to openly post and read text messages that are organized into over 80,000 different newsgroups and classified by subject matter.[20] Although the vast majority of these newsgroups are harmless and lawful, some are used by child pornography offenders to communicate with each other.

There are also Web-based bulletin boards that allow users to post brief messages and discussions, including links to child pornography websites.[21] In recent years, law enforcement officials have also discovered that a number of

---

[14] Noted as the first decentralized peer-to-peer network, Gnutella now refers to the open protocol used by the various clients.

[15] Jerry Ropelato, "Internet Pornography Statistics" (2004), available online at: http://www.internetfilterreview.com/internet-pornography-statistics.html.

[16] Jenkins, *supra*, note 6 at 82-83.

[17] Quayle and Taylor, *supra*, note 3 at 868.

[18] Tony Krone, "International Police Operations Against Online Child Pornography," (2005) 296 Trends and Issues in Criminal Justice 1 at 4, available online from the Australian Institute of Criminology at: http://www.aic.gov.au.

[19] Jenkins, *supra*, note 6 at 54.

[20] February 2003 report of the United States General Accounting Office, "Peer-to-Peer Networks Provide Ready Access to Child Pornography" available online at: http://www.gao.new.items/d03351.pdf.

[21] *Ibid* at 64.

people are using peer-to-peer (P2P) file-sharing networks for the distribution of child pornography. Many child pornography enthusiasts have flocked to P2P file sharing networks because they are free so users do not have to provide credit card details, which leads them to believe they cannot be traced. The explosion in file sharing, driven by the demand for music files, has also made the technology widely accessible and easy to use. The distributed nature of P2P networks makes them a highly robust and efficient means to share content because there is no single point of failure in the network. For criminals, these networks are particularly useful because there is no data stored on a central server that could be accessed by law enforcement.

It is also noteworthy that the Internet enables pedophiles to organize themselves into online networks for the purpose of trading child pornography and communicating with each other.[22] Typically providing an important source of advice, encouragement and support for pedophiles, **virtual pedophile communities** are well-organized and extend across international boundaries.[23] These communities are important because, prior to the Internet, pedophiles were a socially isolated group with few social support networks. Now online networks allow for the normalization of the pedophile's sexual interest in children and facilitate the reduction of outside social contacts that might challenge the interest.

The Internet enables predators to bond with each other by offering advice and encouragement, as well as sharing images and stories of their sexual encounters with children.[24] These individuals frequently trade images with each other as a means of establishing trust and respect and take copies of images from their private collections to share with others.[25] The groups play an important role in sexual fantasy and arousal as well as enabling members to feel less stigmatized, to rationalize what they are doing and to view it as normal and acceptable rather than as abusive.[26]

Reputation and trust are highly important within these virtual networks, as I discussed in Chapter 3 with respect to the online communities devoted to identity theft and fraud. We can therefore observe that the Internet facilitates interaction between cyber-criminals in much the same way as it is used to enable the commission of digital crimes. For example, the Wonderland Club, which had 180 members in 21 countries, enabled participants to view live sex acts performed by adults with children that were transmitted live in real time to viewers around the world. Membership in this elite and sophisticated child pornography network was only open by invitation, upon the payment of 10,000 pornographic images of children, from infants to puberty, which were then encrypted and exchanged on the Internet.

---

[22] Rachel O'Connell, "Paedophiles Networking on the Internet," in Carlos A. Arnaldo, *Child Abuse on the Internet, Ending the Silence* (New York: Berghahn Books, 2001) at 67.

[23] Ropelato, *supra*, note 15 at 5.

[24] Ethel Quayle and Max Taylor, "Child Pornography and the Internet: Perpetuating a Cycle of Abuse" (2002) 23 Deviant Behaviour 331 at 331.

[25] Quayle and Taylor, *supra*, note 3 at 866.

[26] *Ibid* at 867.

Canada's tipline for reporting the online sexual exploitation of children, otherwise known as Cybertip.ca, recently released a report on the thousands of public reports submitted to it between September 26, 2002, and March 31, 2009. The report provides an analysis of 15,662 incidents relating to websites hosting child sexual abuse images and 4,110 unique images. It demonstrates that there is a significant online commercial market for child pornography materials. As many as 13.8% of the images were hosted on commercial websites (45.1% of which were hosted in the United States), with the remaining found on thumbnail galleries (41.4%), forums (16.1%), image hosting websites (11.5%), on a portal page (8.0%), on a social networking website (6.9%) or on a blog (2.2%). Moreover, 82% of the images assessed by Cybertip.ca depict very young prepubescent children under the age of 12.

Most concerning is the severity of the images, with 35% of all images depicting serious sexual assault (and 68.5% of these images depicted a child under 8 years old). Moreover, 77.6% of all Web pages had at least one child sexual abuse image depicting a child under the age of 8 years, with many showing infants or toddlers being assaulted. In addition, 41.3% of the images were found to have at least one adult visible. In the most disturbing cases, the images depicted extreme sexual abuse, including bondage (75.5%), bestiality, torture and defecation. Only 14 drawn or cartoon images were found, at least two of which appeared to be the same image.

Many of the websites were found to be overtly sexual in nature, thereby actively promoting child sexual abuse and exploitation. The average number of child pornography pictures contained on each website was between 20 and 30; and the majority of the websites (54.8%) purported to accept credit cards for payment. Most (85.1%) sold monthly memberships, with payments ranging from $4 to $490 (the average being $53 per month). The table in Figure 4.1 illustrates the various forms of payment currently accepted on commercial child pornography websites.

Figure 4.1 Form of Payment Purportedly Accepted on Commercial Child Sexual Abuse Websites

Traditional credit card payment	568	**56.4%**
Online payment systems	335	**33.3%**
Cash transfer from a traditional bank or institution	61	**6.1%**
Other or specific type unknown (e.g. email request)	41	**4.1%**
Telephone or text message	2	**0.2%**
TOTAL	**1.007**	

Source: Cybertip.ca

In addition, child pornography DVDs were found being sold for as much as $1,900, as well as child pornography image sets. The availability of this commercial material emphasizes the market value and significant, widespread demand for child sexual abuse content around the world.

It is important to note that child pornography images are produced by a variety of different means. In many cases, the child knows the offender who is producing the image, as he or she is either a relative, neighbour, acquaintance or trusted authority figure. Indeed, a number of child pornography cases reported in Canada involve the production of the materials within the family unit.[27] In most of these cases, the offender is father or step-father and the victim is a girl, ranging in age from young prepubescent children to teenagers. In some cases, the offender exclusively abuses his own children; however, in other cases, he also targets the young friends of his children.

In some instances, offenders seduce or coerce children into making their own sexually explicit images using technological devices such as Web cameras or cell phones. For instance, children are sometimes pressured or coerced into producing sexually explicit images of themselves by unknown strangers who lure them into exploitative sexual relationships through the Internet. And, in another kind of situation, children are commercially exploited by people outside of their

---

[27] In *R. v. P. (G.E.)* (2004), [2004] N.S.J. No. 496, 2004 CarswellNS 529 (N.S. C.A.), the accused ran a prostitution business and website (streaming images of the abuse live over the Internet) with girls, including his 15-year-old daughter. In *R. v. H. (M.)* (2002), 2002 CarswellBC 759, [2002] B.C.J. No. 771 (B.C. C.A.), the accused surreptitiously video taped his 13-year-old step-daughter in the bathroom and in the bedroom; in *R. c. M.(L.)* (2008), 2008 CarswellQue 4417, [2008] S.C.J. No. 31 (S.C.C.), the accused abused his own 4-year-old daughter and her 4-year-old friend and produced child pornography during these encounters, which he sold for financial gain. Similarly, in *R. v. P. (C.)* (2008), 2008 CarswellNB 502, [2008] N.B.J. No. 390 (N.B. C.A.), the accused possessed hundreds of child pornography images and videos, including pictures of his two daughters and a friend, who were all 8 or 9 years of age at the time the images were recorded. In *R. v. B. (T.L.)* (2007), 2007 CarswellAlta 504, [2007] A.J. No. 439 (Alta. C.A.), the accused female sexually assaulted her 6-year-old son at the request of her Internet boyfriend who sent child pornography to her. In *R. v. R. (A.)* (2007), 2007 CarswellOnt 6985, [2007] C.J. No. 4205 (Ont. C.J.), the accused made photos and videos of his granddaughter in nude and semi-nude poses from the time that she was 6 years old and also possessed a large collection of other child pornography; in *R. v. J. (R.B.)* (2006), 2006 CarswellAlta 1829, [2006] A.J. No. 1726 (Alta. Prov. Ct.), the accused recorded the sexual assault of two of his daughters using a Webcam and possessed a large collection of other child pornography; in *R. v. M. (B.C.)* (2008), [2008] B.C.J. No. 1774, 2008 CarswellBC 1966 (B.C. C.A.), the accused sexually assaulted his common-law wife's two daughters and produced photos and videos of himself engaged in sexual activity with one of the girls; in *R. v. B. (A.)* (2006), 2006 CarswellOnt 3835, [2006] O.J. No. 2543 (Ont. S.C.J.), the offender sexually assaulted his 16-year-old step-daughter and took pornographic pictures of her; in *R. v. M. (D.S.)* (2001), 2001 CarswellBC 1964, [2001] B.C.J. No. 1913 (B.C. S.C.), the accused surreptitiously video-taped his 15-year-old step-daughter nude and partially nude after a shower; in *R. v. S. (V.P.)* (2001), 2001 CarswellBC 990, [2001] B.C.J. No. 930 (B.C. S.C.), the accused took pornographic images of his step-daughter; in *R. v. W. (R.)* (2001), 2001 CarswellOnt 2497, [2001] O.J. No. 2810 (Ont. S.C.J.) the accused sexually abused his three children over many years and created a written story in which one of his daughters is depicted as a sex slave. The details include incidents of rape, torture, forced sex with animals, prolonged periods of bondage, intercourse, non-consensual intercourse and fellatio with friends of the father as well as friends of the daughter; in *R. v. W. (L.A.)* (2006), [2006] S.J. No. 689, 2006 CarswellSask 689 (Sask. Prov. Ct.), the accused female produced child pornography with her 9-year-old daughter and distributed it to a man she met on the Internet.

intimate circle of family members or care-givers and used to make child pornography images that are sold for financial gain.

Current information about the number of child pornography incidents in Canada is available from Statistics Canada, which collects police-reported crime statistics through its Uniform Crime Reporting Survey (UCR).[28] The latest UCR survey indicates that there were 1,408 child pornography incidents in Canada in 2008, which is a 2,536% increase from only 55 incidents in 1998. Most of those incidents occurred in Quebec (422), followed by Ontario (389), British Columbia (223) and Alberta (129). It is important to note that technology facilitates the rapid collection of countless digital images; thus, each of these incidents could involve tens or even hundreds of thousands of child sex abuse images. However, it is surprising that there were only 408 persons charged with child pornography offences across Canada in 2008, of which 393 were adults.[29]

THE LEGAL DEFINITION OF CHILD PORNOGRAPHY

While child pornography is an old and deeply rooted problem in our society, the laws to combat it are surprisingly new. It was not until 1993 that Parliament created a number of new offences relating to child pornography in s. 163.1 of the *Criminal Code*.[30]

This provision supplemented the existing laws making it an offence to make, print, publish, distribute or circulate obscene materials, which was already prohibited by s. 163 of the *Code*. Under that section, the legal analysis turned on the subjective meaning of "dominant characteristic" and "undue exploitation of sex."

Pornography had never before been defined in the *Code* and there had not been a precise list of the materials that should be regulated.[31] The definition of child pornography, set out in s. 163.1(1), reads as follows:

163.1(1) In this section, "child pornography" means:
    (a) a photographic, film, video or other visual representation, whether or not it was made by electronic or mechanical means,

---

[28] UCR data reflect reported crime that has been substantiated by police agencies throughout Canada. However, the UCR Survey collects information only on those crimes that come to the attention of the police. The UCR data do not include all crimes in Canada because some crimes are never detected and others are never brought to the attention of the police. Responding to this survey is mandatory. Data are collected directly from survey respondents and extracted from administrative files. The response rate in terms of police respondents complying with the UCR Survey is virtually 100 per cent. There are more than 1,200 separate police detachments responding to the survey, comprising 204 different police forces.

[29] Manitoba had the highest number of charges brought (24) with respect to the number of actual incidents (51), which means that charges were brought in 47% of cases; whereas Quebec had the lowest ratio (17%) with respect to the number of charges brought (70) when compared with actual incidents (422). In Saskatchewan, there were only 26 charges brought with respect to 58 actual incidents (45%); in British Columbia there were 73 charges brought with respect to 223 actual incidents (33%); in Ontario, there were 153 charges brought with respect to 389 actual incidents (39%); and in Alberta, there were 31 charges brought with respect to 129 actual incidents (24%).

[30] S.C. 1993, c. 46, s. 2, amended S.C. 2002, c. 13, s. 5; 2005, c. 32, s. 7

[31] "Guide to the Federal Government's Response to the Reports on Sexual Abuse of Children, Pornography and Prostitution" Ottawa: Government of Canada, 1986 at 28.

(i) that shows a person who is or is depicted as being under the age of eighteen years and is engaged in or is depicted as engaged in explicit sexual activity, or

(ii) the dominant characteristic of which is the depiction, for a sexual purpose, of a sexual organ or the anal region of a person under the age of eighteen years; or

(b) any written material or visual representation that advocates or counsels sexual activity with a person under the age of eighteen years that would be an offence under this Act.

Notice that the child pornography provisions were not limited to material produced by using real children. The provision applies to visual representations of real children and to representations of imaginary children. This means that an image depicting sex involving real child sexual abuse is treated in the same way as a sketch, drawing, painting or sculpture. The Supreme Court of Canada would create a judge-made exception to this rule for self-created expressions, such as stories, drawings or paintings, which are privately held by their creator. These works only fall under the definition of child pornography if they are shown to others or passed around.[32]

In Canada, a "child" for the purposes of child pornography is defined as someone under the age of 18 years. The definition is designed to cover representations involving persons either under the age of 18 or depicted as being under the age of 18. In this sense, if the "child" in the image is actually an adult who is depicted as being under the age of 18 years, the image may constitute child pornography. Note as well that written texts were included in the provision if they advocated or counselled the commission of a sexual offence against a child. The definition has since been expanded and in its current form covers fictional representations and any written materials that describe sexual activity with a person under the age of 18 years regardless of whether they "counsel" or "advocate" such activity.[33]

CHILD PORNOGRAPHY AND FREEDOM OF EXPRESSION

Canada's commitment to freedom of expression has historically been rooted in the following values and convictions: that seeking and attaining truth is an inherently good activity; that participation in social and political decision-making is to be fostered and encouraged; and that diversity in forms of individual self-fulfillment and human flourishing ought to be cultivated in a tolerant environment for the sake of both those who convey a meaning and those to whom meaning is conveyed.[34] All of these values are critical to the maintenance of a free and democratic society, which requires the open exchange of ideas and viewpoints.

The Supreme Court of Canada has found that child pornography does not generally contribute to the values that underlie freedom of expression, including the search for truth, self-fulfillment and the contribution to social and political

---

[32] This exception was created by Chief Justice McLachlin in *R. v. Sharpe*, [2001] 1 S.C.R. 45, as discussed below.

[33] *Criminal Code, supra*, note 30 at s. 163.1(1)(c).

[34] *Irwin Toy v. Quebec (A.G.)*, [1989] 1 S.C.R. 927 at para. 53.

discourse.[35] However, unlike in other jurisdictions such as the United States, where it has been found that child pornography is not protected speech,[36] in Canada it is constitutionally protected. Section 2(b) of the *Charter* guarantees everyone the "fundamental freedoms" of thought, belief, opinion and expression, including freedom of the press and other media of communication. Section 52 of the *Constitution* provides that the *Charter* is part of the supreme law of Canada and any law that is inconsistent with it is of no force or effect, with respect to the inconsistency.

Yet our freedom of expression is not absolute, and Parliament or a provincial legislature may limit expression to prevent harm to vulnerable members of our society. Thus, while the offensive nature of child pornography might limit its constitutional worth, it does not negate it altogether.[37] Similar findings have been reached by the Supreme Court of Canada with respect to other forms of offensive speech including obscenity,[38] hate propaganda[39] and defamatory statements.[40]

The onus of proving that a limit on a right or freedom guaranteed by the *Charter* is reasonable and justified in a free and democratic society rests upon the party seeking to uphold the limitation.[41] In *R. v. Oakes*, the Supreme Court of Canada set out the analytical framework for determining whether the violation of a *Charter* right can be justified under s. 1. The analysis, which is commonly referred to as the **"Oakes test,"** provides that a constitutional guarantee can be limited if two conditions are met. First, the objective, which the legislative measures are intended to serve, must be sufficiently important to warrant overriding a constitutionally protected right or freedom.[42] It must relate to "pressing and substantial" concerns in a free and democratic society before it can be characterized as sufficiently important.[43] Second, the means chosen to attain this objective must be reasonable and demonstrably justifiable in a free and democratic society. This involves a proportionality test in which the courts must balance the interests of society against those of individuals and groups.[44]

There are three important aspects of the proportionality test.[45] First, the measures enacted (giving rise to the *Charter* violation) must be carefully designed to achieve the objective in question. In other words, they must be rationally connected to the objective.[46] Second, the means chosen should impair the right or freedom "as little as possible." The legislation, in other words, must limit the right no more than reasonably necessary to achieve its objective. Third, there

---

[35] *Sharpe, supra,* note 32 at para. 24.
[36] *New York v. Ferber*, 458 U.S. 747 (U.S.N.Y., 1982).
[37] *Sharpe, supra,* note 32 at para. 27.
[38] *R. v. Butler*, [1992] 1 S.C.R. 452 (S.C.C.), reconsideration refused [1993] 2 W.W.R. lxi (S.C.C.).
[39] *R. v. Keegstra*, [1990] 3 S.C.R. 697 (S.C.C.).
[40] *Hill v. Church of Scientology of Toronto*, [1995] 2 S.C.R. 1130 (S.C.C.).
[41] *R. v. Oakes*, [1986] 1 S.C.R. 103 (S.C.C.), at para. 66.
[42] *R. v. Big M Drug Mart Ltd.*, [1985] 1 S.C.R. 295 (S.C.C.) at 352.
[43] *Oakes, supra,* note 41 at para. 69.
[44] *Ibid* at para. 70.
[45] *Ibid* at para. 71.
[46] This means that they must not be arbitrary, unfair or based on irrational considerations. *Ibid* at para. 70.

must be proportionality between the effects of the measures, which are responsible for limiting the *Charter* right or freedom, and the objective being sought. This means that legislation infringing a *Charter* right might still be found to be constitutionally valid if the benefit of overriding the right outweighs the costs. In all s. 1 cases the burden of proof rests with the Crown to show on a balance of probabilities that the violation is justifiable.[47]

One of the most vital objectives for criminalizing child pornography is to prevent harm to children. This principle can be traced back to John Stuart Mill's classic essay, *On Liberty,* which defines freedom of expression within a broader theory of liberty. In what has become known as the "Harm Principle," Mill confines the scope of individual liberty to activities that do not harm others. In other words, the harm principle states that where harm to others is involved, individuals may be subjected to state coercion and control.

At the same time, however, the limitation must be reasonable and justified, particularly considering the competing rights and values that exist in society. This means that laws prohibiting the possession, creation or distribution of child pornography must not catch materials that engage the core values promoted by freedom of expression, such as individual self-fulfillment, or which pose little or no risk of harm to others. In other words, if the conduct is private and personal, where no harm is involved, then the individual is protected from state interference.

This raises a number of questions to think about. What kinds of harm might be caused by child pornography? To whom is this harm caused? How significant is the harm suffered by this individual or individuals? How do we measure the harm? And, if harm can be suffered by the children who are used to make real child pornography images, how do we define who is a child? In Canada, a "child" is defined as someone under the age of 18 years. But not all sexual activities involving children under this age are illegal, particularly given that the age of consent in Canada is 16. As a result, sexual activity involving a 16-year-old is not necessarily harmful or abusive.

R. v. SHARPE AND SUBSEQUENT LEGISLATIVE INITIATIVES

In the seminal case of *R. v. Sharpe*,[48] the Supreme Court of Canada weighed in on a constitutional challenge to the law governing child pornography. Although the decision was controversial, the court's interpretation of the definition of child pornography set out in s. 163.1 of the *Code* continues to apply today.

John Robin Sharpe was charged under s. 163.1(4) of the *Code* with simple possession and possession for the purposes of transmission and sale of both his own written work and hundreds of images, including computer disks and photographs, of teenage boys. He had also written a collection of stories that involved sadomasochistic acts between children, typically under the age of 10, with each other and with adults. At trial, he was convicted of the charges in relation to the images that depicted the commission of sexual offences against boys under the age of 14. This material was considered illegal because it involved

---

[47] *Sharpe, supra*, note 32 at para. 140.
[48] *Sharpe, supra*, note 32.

harm to actual children in production. However, he was acquitted on the charges in relation to the stories he had written.

Mr. Sharpe argued that the prohibition of simple possession of child pornography violated the guarantee of freedom of expression in s. 2(b) of the *Charter*. The issue was whether this restriction was justified under s. 1, given the harms that child pornography causes to children. Mr. Sharpe acknowledged that child pornography causes some harm to children and accepted that this justifies criminalizing the possession of some forms of these materials. However, he argued that s. 163.1(4) violated the freedom of expression guarantee under s. 2(b) of the *Charter*.

The trial judge held that s. 163.1(4) was unconstitutional.[49] Shaw J. concluded that the effectiveness of s. 163.1 in protecting children from harm was so negligible that it did not justify the substantial infringement of freedom of expression.[50] He found that the invasion of freedom and personal privacy is "profound," that it extends to all persons, including those who make no harmful use of child pornography, but who use it for very private purposes, and that the violations were not outweighed by the limited beneficial effects of the sweeping prohibition. The British Columbia Court of Appeal upheld this finding.[51] Southin J.A. found that highly compelling evidence of necessity is required to justify the prohibition of simple possession and that the legislation targetted too much material that was not likely to cause harm to children.[52] Rowles J.A. also found the legislation to be overly broad because it caught more material than necessary to achieve the objective of reducing harm to children.[53]

At the Supreme Court of Canada, a majority of 6-3, with Chief Justice McLachlin writing for the majority, held that s. 163.1 of the *Code* violated freedom of expression under s. 2(b) of the *Charter*. In particular, the Court conceded that the offence prohibiting the simple possession of child pornography infringed s. 2(b). The question was whether it could be saved as a "reasonable limit" within the framework of s. 1 of the *Charter*. The primary concern was whether the legislation failed the minimal impairment branch of the *Oakes* test and was overly broad.

As a matter of principle, legislative provisions that are inconsistent with a *Charter* guarantee are invalid.[54] However, the court can sometimes save legislation by reading in an interpretation that is more consistent with the *Charter*.[55] In this case, the Chief Justice "read-in" two limitations to the definition of child pornography, so that the violation of freedom of expression could be saved under s. 1. McLachlin C.J.C. held that s. 163.1 of the *Code* should be read as though it contains an exception for: self-created expressive material intended

---

[49] *R. v. Sharpe* (1999), 169 D.L.R. (4th) 536 (B.C. S.C.).

[50] *Ibid* at paras. 49-51.

[51] *R. v. Sharpe* (1999), 175 D.L.R. (4th) 1 (B.C. C.A.).

[52] *Ibid* at paras. 124 and 128.

[53] *Ibid* at para. 205.

[54] Jamie Cameron, "Abstract Principle v. Contextual Conceptions of Harm: A Comment on R. v. Butler" (1992) 37 McGill Law Journal 1135 at 1143.

[55] *Ibid*.

for private use, held by the accused exclusively for personal use; and private recordings of lawful activity created and held by the accused purely for private use, such as the lawful recording of the consensual sexual activity of two teenagers.

The reason for this decision is complex. The majority found that the inclusion of simple possession within the prohibition would fail the minimal impairment branch of the *Oakes* test by criminalizing the private possession of works of the imagination, including stories, drawings and diaries as well as visual representations, such as photographs, created by the participant(s) and intended only for personal use. The majority concluded that the value of the expression implicated in these works is significant as it touches on self-actualization and personal fulfillment. Moreover, the risk of harm posed to children by these materials was said to be low because no real children are involved in the production of imaginary works and the children who are involved in the production of the second class of works are willing participants.

However, the Chief Justice recognized that there were a number of ways that child pornography, both real and imaginary, could cause indirect or attitudinal harm to children. The most apparent and direct form of harm that child pornography produces is that it sexually exploits the children used in its production. The link between the production of real child pornography and harm to children is beyond question.[56] Criminalizing possession can also help to quash the market for these materials and aid in the detection and prosecution of those who produce and distribute it. But what about the more difficult cases when no child sexual abuse is involved, such as with the production of imaginary works?

The Chief Justice maintained that imaginary representations could cause attitudinal harm, or might fall into the hands of someone who might use them in a way that harms children.[57] The Chief Justice found that the possession and viewing of child pornography gave rise to a "reasoned apprehension" of harm because:

- it can generate and reinforce cognitive distortions whereby people might view sex with children as normal;[58]
- it can "fuel fantasies and may incite offences in the case of certain individuals;"[59] and
- it can be used for the grooming and seduction of children, to entice them into sexual activity.[60]

The court also found that some of these risks did not apply in cases where imaginary works or self-created photographs or videos were privately held and not distributed to others. As a result, the majority decided to read in the two

---

56 *Ibid* at para. 92.
57 *Ibid* at para. 100.
58 *Ibid* at para. 88.
59 *Ibid* at para. 89.
60 *Sharpe, supra,* note 32 at para. 91.

exceptions to s. 163.1 of the *Code* for the purpose of the production and possession offences.

The perceived correlation between possession of child pornography and the indirect harms identified by the Chief Justice has been controversial. Some people believe that those who collect child pornography are likely, as a result of consuming these materials, to engage in child molestation. However, there is little, if any, empirical data that demonstrates child pornography actually *causes* sexual abuse.[61] If there is no verifiable causal connection between imaginary child pornography and actual child sexual abuse, the harm flows not from the expression itself but from the idea that it might encourage the commission of harmful acts.

The relationship between pornography and sex offending has been the subject of extensive scholarly debate. However, the evidence of a causal link between child pornography use and sex offending remains unclear.[62] The studies into Internet child pornography offending are extremely limited and further research is needed to explain why such a diverse range of people are interested in accessing these materials online.

Some Canadian legal scholars, such as Bruce Ryder, have argued that by targetting imaginary images and treating them in the same way as real child sexual abuse images, child pornography law "causes harm to society by suppressing thoughts and expression concerning child and youth sexuality that involved no harm in production, fall short of advocating harm and that have at best a tenuous connection to the commission of harmful acts."[63] In other words, child pornography law criminalizes a wide range of expressive works without demonstrating evidence of a risk of harm. Ryder believes that an offence focused on targetting real child sex abuse images would be an improvement from both regulatory and constitutional perspectives.

According to Ryder, "[t]he 'indirect harms' that allegedly arise from this kind of material are too speculative and uncertain to support a criminal prohibition."[64] The possibility that they might be used to generate or reinforce cognitive distortions in the minds of some individuals or fuel fantasies that may be acted on in a small handful of cases is not an appropriate rationale for suppressing them altogether. Indeed, other heinous crimes, such as murder, have been inspired by significant literary works, including the Holy Bible.[65] However, few would suggest that this is a sufficient reason for banning the possession of these materials by anyone.[66] On this basis, Parliament could suppress virtually any unpopular ideas, words or images alleged to cause someone to engage in bad acts. The Court's rationale also runs counter to the reasons for protecting freedom

---

[61] Michael Seto, Alexandra Maric and Howard E. Barbaree, "The Role of Pornography in the Etiology of Sexual Aggression," (2001) 6 Aggression and Violent Behavior 35 at 36.

[62] Seto, Maric and Barbaree, *ibid* at 36.

[63] Bruce Ryder, "The Harms of Child Pornography Law," (2003) 36 University of British Columbia Law Review 101 at 103.

[64] *Ibid* at 125.

[65] Arnold H. Loewy, "Taking Free Speech Seriously: The United States Supreme Court and Virtual Child Pornography," (2003) 1 First Amendment Law Review 6 at 8.

[66] D. Howitt, *Paedophiles and Sexual Offences Against Children* (Chichester, England: Wiley, 1995).

of expression, which is to facilitate the open exchange of ideas and viewpoints, even those perceived as unpopular or offensive.[67]

The Court's decision in *Sharpe* both shocked and infuriated many members of Parliament as well as the general public. The social and political controversy led to unprecedented Parliamentary initiatives, even before the decision reached the Supreme Court of Canada. The Reform Party proposed that s. 163.1(4), which had been struck down by the British Columbia Supreme Court, be re-enacted using the notwithstanding clause found in s. 33 of the *Charter*, which permits legislatures to override the *Charter* decisions of the courts for a limited 5-year time period, which can be indefinitely renewed.[68] This initiative was narrowly defeated in a 143-129 vote.

Parliament further expanded the child pornography laws in 2002. Bill C-15A was introduced into the House of Commons in March 2001, and passed into law in June 2002, to address the specific problem of Internet child pornography.[69] This Bill made it illegal to "transmit" child pornography from one person to another; to "make available" child pornography by posting it on a website and offering information about where to find it; to "export" child pornography; or "possess child pornography for the purpose of transmitting, making available or exporting it." It also made it an offence to knowingly access child pornography, which targets individuals who are accessing and viewing child pornography online but not actually downloading or possessing it. The amendment also enabled the court to order that a child pornography image be deleted or destroyed by either the "custodian" of the computer system, such as an ISP, or by the court itself. These provisions are necessary to target offenders who use the Internet to access and disseminate child pornography. They can also be used to remove child pornography images from the Internet and take them out of circulation.

Motivated by public outcry, Parliament introduced new legislation again in 2004.[70] It made a number of changes to Canada's child pornography laws, which are currently set out in s. 163.1 of the *Code*.[71] It eliminated exemptions for material with "artistic merit or an educational, scientific or medical purpose" and replaced it with new defence. Section 163.1(6) of the *Code* now provides that no person can be convicted under this section if the material at issue "has a legitimate purpose related to the administration of justice or to science, medicine, education or art" and "does not pose an undue risk of harm to persons under the age of

---

[67] *Sharpe, supra,* note 32.

[68] Stan Persky and Dixon J., *On Kiddie Porn: Sexual Representation, Free Speech and the Robin Sharpe Case* (Vancouver: New Star Books, 2001) at 125.

[69] S.C. 2002, c. 13.

[70] S.C. 2005, c. 31.

[71] It also added a voyeurism offence, contained in s. 162(1) of the *Code,* which prohibits the secret observation (by any means) or recording of any person, in circumstances where there is a reasonable expectation of privacy, in one of three situations: when the person observed or recorded is in a place where a person is expected to be in a state of nudity, or engaged in sexual activity (such as bedroom, bathroom or changing room); or when the person is in a state of nudity or engaged in sexual activity and the purpose is to observe or record the person in such a state or activity; or when the observation or recording is done for a sexual purpose. The intentional distribution of voyeuristic material is also prohibited.

eighteen years." The phrase "legitimate purpose" is subjective and does not provide any basis for determining which works will fall under the definition of "child pornography."

The maximum penalty for all child pornography offences was also increased from 6 to 18 months on summary conviction, and the commission of a child pornography offence with intent to profit must be considered as an aggravating factor for sentencing purposes. In addition, all child pornography offences are now subject to a mandatory minimum sentence of imprisonment and, as such, are no longer eligible for a conditional or "house arrest" sentence.[72] The change in the sentencing requirements is important because the sentences granted for child pornography offences have been inconsistent and inexcusably lenient, with conditional sentences awarded in many serious cases involving the possession and distribution of real child pornography.

For instance, in *R. v. Batshaw*,[73] the accused plead guilty to a charge of possession of child pornography. The computer images showed children, some as young as 6 to 8, engaged in explicit sexual activity with adults. In some images, the children were clearly in pain. The Manitoba Court of Appeal upheld a conditional sentence of 15 months as appropriate. The offender's youthfulness, lack of any record and the fact that he was a student working in a restaurant and hoping to become a psychologist were reasons for this light sentence. In *R. v. Paton*,[74] the accused was found in possession of child pornography on his computer. A video of the accused having intercourse with a child was also found and the child appeared to be unconscious during part of the intercourse. The accused received a conditional sentence of 6 months for the possession of child pornography and 18 months conditional sentence for sexual assault. The Court observed that the assault was not of a violent nature. The accused was also undergoing treatment and was said to represent a low risk to the public.[75]

---

[72] Making and distributing child pornography are now punishable, on an indictable offence, by a minimum term of imprisonment of 1 year and a maximum term of 10 years. On summary conviction, an individual who is convicted of making or distributing child pornography can be convicted of a minimum term of imprisonment of 90 days and a maximum term of 18 months. Those convicted of possessing and accessing child pornography (on a computer, regardless of downloading it) are liable to imprisonment for a maximum term of 5 years and to a minimum punishment of imprisonment for 45 days and on summary conviction are liable to imprisonment for a maximum of 18 months and a minimum term of 14 days.

[73] (2004), 186 C.C.C. (3d) 473 (Man. C.A.).

[74] (2005), [2005] Nu.J. No. 7, 2005 CarswellNun 7 (Nun. C.J.).

[75] See also: In *R. v. Cohen* (2001), 2001 CarswellOnt 1440, [2001] O.J. No. 1606 (Ont. C.A.), the Ontario Court of Appeal imposed a conditional sentence of 14 months instead of a jail term on charges of possession and distribution of child pornography. The fact that the accused was a husband and father with no criminal record, that he was not a pedophile, that he was not involved in pornography production and was not a threat to the public, and that he had lost his job and been forced to move from the community led to the finding that an error in principle had been made. In *R. v. Weber* (2003), 2003 CarswellOnt 3218, [2003] O.J. No. 3306 (Ont. C.A.), the offender was convicted of three charges of distribution of child pornography and one charge of possession of child pornography. He was given a fourteen month conditional sentence. The Ontario Court of Appeal affirmed the sentence and the trial judge's reliance on the earlier decision in *Cohen* where the facts were similar and a 14 month conditional sentence was imposed. See also *R. v. North*

The mandatory minimum penalty recognizes that child pornography offences, including the production, distribution and possession of child pornography, all contribute to the general problem of child pornography in contemporary society. Those who access and download the images encourage the production and distribution of child pornography by creating a ready market for it and the production of child pornography often involves direct harm to children. Through the imposition of more severe sanctions, Canadian judges can help stop the production and collection of child pornography, and this may substantially reduce the market for it. This would stifle the motivation to produce child pornography, thereby serving Parliament's goal of protecting children from exploitation and harm.

CHILD PORNOGRAPHY LAWS IN THE UNITED STATES

The federal statute governing child pornography in the United States is 18 USC 2252. It was initially enacted as part of the *Protection of Children Against Sexual Exploitation Act*.[76] It prohibits knowingly transporting or shipping in interstate commerce any visual depiction of a minor engaging in sexually explicit conduct; receiving or distributing such depictions; or reproducing such materials for distribution in interstate or foreign commerce.[77] It also prohibits possessing, selling or having possession with intent to sell child pornography.[78]

Congress passed the *Child Pornography Prevention Act* (CPPA)[79] in 1996 in response to concerns that technology was evolving to the extent that it was possible to create child pornography by electronic or mechanical means, such as innocent images of children modified or "morphed" into sexually exploitative images through the use of computer technology. Morphed images are often indistinguishable from those depicting real people or events. Using computer software, an individual can modify an innocent image of a child, such as a picture of a child in a playground or a public beach, to produce a sexual image. An image of a child can be superimposed onto another picture, such as by combining an image of a child holding a toy with an image of a man to make it appear that the child is holding the man's penis.[80] It is also possible to digitally alter adult pornography such that genitals and breasts can be removed or shrunk, pubic hair can be erased, and other body parts adjusted, to create a realistic sexual image of a child at little cost.[81] These images can then be replicated and disseminated to others without reducing their quality over time.

(2002), 3 Alta. L.R. (4th) 290 (Alta. C.A.) where the Alberta Court of Appeal found that in a case where there was an extensive child pornography collection, the goals of denunciation and deterrence required a conditional sentence of 12 months, plus 2 years probation.

[76] Pub. L. No. 95-225 (1978).

[77] *Ibid*, see 2252(a)(1)-(2).

[78] *Ibid*, see 2252(a)(3)-(4).

[79] Pub. L. No. 104-208 (1996).

[80] Taylor, *supra*, note 25 at 8.

[81] Sarah Sternberg, "The Child Pornography Prevention Act of 1996 and The First Amendment: Virtual Antitheses," (2001) 69 Fordham Law Review 2783 at 2788.

Since the images are not real, because the exploitative events that they depict did not actually happen or the person in the image does not exist in real life, they might be regarded by some people as harmless.[82] However, they are capable of being used to victimize children and this is primarily why Congress was so concerned about them. CPPA was designed to expand the child pornography laws to include these digitally created forms of child pornography. However, in 1999, the United States Supreme Court struck down the law that expanded the definition of child pornography to encompass "any visual depiction" that "is or *appears to be* a minor engaging in explicit sexual conduct."[83]

In *Ashcroft v. Free Speech Coalition*, the Court ruled that the "appears to be" language was overbroad and unconstitutional under the First Amendment.[84] The majority opinion written by Justice Kennedy stated that the harm to actual children, which is the singular rationale behind the child pornography provisions in the United States, is absent when a virtual child is depicted in the image. The Court also found that the argument that these materials might cause indirect harm to children was too remote to support a ban on constitutionally protected speech, particularly "the government seeks to control thought or to justify its laws for that impermissible end."[85]

However, the problem with the exclusion of virtual images from the definition of child pornography in the United States was that a number of offenders have had indictments dismissed or convictions overturned because of the government's inability to prove that they knowingly possessed real child pornography. In possession cases, defendants took advantage of the fact that the government must prove that an image is of an *actual* child and that the defendant *knew* it was of a real child to sustain a child pornography conviction and argued that they had no way of establishing whether the image was real or virtual.[86] The *Protect Act of 2003* made a number of amendments to the child pornography provisions of Chapter 10 of the US Federal Code entitled "Sexual Exploitation and other abuse of children," which includes child pornography related offences. Section 502, entitled "Improvements to prohibition on virtual child pornography," deals with the problem of excluding virtual images.

The amendment to section 2256(8) of title 18 of the United States Code reads as follows:

> 2256(8) 'child pornography' means any visual depiction, including any photograph, film video, picture or computer or computer-generated image or picture, whether

---

[82] Taylor, *supra*, note 25 at 8.

[83] 18 U.S.C. 2256(8)(B) (1994 & Supp. V. 1999) (emphasis added).

[84] *Ashcroft v. Free Speech Coalition*, 122 S. Ct. 1420 (2002).

[85] *Ibid* at 253-254.

[86] *U.S. v. X-Citement Video, Inc.*, 513 U.S. 64 (U.S. Cal., 1994) which provided that the government must establish that the image is of an actual child and that the defendant knew it was of a real child. See also *United States v. Reilly*, 2002 U.S. Dist. LEXIS 19564 (S.D.N.Y., 2002) where the defendant was permitted to withdraw his guilty plea of receiving child pornography because the state had not proven that he knew the images he received were of real children. See also *U.S. v. Hilton*, 363 F.3d 58 (1st Cir. C.A. (Me.), 2004) which required the government to introduce evidence proving that the pictures were real.

made or produced by electronic, mechanical, or other means, of sexually explicit conduct, where –

  (A) the production of such visual depiction involves the use of a minor engaging in sexually explicit conduct;

  (B) *such visual depiction is a digital image, computer image, or computer-generated image that is, or is indistinguishable from, that of a minor engaging in sexually explicit conduct;*[87] or

  (C) such visual depiction has been created, adapted, or modified to appear that an identifiable minor is engaging in sexually explicit conduct.

Section 2256 is also amended by the addition of a new paragraph to explain the meaning of the word "indistinguishable:"

Section 2256(11) – the term 'indistinguishable' used with respect to a depiction, means virtually indistinguishable, in that the depiction is such that an ordinary person viewing the depiction would conclude that the depiction is of an actual minor engaged in sexually explicit conduct. This definition does not apply to depictions that are drawings, cartoons, sculptures, or paintings depicting minors adults.

CHILD PORNOGRAPHY AND BORDER SEARCHES

Security and privacy are important social and political goals and paramount in the current debate about the constitutionality of border searches of electronic storage devices. The question of whether the government can conduct a border search of the information on a traveller's laptop computer is a complex issue because technological advances have enabled business and leisure travellers to store vast amounts of private information within a variety of electronic storage devices, including laptop computers, personal organizers, cellular telephones and CDs.[88] Given these new realities, it is significant that the United States Court of Appeals for the Ninth Circuit recently released its judgment in what is undoubtedly its most controversial laptop border search case.[89]

For the purposes of the Fourth Amendment, an international airport terminal is the "functional equivalent" of a border; thus, passengers travelling to the United States from international flights are subject to border searches.[90] Since the founding of the United States, Congress has granted broad authority to customs officials to conduct searches and seizures at the border without obtaining a warrant or establishing probable cause.[91] In other words, border searches lacking prior authorization and based on a lower standard than probable cause are justified by the national interests of the sovereign state in preventing the entry of undesirable

---

[87] Emphasis added; this part was added by section 502 of the Protect Act, 2003. Note that this subsection used to include the following wording: "such visual depiction is, or appears to be, of a minor engaging in sexually explicit conduct." However, a ban on sexually explicit images that appeared to depict minors was found to be unconstitutionally overbroad because it prohibits speech that is neither child pornography nor obscene: See *Ashcroft v. Free Speech Coalition*, *supra*, note 84.

[88] *U.S. v. Arnold*, 454 F.Supp.2d 999 (C.D. Cal., 2006).

[89] *U.S. v. Arnold*, 523 F.3d 941 (9th Cir. C.A. (Cal.), 2008) at 948.

[90] *Almeida-Sanchez v. U.S.*, 413 U.S. 266 (U.S. Cal., 1973.) at 273; and *U.S. v. Okafor*, 285 F.3d 842 (9th Cir. C.A. (Cal.), 2002) at 845.

[91] *U.S. v. Montoya de Hernandez*, 473 U.S. 531 (U.S.Cal., 1985), at 537.

persons and prohibited goods and in protecting its tariff revenue.[92] These important state interests, combined with the individual's lowered expectation of privacy at an international border, render border searches reasonable under the Fourth Amendment.[93]

Prior to *U.S. v. Arnold*,[94] only four circuit courts applied the United States Supreme Court's rulings on the border search exception to electronic storage devices. The central theme of these cases is that warrantless border searches of electronic storage devices are constitutionally permissible when they are preceded by reasonable suspicion. For example, in *U.S. v. Ickes*,[95] the defendant was attempting to enter the United States from Canada when United States Customs Agents searched his van.[96] Ickes told the customs agent that he was returning from vacation; however, the agent was puzzled because his van appeared "to contain everything he owned." Ickes' van was subjected to a routine inspection, whereupon the customs agent discovered a video camera containing a tape of a tennis match that focused on "a young ball boy."[97] This led customs officials to conduct a more thorough investigation of the van, which led them to discover marijuana seeds and pipes, along with several albums containing photographs of prepubescent boys, who were mostly nude or semi-nude.[98] At this point, Ickes was detained, and the agents discovered two outstanding warrants in his name. While Ickes was in custody, the customs agents continued to search the van and they confiscated a computer and approximately 75 disks containing additional child pornography, including a video of Ickes fondling the genitals of two young children.[99]

Ikes was charged with transporting child pornography, in violation of 18 U.S.C. 2252(a)(1). He filed a motion to suppress the contents of the computer and the disks, alleging that the warrantless search violated his First and Fourth Amendment rights. The District Court denied Ickes' motion, holding that the search fell under the border search exception to the Fourth Amendment warrant requirement.[100] The Fourth Circuit held that a laptop border search preceded by reasonable suspicion was not intrusive and did not violate the Fourth Amendment.

In *U.S. v. Romm*, the Ninth Circuit affirmed a laptop border search based on reasonable suspicion.[101] Once again, the court did not need to address the issue of whether the search was routine or non-routine because it was preceded by reasonable suspicion. In that case, Stuart Romm flew from Las Vegas, Nevada, to Kelowna, British Columbia, on business.[102] At the British Columbia airport,

---

[92] *Ibid*.

[93] *U. S. v. Thirty-Seven (37) Photographs*, 402 U.S. 363 (U.S., 1971), at 376, rehearing denied 403 U.S. 924 (U.S. Cal., 1971); *Montoya de Hernandez, supra*, note 91 at 538.

[94] *Supra*, note 89.

[95] *U.S. v. Ickes*, 393 F.3d 501 (4th Cir. 2005).

[96] *Ibid* at 502.

[97] *Ibid*.

[98] *Ibid* at 503.

[99] *Ibid*.

[100] *Ibid*.

[101] *U.S. v. Romm*, 455 F. 3d 990 (9th Cir. 2006).

[102] *Ibid* at 994.

Canadian Customs Agents discovered that Romm had a criminal record and was on probation so they stopped him for questioning.[103] They asked him to turn on his laptop and noticed that he had several child pornography websites in his "internet history." The customs agents asked him if he had violated the terms of his probation by visiting these websites and Romm answered, "Yes. That's it. My life's over." Romm was then denied entry into Canada and was placed under detention until the next flight to Seattle. The Canadian Customs Agents informed United States Customs in Seattle that Mr. Romm had been denied entry and possibly had child pornography on his computer. At the Seattle-Tacoma airport, Romm was interviewed by United States Immigration and Customs Enforcement officers who told him they needed to search his computer. He denied having any child pornography on his laptop; however, the customs agents found that the computer contained ten images of child pornography, which Romm had deleted from his hard drive.[104] The Ninth Circuit found that a laptop computer search could be characterized as routine and thus did not need to be preceded by reasonable suspicion.[105]

It is critical to note that in each of these cases, customs officials had reasonable suspicion and the courts found it unnecessary to decide whether the searches were too intrusive to be characterized as routine. In other words, the courts of appeal did not simply find that the searches of the computer equipment were reasonable simply because they occurred at the border. In each case, the court relied on the presence of reasonable suspicion to conclude that the searches were reasonable. *Arnold* marks a significant departure from these earlier decisions because it was the first genuinely suspicionless search case to come before a Circuit Court.[106]

On July 17, 2005, Michael Arnold arrived at Los Angeles International Airport after a nearly 20-hour flight from the Philippines.[107] Once he collected his luggage from the baggage claim, he proceeded to customs. He was selected for secondary questioning and asked general questions about his vacation. The customs official then inspected Arnold's luggage, which contained his laptop computer, a separate hard drive, a computer memory stick (also called a flash drive or USB drive) and six CDs. She instructed Arnold to turn on the computer. When they found that the folders contained images of two nude women, the

---

[103] *Ibid.* Note that in an unrelated Florida state court prosecution, Romm pleaded *no contendere* to two counts of promoting sexual performance by a child and one count of child exploitation by means of a computer.

[104] *Ibid.* When Romm viewed the images online and enlarged them on his screen, his computer automatically saved copies of them to the **Internet cache**. The cache is a set of files on the user's hard drive. The Internet cache or "Internet temporary folder" is a set of files kept by a Web browser to avoid having to download the same files repeatedly. Essentially, it speeds up future visits to sites because it enables the images to be re-displayed quickly when you go back to them. All of the child pornography images found on Romm's computer had been deleted from the computer's recycle bin, which is an area of the hard drive where Windows stores files that the user deletes. See *ibid* at 995-996.

[105] *Ibid* at 997.

[106] *Supra,* note 88.

[107] *Ibid* at 1001.

customs agents called in special agents with the United States Department of Homeland Security, Immigration and Customs Enforcement (ICE). The ICE agents examined Arnold's computer and found numerous images depicting what they believed to be child pornography. The ICE agents seized the computer and storage devices, released Arnold and obtained a warrant two weeks later. Arnold was indicted for transportation of child pornography and for possession of a computer hard drive and compact disks containing images of child pornography.[108] He moved to suppress evidence seized by customs officers, contending that the warrantless search of his laptop computer violated his Fourth Amendment rights.[109]

On October 2, 2006, the United States District Court for the Central District of California held that the government's border search of information stored on Arnold's computer hard drive or electronic storage device violated the Fourth Amendment.[110] Judge Pregerson reasoned that because the border search of a laptop computer implicates the dignity and privacy interests of the individual, it is intrusive and must be preceded by reasonable suspicion.[111] However, on April 21, 2008, the Ninth Circuit reversed this decision and ruled that reasonable suspicion is not needed for customs officers to examine the electronic contents of an international traveller's laptop.[112]

Arnold argued that the District Court was correct to find that reasonable suspicion was required to search his laptop at the border because it is "fundamentally different" from traditional closed containers and more closely analogized to a home or the human mind, given its ability to store vast amounts of information and its ability to record ideas, chat logs and Web-surfing habits.[113] The Ninth Circuit rejected this argument and reasoned that it makes no difference that a laptop computer has the capacity to hold vast amounts of personal or confidential information. Judge O'Scannlain, who wrote the unanimous decision for the court, observed that "Arnold has failed to distinguish how the search of his laptop and its electronic contents is logically any different from the

---

[108] *Ibid* at 999.

[109] *Ibid*. Note that the border search doctrine allows broad discretion for United States customs officers to search the belongings of international travelers. In most cases, these searches will be constitutional if they are routine or proceeded by reasonable suspicion. As I will explain below, routine searches, such as the search of a traveler's luggage or handbag can be conducted without suspicion; however, the non-routine search of a person, such as a body-cavity or x-ray search, must be preceded by reasonable suspicion of illegal conduct. As the search becomes more intrusive, in terms of the invasion of individual dignity and privacy, a higher level of suspicion is required.

[110] *Ibid*.

[111] *Ibid* at 1003. The government had failed to establish that the customs officers had reasonable suspicion to conduct the search. The government appealed the District Court's order granting the motion to suppress.

[112] *Arnold, supra*, note 89 at 946.

[113] *Ibid* at 944.

suspicionless border searches of travellers' luggage that the Supreme Court and we have allowed."[114]

Some might argue that there is little reason to protect the privacy interests of those who import electronic contraband, such as child pornography, into the United States and that law abiding citizens do not need to worry about the government's ability to conduct warrantless border searches of electronic storage devices.[115] However, more than 500 million people annually cross our borders at legal entry points.[116] These travellers are more frequently bringing electronic storage devices with them across international boundaries. Although the individual traveller's reasonable expectation of privacy is considerably lower at the border, he or she does have a legitimate expectation that some information or personal items will be granted constitutional protection.[117] Constitutional concerns are raised much more clearly with respect to electronic storage devices than luggage, pockets and handbags, which are also routinely searched in airports because electronic storage devices can contain a wide range of private and personal information, including passwords and PINs, medical or banking records, income tax information, client information, letters, pictures and personal diaries.[118]

THE ROLE OF THIRD PARTIES – ISPS AND INDIVIDUALS

Individuals and Mandatory Child Pornography Reporting Laws in Canada

On June 12, 2008, Manitoba became the first Canadian province to enact a law requiring anyone who encounters child pornography to report it to police. The definition of child pornography in the *Child and Family Services Act*[119] mirrors the definition in the *Criminal Code*. The legislation also stipulates that no person will be required or authorized to seek out child pornography and that an informant's identity will be kept confidential except as required in judicial proceedings or by consent (it is also illegal to retaliate against an informant). Penalties for violating the provisions of the act include a maximum fine of $50,000 and/or imprisonment of not more than 24 months.

---

[114] *Ibid* at 947. The court also found that Arnold's analogy to "a search of a home based on a laptop's storage capacity is without merit." Relying on *California v. Carney* 471 U.S. 386 (1985), the Ninth Circuit observed at 947 that "[t]he Supreme Court has rejected applying the Fourth Amendment protections afforded to homes to property which is "capable of functioning as a home" simply due to its size, or, distinguishing between " 'worthy' and 'unworthy' containers. . .beyond the simple fact that one cannot live in a laptop, *Carney* militates against the proposition that a laptop is a home. . .as Arnold himself admits, a laptop goes with the person, and, therefore is 'readily mobile. . .[s]econd, one's expectation of privacy [at the border]' . . . is significantly less than that relating to one's home or office."

[115] These issues are discussed in Daniel J. Solove, "I've Got Nothing to Hide and Other Misunderstandings of Privacy," (2007) 44 San Diego Law Review 745 at 747.

[116] *U.S. v. Cortez-Rocha* 394 F.3d 1114 (4th Cir. 2004) at para. 48.

[117] *Montoya, supra,* note 91 at 539-540.

[118] *Arnold, supra,* note 89.

[119] C.C.S.M. 1985-86, c. C80.

In a similar vein, Nova Scotia's *Child Pornography Reporting Act*[120] received Royal Assent on November 25, 2008. It requires "any person who reasonably believes that a representation or material is child pornography" to "promptly report to a reporting entity any information, whether or not it is confidential or privileged, that the person has respecting the material." The definition of child pornography is also the same as that set out in the *Criminal Code*. The other provisions described above, with respect to the requirement to keep the identity of the informant confidential and the provision of immunity to the informant, unless the report is false or malicious, are also set out in the legislation. However, the penalty for failing to make a report is merely a fine of not more than $2,000 or imprisonment of not more than 6 months, or both.

Ontario's *Act to Amend the Child and Family Services Act to Protect Ontario's Children*,[121] which received Royal Assent on December 10, 2008, requires "any person who reasonably believes that a representation or material is, or might be, child pornography shall promptly report the information to an agency, organization or person designated by regulation." It too adopts the definition of child pornography contained in the *Code* and provides that a person convicted of failing to report is liable to a maximum fine of $50,000 or to imprisonment of not more than 2 years, or both.

While no one can argue that those who advocated for the introduction of mandatory reporting laws did not have the very best intentions in mind, noble intentions do not always make good law. In fact, there have been a number of criticisms launched against the mandatory reporting of child abuse and there is a lack of empirical evidence to support the effectiveness of this regime. Moreover, it is clear that the new mandatory reporting laws suffer from a number of critical defects.

At the very core of mandatory reporting laws are two broad obligations: the duty to protect and the duty to warn.[122] The essential goal is to help rescue vulnerable children from their abusers and to prevent child abuse cases from leading to severe injury or even death. Indeed, if there is a serious risk of immediate or ongoing harm to a child, intervention by the state may be required. Given these vital imperatives, those in favour of mandated reporting argue that abolishing it would seriously undermine children's rights to safety and increase their risk of harm.[123]

However, the mandatory reporting laws are not only about child protection. What is, in fact, the *pith and substance* of this legislation? In my opinion, the law constitutes an impermissible attempt by the provinces to regulate in the area of criminal law. Making this determination involves determining the essential subject matter of the legislation and then assigning it to one of the classes of subjects in respect of which the federal and provincial governments have distinct

---

[120] S.N.S. 2008, c. 35.

[121] S.O. 2008, c. 21.

[122] Seth C. Kalichman, *Mandated Reporting of Suspected Child Abuse: Ethics Laws and Policy* (American Psychological Association, 2000) at 43-44.

[123] B. Mathews and D.C. Bross (2008) 32 Child Abuse and Neglect 511 at 514.

legislative authority pursuant to ss. 91 and 92 of the *Constitution Act, 1867*.[124] There is no single test for the law's pith and substance; indeed, the analysis must be undertaken in a broad and flexible manner with a view to determining the legislation's dominant purpose and thus its constitutional validity.

The goals of mandatory reporting are clear: to save children from sexual abuse and to reduce the production, reproduction and distribution of child pornography. However, the fact that the law extends to imaginary forms of child pornography, for which direct harm to children is very minor or non-existent, it is clear that the legislation is not simply about child protection. Given that the Acts are broadly aimed at targetting all forms of child pornography, including those produced without any harm to children whatsoever (particularly given that such forms of expression are legal when they are privately held by the individual), it is difficult to see how it is an appropriate exercise of provincial power, especially given that it deals with public security, order and morality.[125]

Section 91(27) of the *Constitution Act, 1876* gives the federal Parliament exclusive legislative jurisdiction over criminal law, in the broadest sense of the term.[126] It goes without saying that the prohibition of child pornography, with penal consequences, has long been considered a subject for the criminal law. Although Canada's child pornography provisions were not enacted until 1993, representations of sex with children were formerly prohibited pursuant to the obscenity law provisions of the *Criminal Code*.[127] It is also relevant that the duplication of *Criminal Code* language can also raise an inference that the province has stepped into territory traditionally occupied by the federal government.[128] Here, the definition of child pornography set out in the Act mirrors that set out in s. 163.1 of the *Code*. This strongly raises the inference that the province has acted beyond its constitutional bounds.

Recall that the child pornography provisions were not limited to material produced by using real children. The provision applies to visual representations of real children and to representations of imaginary children. This means that an image depicting sex involving real child sexual abuse is treated in the same way as a sketch, drawing, painting or sculpture. In order to make general mandatory reporting laws effective, members of the general public would benefit from training in the recognition of child pornography (i.e., what exactly child pornography is and what it is not) and in the reporting process itself. Training also needs to notify the general public about their reporting responsibilities, what constitutes reasonable suspicion and what to expect when a report is made. There is also a risk that the Canadian mandatory reporting systems will be overburdened

---

[124] *R. v. Morgentaler* (1993), [1993] S.C.J. No. 95, 1993 CarswellNS 19 (S.C.C.), at para. 23.

[125] This comports with the classic formulation of the scope of the test for criminal law set out by Rand J. in *Reference re Validity of s. 5(a) of Dairy Industry Act (Canada)*, (1948), [1949] S.C.R. 1 (S.C.C.) (the Margarine Reference).

[126] *Attorney General for Ontario v. Hamilton Street Railway Co.*, [1930] A.C. 524 (P.C.) at 529.

[127] *Butler, supra*, note 38 at para. 60. See also *R. v. Westendorp*, [1983] 1 S.C.R. 43 (S.C.C.).

[128] *McNeil v. Nova Scotia (Board of Censors)*, [1978] 2 S.C.R. 662 (S.C.C.) at 669; *Rio Hotel Ltd. v. New Brunswick (Liquor Lisencing Board)*, [1987] 2 S.C.R. 59 at 70-71.

with notifications about child pornography and that this will put further strain on the system, leading it to become increasingly inefficient and ineffective.

The harm from this overemphasis on reporting and investigation is that the system is almost certain to be overwhelmed and policy-makers, as well as the general public, are likely to be distracted from the core issues at stake. Instead, focus is placed on investigating and prosecuting individual consumers on a case-by-case basis. The difficulty of this approach is compounded by the impossibility of the constant monitoring of individuals by their friends, colleagues, acquaintances and family members, which renders this policy approach unlikely to be effective at targetting the widespread circulation of these materials on the Internet.

It is noteworthy that similar problems have been discovered with respect to the mandatory reporting of child abuse. The most egregious mistake that the designers of that system made was to grossly underestimate the number of complaints that would be brought forward.[129] Since they underestimated the number of complaints, they failed to allocate sufficient resources to go along with the mandatory reporting laws. The result is that a large number of complaints have been made against families, all of which must be investigated and managed, which necessarily causes unnecessary hardship for the families who are forced to undergo intrusive investigations into their private lives. The increase in both substantiated and unsubstantiated cases also places a burden upon the scarce resources allocated to child protection and child welfare by the state.[130] Every year, a substantial amount of human and fiscal resources are devoted to child protection investigations, which could otherwise be spent on prevention and treatment. Since only a fraction of the complaints are substantiated each year (26% in the United States and 52% in Australia),[131] it is apparent that the mandatory reporting of child abuse laws has had serious negative unintended effects.

As I discussed earlier, Canada already has a highly successful child pornography reporting system in place. In 2004, Cybertip.ca was adopted as a partner to Canada's National Strategy for the Protection of Children from Sexual Exploitation on the Internet, and, in 2005, it was officially launched as Canada's national tip-line. Cybertip.ca receives reports about the sexual exploitation of children online, which includes child luring and child pornography. On average, it receives more than 700 tips per month.[132]

---

[129] Gary B. Melton, "Mandated Reporting: A Policy Without Reason" (2005) 29 *Child Abuse & Neglect* 9 at 10-13.

[130] N. Trocmé, M. Tourigny, B. MacLaurin, and B. Fallon, "Major findings from the Canadian Incidence Study" (2003) 27(12) Child Abuse and Neglect 1427-1439 [.pdf] report on low levels of severe harm identified as a result of child protection reports in Canada. See also B. Mathews and M.C. Kenny, "Mandatory Reporting Legislation in the United States, Canada and Australia: A Cross-Jurisdictional Review of Key Features, Differences and Issues" (2008) 13(1) Child Maltreatment 50-63.

[131] Berrick, Jill Duerr, and Neil Gilbert, *With the Best of Intentions: The Child Sexual Abuse Prevention Movement* (New York & London: Guilford Press, 1991) at 168.

[132] Jennifer Loughlin and Andrea Taylor-Butts, "Child Luring Through the Internet," Statistics Canada, March 2009, Vol. 29(1) at 9.

In 2005, when it was officially launched as a national tip-line, Cybertip.ca received five times (5,595) the number of reports it received in the previous year (956) and in 2008 it received as many as 7,846 reports. Between its launch in 2002 and January 2008, Cybertip.ca received 21,000 tips, of which 90% related to child sexual abuse images on the Internet and 8% related to online child luring.[133] Approximately 85% of Cybertip's reports are forwarded to international law enforcement agencies outside Canada.[134] While we cannot necessarily assume that all of the tips are accurate and reliable, the increase in the number of tips indicates that a larger number of online child pornography images are being reported. In addition, by January 2008, Cybertip.ca assisted in 42 arrests and the removal of 2,850 websites from the Internet.

ISPs and Filtering and Blocking

In November 2006, a group of Canada's largest ISPs, including Bell, Rogers, Shaw and Telus,[135] joined with Cybertip.ca to launch a new initiative to block Internet child pornography. Cleanfeed limits the public's exposure to online child pornography by voluntarily blocking images hosted outside of the country. To date, over 10,000 illegal images of children have been blocked through this process. Cybertip.ca receives complaints regarding websites hosting child pornographic images. Analysts assess the information and potentially illegal websites are forwarded to the appropriate law enforcement agency. Foreign-hosted URLs associated with child pornography are compiled onto a list and provided to participating ISPs. The ISPs then automatically block access to addresses on the list.

The system is designed to only prevent access to Internet addresses that contain child pornography images. Additionally, only websites displaying the most heinous forms of child pornography, including images of prepubescent children being assaulted or who are posed in a sexualized manner, are added to the list and only foreign websites are blocked. This reduces the chance of blocking content that is legal under Canadian law. There is also an appeal process to deal with cases where a site with no illegal content is mistakenly filtered by an ISP.

It is important to keep in mind that the Cleanfeed initiative is voluntary and not a legal requirement. As private entities, ISPs are not required by law to provide service to everybody on equal terms. An ISP has the right to cancel or refuse service to anyone and to filter out whatever content it deems objectionable. Customers who disagree with an ISP's practices can freely switch to another service provider. Further, only URLs hosted outside Canada are added to the list. Law enforcement officials proceed with their normal course of investigation for sites hosted within Canada. If the content is hosted in Canada, the *Code* enables

---

[133] See http://www.cybertip.ca.

[134] *Ibid.*

[135] Michael Geist, "Project Cleanfeed Canada," November 24, 2006, available online at: http://www.michaelgeist.ca.

a judge to determine whether it meets the legal definition for child pornography and to issue an order for it to be taken down or destroyed.[136]

THE NEED FOR INTERNATIONAL COOPERATION

Online child pornography is a particularly difficult type of crime to confront on an international scale because it requires many countries to agree on a variety of difficult questions. For example, the very idea of what constitutes "child pornography" is a controversial issue. Owning pedophilic materials is not illegal in Sweden, although it is a crime to market or transmit them, whereas in areas of the Middle East, a picture of a girl in a bikini is considered scandalous.[137] The lack of an international consensus on these issues has led to inconsistent standards and practices around the world and a lasting difficulty in defining what types of material should be prohibited.

If many countries are not combatting child pornography, this creates a large number of safe havens for criminals to exploit. An individual running a child pornography website can simply relocate his criminal enterprise to a jurisdiction that does not criminalize these materials. Another problem is that the volume of child pornography circulating on the Net is so large that law enforcement agents in only a few countries cannot possibly investigate and prosecute offenders on their own, particularly when they are faced with conflicting regulations in multiple jurisdictions worldwide. As I discussed above, child pornography images can be hosted anywhere in the world. In fact, a recent review of the child pornography website and image hosting countries by Cybertip.ca found that nearly 60 countries were hosting this type of content. According to Cybertip.ca, the images they analyzed were hosted on at least 7,367 different IP addresses and of the 12,696 websites they looked at, there were 10,436 different entries for host country information! The table in Figure 4.2 illustrates the top child pornography image and website host countries around the world.

---

136 *Criminal Code, supra*, note 30 at s. 164.1.
137 Frances Cairncross, *The Death of Distance* (Boston: Harvard Business School Press, 1997) at 183.

Figure 4.2: Top 15 Image and Website Host Countries

TOP 15 IMAGE HOST COUNTRIES		TOP 15 WEBSITE HOST COUNTRIES	
United States	57.3% (4,222)	United States	49.2% (6,359)
Canada	12.6% (929)	Russia	20.4% (2,636)
Russia	7.5% (550)	Canada	9.0% (1,165)
Netherlands	3.6% (264)	Japan	4.3% (557)
Spain	3.4% (250)	South Korea	3.6% (471)
Thailand	3.0% (220)	Netherlands	3.4% (444)
China	2.1% (156)	Germany	1.1% (145)
Germany	1.7% (122)	China	1.1% (143)
Japan	1.2% (88)	Spain	0.8% (108)
United Kingdom	1.0% (72)	Hong Kong	0.7% (85)
Czech Republic	1.0% (71)	Panama	0.6% (81)
South Korea	0.9% (63)	United Kingdom	0.6% (78)
Panama	0.7% (48)	France	0.5% (63)
Portugal	0.6% (47)	Thailand	0.4% (57)
France	0.6% (44)	Belize	0.3% (43)

Source: Cybertip.ca

Cybertip.ca reports that there were 929 images hosted on unique IP addresses in Canada. As many as 64.5% of these images depicted children under 8 years old. The majority of the images (47.1% or 438) were hosted by a website designed to enable the public hosting of images. The remaining images were being hosted on the following venues: 24.8% (230) were hosted on a website that sells member information to or provides links to websites hosting child pornography images; 8.2% (76) of the images were hosted on a website made available from within Canada that allows users to create personalized social networking websites; 4.6% (43) were hosted by a webhost and 13.7% (127) were hosted on at least 13 different services from within Canada.

The Importance of International Conventions

The Council of Europe's *Convention on Cybercrime*[138] is the first multilateral treaty aimed at facilitating international cooperation in the prosecution of computer crimes. It was signed in Budapest on November 23, 2001, by member states of the Council of Europe and by several non-member states, including Canada, Japan, South Africa and the United States, that participated in its development.[139] The Convention entered into force on July 1, 2004. As of March

---

[138] The Council of Europe's Convention on Cybercrime, Budapest, 23.XI.2001, available online at: http://conventions. Coe.int/Treaty.en.Treaties/HTM/185.htm.

[139] Laura Huey and Richard S. Rosenberg, "Watching the Web: Thoughts on Expanding Police Surveillance Opportunities under the Cyber-Crime Convention," (2004) Canadian Journal of Criminology and Criminal Justice 597.

12, 2008, there were 43 signatory states.[140] Of the 43 countries that signed the Convention, 22 countries have ratified it and entered it into force, including the United States but not Canada.[141] Parliament must ratify the Convention in order for it to take effect in Canada. The reasons why Canada has not yet ratified this important treaty are discussed in Chapter 10.

Article Nine of the Convention requires signatory states to adopt legislative and other measures to establish criminal offences under their domestic law for the following conduct:

- producing child pornography for the purpose of distribution through a computer system;
- offering or making available child pornography through a computer system;
- distributing or transmitting child pornography through a computer system;
- procuring child pornography through a computer system; and
- possessing child pornography in a computer system.

This Article is essential because it establishes a comprehensive framework for the prosecution of child pornography offences throughout the world. By enacting a common list of offences into their penal codes, member states will make it easier to combat child pornography on the Internet because they will have a universal basis upon which to approach these crimes. Given that there are vast differences between countries on the question of what constitutes a child, the provision can assist in the investigation and prosecution of online child pornography offences by establishing a universal standard to work from.

Much of the treaty deals with extradition and mutual assistance between nations in investigating and gathering evidence in cybercrime offences. The extradition provisions, contained in Article 24, are critical to the investigation and prosecution of online child pornography offences that can involve the apprehension of suspects who live in one country but are under investigation or are charged in another. This might occur in the case where an individual operates a website from one country and makes child pornography available in another country for a fee. It will help to prosecute child pornographers who set up their operations in countries with weak laws and escape prosecution in the host country, as well as those to whom they disseminate their illegal materials. Similarly, the mutual assistance provisions contained in Article 25 obligate countries to help out other countries in cross-border investigations to the "widest extent possible." This can include drafting mutual assistance treaties with specific nations or responding to requests for mutual assistance from states with respect to investigations. This is important because the physical evidence needed to arrest and prosecute a child pornography suspect can be located anywhere in the world.

---

[140] US Department of State, Fact Sheet, Office of the Spokesman, Washington, DC, September 29, 2006, available online at: http://www.state.gov.
[141] Council of Europe Treaty Office, available online at: http://conventions.coe.int.

The Need for an International Law Enforcement Network

Given the inter-jurisdictional nature of child pornography offences, there is an essential need to coordinate law enforcement agencies at the international, federal, provincial and local levels. International police organizations like the International Criminal Police Organization (Interpol) can facilitate inter-jurisdictional cooperation by providing an international network for police forces to exchange information quickly and cooperate in the policing of cyberspace.[142] This is critical because the online transmission of child pornography is often perpetrated through many countries at once and, in order to investigate and prosecute offenders, assistance between law enforcement in multiple jurisdictions is often needed. Assuming that one or more countries is unable or unwilling to assist, based on a lack of financial or technical resources or a simple political disinterest in the crime, formal oversight bodies and mutual assistance agreements can be of enormous benefit.

Due to the international nature of child pornography offences, investigators need to know their own laws and also be familiar with the relevant laws of other jurisdictions. Ideally, multi-jurisdictional or multi-national law enforcement teams will be created to specialize in this area and work together internationally. We have already witnessed the success of this approach with the creation of the **Virtual Global Taskforce**, or **VGT**.[143] The VGT is an international alliance of law enforcement agencies that includes the National Crime Squad in the United Kingdom, the High Tech Crime Centre in Australia, the Royal Canadian Mounted Police, the United States Department of Homeland Security in the United States and Interpol. VGT members have met in Australia, Ireland, the United Kingdom and Canada to discuss how to combat Internet child exploitation and share information and ideas.

In addition, international law enforcement efforts have been enormously enhanced by the **Child Exploitation Tracking System (CETS)**, which is a technological resource that was recently developed and funded by Microsoft Canada Co., as well as several international police agencies, in conjunction with the RCMP and the Toronto Police Service.[144] CETS is critical to our ability to stamp out the worldwide market for child pornography because it can enable police in various countries around the world to conduct investigations over the Internet that span multiple legal jurisdictions; to identify suspects in multiple countries and investigations at once; to facilitate cooperation between investigating officers in the same country, as well as in other nations; and, because it enormously improves the technical capabilities of law enforcement officials to combat child pornography crimes. It is important to note that CETS began as an informal initiative and that it operates independently from the Cybercrime Convention.

---

[142] Susan W. Brenner and Joseph W. Schwerha, "Introduction – Cybercrime: A Note on International Issues," (2004) 6 Information Systems Frontiers 111 at 112.

[143] See http://www.virtualglobaltaskforce.com/what_we_do.asp.

[144] See Government of Canada National Child Exploitation Coordination Centre Website, available online at: http://ncecc.ca/cets_e.htm.

CETS began with an email written in 2003 by Detective Sgt. Paul Gillespie, head of the child exploitation team of Toronto's Sex Crimes Unit. Gillespie emailed Microsoft Chairman Bill Gates, asking if his company could assist the police to combat online child pornography.[145] Gates responded by asking Frank Clegg, then-president of Microsoft Canada, to work with Gillespie's team on an innovative database program that would store and retrieve large amounts of data, such as arrest records, email addresses, aliases, credit card information and intelligence reports.[146] To date, Microsoft has invested more than $4.5 million, and employed some of its best software engineers to develop the necessary resources and technology for the system.[147] By early 2007, it had assisted with 64 arrests and the identification of 43 victims worldwide.[148]

The system enables police to capture, share and search information since it links police forces and quickly finds common elements in their investigations. It allows the police to visualize linkages between suspects and criminal organizations. By sharing information over a secure network, police officers can identify connections between investigations that refer to the same people or online identities. Police agencies throughout Canada and around the world can now manage and analyze large volumes of information in powerful new ways, such as cross-referencing data relationships and using social-network analysis to identify communities of offenders and determine who is significant in these relationships.[149] This allows police to find the leaders of large-scale child pornography operations and target the key players.

It also enables police to store and retrieve enormous amounts of inter-related information about various cases and suspects and analyze it as a whole, instead of trying to access individual sites and collect the information themselves and trying to match it and find connections. CETS also provides real-time chats and newsgroups so that officers from around the country, and in different countries once this feature is activated, can share information and best practices techniques, such as how to get warrants to catch predators online. Law enforcement officials using CETS can also post images onto global bulletin boards and ask other police forces to help find the children in the images. Prior to CETS, police services were manually sorting through files and photos, making it almost impossible to share information.

Given the inter-jurisdictional nature of online child pornography offences, the ability to share and cross-link information between police forces in multiple

[145] "RCMP, Toronto Police Service and law enforcement from across Canada unite to fight the online sexual exploitation of children - Microsoft Canada President David Hemler and national police services join launch of Canadian-developed Child Exploitation Tracking System (CETS)," available online at RCMP website: http://www.rcmp-grc.gc.ca/news/2005/n_0510_e.htm.
[146] Lee Craig, "Arming Police With High-Tech Tools," April 18, 2006, University of Alberta, *Express News*, available online at: http://www.expressnews.ualberta.ca/article.cfm?id=6549.
[147] "Tool Thwarts Online Predators," April 7, 2005, available online on Microsoft website at: http://www.microsoft.com/presspass/features/2005/apr05/04-07CETS.mspx.
[148] Julian Sher, *Caught in the Web: Inside the Police Hunt to Rescue Children from Online Predators* (New York: Carroll and Graf Publishers, 2007) at 271.
[149] *Ibid.*

jurisdictions is critical. Microsoft and the Toronto Police Service (which jointly share ownership of the program) will now implement CETS in any country in the world that asks for it, free of charge. Several countries are already actively promoting CETS and it has recently been implemented in Europe and Asia. Indonesian police worked with the United States Department of Justice to build their program, which was recently launched in June of 2006, and 'ndonesian police officers travelled to Toronto to see how CETS was being used there.[150] CETS is now also in various stages of development and implementation in the United States, Britain, Brazil, Italy, Spain and Australia, and several other European countries have expressed interest in it.[151]

CHILD LURING

The anonymity of the Internet makes it easier for child sexual predators to locate and communicate with children than in the past. As such, we have recently witnessed the emergence of a new kind of crime, known as "child luring," whereby adult sexual predators seek to gain the trust of their targetted victims through online chats and then entice them into sexual activity over the Internet or in person.

Following the addition of the luring offence to the *Code* in 2002, the number of incidents reported to the police has been on the rise.[152] Child luring offenders are different than child pornography offenders, although both groups frequently use the Internet to facilitate their crimes.[153] The concern is that child sexual predators are now using the Internet to gather information about children for a potential sexual assault (e.g., phone number, address, school, hobbies and interests) or to lure them into a real-life meeting where an actual sexual assault can take place.[154]

While the Internet has provided child sexual predators with increased access to children to lure into sexually exploitative situations, there is very little data available on child luring in Canada. The information that does exist includes only the incidents that have been reported to police in recent years. Thus, it is extremely difficult to understand the full extent and nature of child luring offenders and victims in Canada. This problem is compounded by the fact that very few child luring incidents are reported to the authorities.[155] Further research is clearly needed in this area to better understand the online sexual exploitation of children.

The Nature of Child Luring Incidents

The anonymity and ease of access to a wealth of sensitive information about children make these social networking sites attractive to child sexual predators.

---

[150] Dan Nystedt, "Indonesia Joins Microsoft to Battle Child Predators," June 28, 2006, available online at: http://www.Webwereld.nl.

[151] Jack Kapica, "Cybercops on the Move," October 17, 2006, *The Globe and Mail*, available online at: http://www.theglobeandmail.com/blogs/cyberia.

[152] *Criminal Law Amendment Act, 2001*, S.C. 2002, c. 13, s. 172.1.

[153] Seto, *supra*, note 2 at 61.

[154] *Ibid.*

[155] Loughlin and Taylor-Butts, *supra*, note 132 at 7.

In the years 2006 and 2007, a total of 464 incidents of child luring were reported by police services in Canada.[156] This figure represents an average of about 3 incidents of child luring per 10,000 young people across Canada under the age of 18 reported to police per year.[157] In three-quarters of these cases, child luring was the only violation. The remaining one-quarter involved one or more additional violations, including the production or distribution of child pornography (31%); invitation to sexual touching (32%); as well as sexual assault; sexual interference; indecent acts; sexual exploitation and procuring prostitution.[158] Between 2004 and 2007, approximately three-quarters of the court cases involving a charge of child luring resulted in a finding of guilt.[159]

Recent research suggests that child luring incidents typically involve adolescents rather than young children. The reason is that very young children are difficult to access online. They use the Internet infrequently for communication, and tend to be supervised when they do; as well, they are not likely to respond to online solicitations in the same way as older children.[160] In the vast majority of cases in which child sexual predators use the Internet to target victims, the offender uses the Internet to develop an intimate relationship with an adolescent. Children who are between the ages of 13 and 17, particularly those who are 13 to 14 years old, are the most likely to share personal information and to engage in risky online behaviour.

By the time the child goes to meet the offender in real life, the perpetrator is expecting to engage in sexual activity. Trickery most often occurs in cases where the offender promises love and romance to the victim to disguise the fact that his interests are predominantly sexual in nature. These relationships often take place in isolation, out of sight from peers, family members and other care-givers and lead children to disclose personal information and feel intimately attached to the predator much more quickly than they would in real life.[161]

Researchers at the National Center for Missing and Exploited Children (NCMEC) reported that during their Youth Internet Safety Surveys, conducted in 2000 and 2005, many adolescents disclosed using the Internet to chat, email or exchange instant messages with strangers and being sexually solicited or approached online, as well as experiencing unwanted exposure to sexual materials.[162] The researchers conducted a survey of 1,500 children between the ages of 10 and 17. Approximately 1 in 7 American children reported receiving

---

[156] *Ibid.*

[157] *Ibid.* Note that these data are from the 2006 and 2007 *Incident-based Uniform Crime Reported Surveys* (UCR2), Statscan (see http://www.statscan.gc.ca/).

[158] *Ibid.*

[159] *Ibid* at 5.

[160] *Ibid.*

[161] *Ibid.*

[162] Janis Wolak, Kimberly Mitchell and David Finkelhor, "Online Victimization of Youth: Five Years Later" (Alexandria, VA: National Center for Missing and Exploited Children, Bulletin #07-06-025, 2006) at 7. The researchers conducted telephone surveys of representative national samples of 1,500 youth Internet users (between the ages of 10 to 17, with a roughly equal number of boys and girls) between 1999 and 2000 and 1,500 youth Internet users in the year 2005 in the United States.

online sexual solicitations, which represented a decline from the year 2000, when approximately 1 in 5 children surveyed reported receiving such solicitations. Sexual solicitations and approaches include requests to engage in sexual activities or talk or give out personal sexual information, which are unwanted and made by an adult, and can also involve offline contact with the perpetrator through the telephone or an in-person meeting.[163] The decline in the number of incidents was attributed to greater awareness of online sexual exploitation by young people and less risk-taking in online behaviour.

Nevertheless, research shows that Canadian young people are engaging in activities that might raise their risk of online sexual victimization, including sharing personal information over the Internet; emailing or posting photos online; chatting online with strangers; and visiting adult websites and chat-rooms.[164] Children who are dealing with emotional problems or who have a history of physical, sexual or emotional abuse are particularly vulnerable to online victimization by sexual predators. It is thought that these children are more likely to venture online looking for attention and affection; more prone to engage in sexually risky behaviour; and less threatened by inappropriate sexual advances directed toward them.[165]

It is important to note that as children get older, they tend to use the Internet in more sophisticated and interactive ways. This places older children at a greater risk of online victimization than younger children who use technology in less complicated ways and who are far less likely to connect with strangers or to use the Internet without adult supervision.[166] Typically, the Internet predator befriends the adolescent victim and tries to make him or her feel comfortable about sharing personal information with a stranger. The offender then introduces sexual discussion into the relationship as a precursor to asking to meet in person or to share sexual images online. As one might expect, violence and abduction are extremely rare in these cases because the adolescent targets tend to be sexually mature and interested in romance.

The factors that make adolescents susceptible to exploitation online are that they are likely to be impulsive and inquisitive. Their sexual curiosity makes them particularly vulnerable to forming "romantic" attachments with online sexual predators. It is important to stress that online predators do not typically prey upon unsuspecting victims on social networking sites but seek out children who are

---

[163] *Ibid* at 3. Note that a detailed discussion of child luring is beyond the scope of this book; however, there are many instances where child pornography and child luring overlap. There are a number of luring offences in the *Criminal Code*, which include: Sexual Exploitation, s. 153(1); Incest, s. 155; Prostitution under 18 years, s. 212(1) and (4); Sex Assault/with weapon/aggravated, ss. 271, 272, 273; Child Pornography, s. 163.1; Sexual Interference, s. 151; Invitation to sexual touching, s. 152; Bestiality under 14 years, s. 160(3); Indecent act, s. 173(2); Abduction under 16 years, s. 280.

[164] Loughlin and Taylor-Butts, *supra*, note 132 at 6.

[165] Janis Wolak, Kimberly Mitchell and David Finkelhor, "Online Victimization of Youth: Five Years Later" (2006) National Center for Missing and Exploited Children, Washington, D.C. at 117 and Melissa Wells and Kimberley Mitchell, "How Do High Risk Youth Use the Internet? Characteristics and Implications for Prevention" (2008) 13(3) Child Maltreatment 227.

[166] *Ibid.*

vulnerable to seduction and manipulation. The children who are most vulnerable to victimization by online child molesters are those who interact with strangers on the Internet, particularly where this involves talking about sex and sending and/or receiving pornography.[167]

It is important to give adolescents the appropriate tools and information to help them make smart decisions and to recognize dangers online. This should include information about the dangers of forming personal relationships with older men, who are more likely to try to seduce vulnerable adolescents into sexual encounters, as well as sharing sexually explicit images of themselves. Adolescents must also be taught to recognize healthy versus unhealthy romantic relationships and given information about how to report inappropriate behaviour online. Ideally, educational materials should stress that it is normal and healthy for adolescents to be curious about romance and sex and not place so much emphasis on the risks of stranger danger. However, it is important for them to be made aware of seduction and manipulation techniques used by predators and the criminal nature of these relationships.

Child Luring and the Law in Canada

Section 172.1 of the *Criminal Code*[168] sets out the offence of luring a child via the Internet as follows:

> 172.1 (1) Every person commits an offence who, by means of a computer system within the meaning of subsection 342.1(2), communicates with
>
> (a) a person who is, or who the accused believes is, under the age of eighteen years, for the purpose of facilitating the commission of an offence under subsection 153(1) [sexual exploitation], section 155 [incest] or 163.1 [child pornography], subsection 212(1) [procuring] or (4) [prostitution of person under eighteen] or section 271 [sexual assault], 272 [sexual assault with a weapon, threats to a third party or causing bodily harm] or 273 [aggravated sexual assault] with respect to that person;
>
> (b) a person who is, or who the accused believes is, under the age of sixteen years, for the purpose of facilitating the commission of an offence under section 280 [abduction of person under sixteen] with respect to that person; or
>
> (c) a person who is, or who the accused believes is, under the age of fourteen years, for the purpose of facilitating the commission of an offence under section 151 [sexual interference] or 152 [invitation to sexual touching], subsection 160(3) [bestiality in presence of or by child] or 173(2) [exposure] or section 281 [abduction of person under fourteen] with respect to that person.

This provision prohibits the use of computers to communicate with a child for the purpose of facilitating the commission of one of the listed secondary offences. The vague wording of this section raises a number of important questions: what if the accused is not communicating with a child but an undercover police officer who is pretending to be a child; what if the accused does not actually arrange a meeting with the child; and what if the accused claims that he never

---

intended to carry out the specified secondary offence or meet with the child? Recently, the courts have helped to define the scope of this provision and have provided answers to these difficult questions. In *R. v. Alicandro*,[169] the court found that a person could be convicted under s. 172.1(1)(c) for communicating with a person (an adult police officer posing as a 13-year-old child) believed to be under 14 for the purpose of facilitating the commission of the offence of exposing his genitals to a child. The important thing to note is the accused's belief that he was communicating with a person under the age of 14. In other words, the offence under s. 172.1(1)(c) is made out regardless of whether the crime is factually possible or not (i.e., it doesn't matter that the "child" was an adult police officer rather than an actual child).

Similarly, in *R. v. Legare*,[170] the Supreme Court of Canada held that s. 172.1(1)(c) creates an *inchoate offence* (i.e., a preparatory crime that captures otherwise legal conduct meant to culminate in the commission of a crime) consisting of three elements:

1. an intentional communication by computer;
2. with a person whom the accused knows or believes to be under 14 years of age;
3. for the specific purpose of facilitating the commission of a specified secondary offence with respect to the underage person.

The case also establishes that the accused does not need to attempt to meet in person for a charge of luring by a computer system to be made out under s. 172.1(1)(c). The key thing to note is that Parliament under s. 172.1(1)(c) enacted an offence of communication, not of physical contact.

It is also noteworthy that Fish J., who wrote the decision for the majority of the Supreme Court of Canada, found that the use of sexually explicit language is not essential in these communications. He noted that adults who use computers to sexualize or groom or trick a child toward being receptive to a sexual encounter often work to gain their trust through seemingly innocent conversations about their home life, friends, personal interests and so on. All of this is designed to foster a sense of trust and security, with a view to furthering the adult's capacity to sexually exploit the child. As such, the content of the communication is not necessarily important: what matters is whether the Crown establishes, beyond a reasonable doubt, that the accused communicated by computer with (a person believed to be) an underage person for the purpose of *facilitating* one of the listed secondary offences.

Online Sting Operations and Child Luring Cases

Generally speaking, there are two ways that undercover investigations are initiated in child luring cases in Canada. Some cases begin with a complaint from a citizen or other agency. In these cases, the police are notified about a possible child luring incident that has come to light in any of the following ways: an

---

[169] (2009), 2009 CarswellOnt 727, [2009] O.J. No. 571 (Ont. C.A.).
[170] [2009] 3 S.C.R. 551 (S.C.C.).

authority figure, such as a parent, finds a disturbing chat log on a child's computer; a social networking site receives a complaint about an adult; a child pornography suspect is arrested and other evidence emerges to suggest he has been committing hands-on abuse; or a child discloses the abuse to another child or an adult.

In these cases, the police go online and seek to target the suspect with a fake online persona (of a fictional child) or an investigator takes over the online identity of the child victim. In cases where a police officer assumes the identity of the child, he or she must learn all about the personal interests and habits of the child, as well as what information has already been disclosed by the child to the suspect. These cases are likely to be challenging because the police must work to convince the suspect that he is still communicating with the child that he is trying to lure.

In other cases, undercover officers pose as 12- or 13-year-old girls in chat-rooms. In these cases, the investigators don't have a particular suspect in mind, but they are simply trying to locate offenders and communicate with them online. Their goal is to take on the persona of a naïve and vulnerable child. Child luring offenders typically engage in public chat then move to private communications (private chat, email, IM). Offenders often arrange, or attempt to arrange, in-person meetings (although this is *not required* for a luring charge). Additionally, offenders sometimes send images of themselves exposed or masturbating and/or invite the "child" to do this. Child pornography is also sometimes found on the offender's computer, which can lead to additional charges.

CONCLUSION

The Internet is now the primary mechanism by which child pornography is distributed. It is also being used by child sexual predators to share images and stories with each other, to document their exploitation of real children, and to form social networks that can facilitate and reinforce cognitive distortions and abusive fantasies. We need to recognize that child sexual abuse is a widespread phenomenon that occurs in the real world.

From this perspective, we need to focus on preventing child sexual abuse from occurring in our communities. We need to educate both adults and children about what constitutes child sexual abuse and child pornography and how to report evidence of child exploitation and abuse. Attention must be paid to educating young children, particularly those under the age of 12, about child sexual abuse. Education in this area must focus on helping children to recognize the signs of victimization and abuse, both online and offline. Children must also be provided with the skills and knowledge to disclose abuse to trusted adults or other authority figures.

We also need to develop strategies aimed at curtailing the circulation of these images online. Given that the Internet is a global phenomenon, very few countries in the world can turn a blind eye to the issue of online child victimization. Canada should focus on developing international standards and protocols to define and respond to child sexual abuse and exploitation, working with banks and ISPs to track down and eliminate commercial child pornography websites, as well as to prosecute and punish those who host and access them. We also need to focus our attention on building partnerships with other law enforcement agencies to internationally share information and resources. Finally, we should also think about how to facilitate suspect identification and evidence gathering in online investigations here at home. More will be said about this in Chapter 10.

QUESTIONS FOR FURTHER THINKING AND DISCUSSION

1. The punishments for distributing imaginary child pornography, including stories, drawings and cartoons are the same for distributing real child pornography images. Does this make sense as a matter of policy?
2. What are the indirect harms identified by the Chief Justice in the *Sharpe* case? Do these harms justify the criminalization of imaginary works?
3. Child pornography is constitutionally protected speech in Canada but the government is also permitted to criminalize it. How can this paradox be reconciled?
4. What are the risks to individuals and society of permitting customs agents to search electronic storage devices at the border without any reasonable suspicion whatsoever?
5. What is Operation Cleanfeed? Are these kinds of initiatives likely to be effective at combatting cybercrime?
6. What are the risks of law enforcement officials engaging in online sting operations in child luring cases?
7. What are the elements of the offence set out in s. 172.1 of the *Criminal Code*?
8. Are the offences of child pornography and child luring related? If so, how?
9. What are the unique characteristics of the children who are typically targetted by Internet child sexual predators? Why might these victims be challenging for law enforcement/prosecution officials to deal with?

5

Bullying, Stalking and Harassment on the Internet

KEY TERMS AND CONCEPTS

- Bodily harm
- Bullying
- *Communications Decency Act* (*CDA*)
- Criminal harassment
- Cyber-bullying
- Cyber-stalking

- Defamation
- Defamatory falsehood
- Defamatory liable
- Hate propaganda
- Identifiable group
- James Keegstra
- Libel

- Publicly incite hatred
- Slander
- Stalking
- Threatening death or bodily harm
- Willfully promote hatred

INTRODUCTION

Cyber-bullying is a new form of harassment occurring among school-aged children. In a nutshell, it is willful and repeated harm inflicted through the medium of electronic text. Cyber-bullies use modern communications technology to cause harm/distress to their targetted victims. They are often known to their victims but hide behind the anonymity provided by technology, such as the Internet. The bullying relationship is characterized by an imbalance of power, such that the victim finds it hard to defend him- or herself and feels powerless against the bully. Both girls and boys engage in cyber-bullying.

In Chapter 4, you learned that child luring and child pornography have existed for decades and have proven to be especially challenging for law enforcement officials in the age of the Internet. Cyber-bullying and cyber-stalking are also problems that have received a great deal of media attention in recent years. However, unlike child pornography and child luring, which have also generated a great deal of public concern and have received widespread attention from the media in recent years, the Canadian government has done little to address the problems of cyber-bullying and cyber-terrorism through the enactment of new legislation.

CYBER-BULLYING: AN OVERVIEW

Bullying is a psychologically disturbing form of social cruelty among adolescents in North America and throughout the world. It has longstanding roots in traditional taunting and name-calling, which typically occurs in the middle-school setting; however, the medium of the Internet has allowed this practice to flourish and created new challenges for parents, teachers and law enforcement officials. Cyber-bullying appeared to emerge out of nowhere in the last several years and has escalated to extremely dangerous, even life-threatening extremes. Further, the anonymity of the Internet has enabled participation by a seemingly limitless number of perpetrators who hide behind pseudonyms and IP (Internet Protocol) addresses, making it very difficult to pinpoint the source of the threat.

Bullying is commonly defined as repeated, aggressive behaviour in which there is an imbalance of power between the parties. It is an aggressive, intentional act carried out repeatedly by an individual or group of individuals over time against a victim who cannot easily defend him- or herself. Cyber-bullying, as its name suggests, is when a person under the age of 18 is threatened, harassed, humiliated, or otherwise targetted by another young person using communication technologies.

Generally speaking, bullying involves physical acts (such as hitting or shoving) as well as verbal abuse (such as taunting or name-calling) as well as more indirect forms of torment such as social exclusion and the spreading of rumours about the target. The verbal harassment that accompanies bullying can also incorporate sexual or racist remarks and homophobic slurs.[1] The key factor that defines this behaviour as bullying is that it occurs repeatedly, and is persistent, unwanted and deliberate, often involving a weaker player within the context of an ongoing social interaction. Since this has been recognized historically as a schoolyard problem, the focus of concern has typically been on bullying in the schools – in the classroom, locker room, hallway, cafeteria, playground, bathroom, and so on – based on the assumption that children must be in close physical proximity in order for bullying to occur.

However, in recent years, technology has transformed the landscape of children's social lives, and interactions between peers now take place more frequently in the digital sphere than in real space. This has enabled bullies to extend the reach of their aggression and threats beyond the real physical world of face-to-face contact to target victims virtually through the use of emails, instant messaging, social networking sites, cellular telephones, and the like. Electronic bullying commonly occurs through email, instant messaging (e.g. MSN, Yahoo

---

[1] Shaheen Shariff and Dianne L. Hoff, "Cyber bullying: Clarifying Legal Boundaries for School Supervision in Cyberspace" (2007) 1(1) International Journal of CyberCriminology 76 at 80.

Messenger), chat-rooms, blogs, Web pages, digital images, social networking sites (e.g. MySpace and Facebook) and text messages sent to cell phones.

One of the reasons for the rapid rise in cyber-bullying is the fact that children's spontaneous outside play has been almost entirely replaced by high-speed Internet, cell phones with cameras and video screens, video games and portable music devices, such as iPods. Even very young children, age 6 years and under, now spend an average of almost 2 hours per day with screen media (i.e., television, movies and computers).[2] As many as 94% or more than 5,000 Canadian students recently surveyed, from grades 4 through 11, have Internet access in the home and 86% have their own email accounts.[3] Furthermore, 37% have their own computer with Internet access (not shared with anyone else); 23% have their own cell phone and 22% have a Webcam for personal use.

Just as we saw with other traditional types of crime that are now being committed online, cyberspace has facilitated communication between the criminal and the victim without the need for physical contact. In other words, crimes that once required complex human interaction are now easily committed remotely and anonymously in cyberspace. In a recent study led by Wendy Craig of Queen's University, researchers interviewed 2,744 Canadian boys and found that 22.3% reported being bullied. Of the 3,051 girls polled, 17% said they had been bullied.[4] Other bullying surveys also suggest that more boys than girls report being victims of bullying and almost all boys named other males as aggressors.[5] A recent self-report survey on delinquency among young people in Toronto reports that 16% of children in grades 7 to 9 reported being bullied on more than 12 occasions in the year prior to the survey.[6]

The ability to hide behind fake screen names or to steal someone else's screen name or identity and communicate as that person provides young people with the opportunity to communicate things that they might be reluctant to express in person. Degrading comments can be posted online and reach far more people than they would in real space; thus, the potential for hurt and humiliation is far greater. Since bullies do not have to "face" their victims, attacks can be more vicious and destructive than in the real world. Moreover, a greater number of children can participate in the bullying through the use of Web pages and social networking sites. Also, parents might not be aware of what is going on or not have the computer skills to monitor their children's activities online.

---

[2] American Academy of Pediatrics, "Policy Statement – Media Violence," (2009) 124(5) Pediatrics 1495 at 1496.

[3] ERIN Research Inc. and Industry Canada, "Young Canadians in a Wired World, Phase II," November 2005, available online at: www.media-awareness.ca/english/research/.

[4] M. Molcho, W. Craig, P. Due, W. Pickett, Y. Harel-Fisch and M. Overpeck, "Cross-national Time Trends in Bullying Behaviour 1994-2006: Findings from Europe and North America" (2009) 54(2) International Journal of Public Health 225.

[5] M. Totten, P. Quigley and M. Morgan, "CPHA Safe School Survey for Students in Grades 4-7" (2004) Ottawa: Canadian Public Health Association and Department of Justice Canada, available online at: http://acsp.cpha.ca/antibullying/english/surveys/4-7_survey.html.

[6] Statistics Canada "Youth Self-Reported Delinquency, Toronto, 2006" Ottawa: Canadian Centre for Justice Statistics, Statistics Canada (2007) Juristat (27): 6.

The convenience of being able to hide behind a computer also frees cyber-bullies from the normative constraints that ordinarily govern behaviour in real space. Through remaining anonymous online, a bully can conveniently harass a victim from the privacy of one's bedroom, without the immediate risk of being identified. The lack of immediate detection and punishment further serves to reinforce the bullying behaviour. Even though chat hosts regularly observe the dialogue in chat-rooms in an effort to monitor and control content, personal messages sent between users, such as email or text messages, are only viewable by the sender and the recipient, thereby outside the bounds of regulatory enforcement.

One of the most devastating effects of being cyber-bullied is the fact that he or she has no way of knowing whether the torment is being perpetrated by one individual or a group of individuals. Moreover, when bullying occurs over the Internet it is often constant and extremely difficult for the victim to escape. Cyber-bullying can also cause extensive harm to the victim; for example, the publishing of hateful or defamatory information about the victim is extremely difficult to control and millions of people can access and download information before it is removed from the Internet. This fact alone provides cyber-bullies with an even greater sense of power over their victims than they previously enjoyed in real space.

New advances in technology have also meant that many young people are connected to their email, phones and Internet at virtually all hours of the day and night. This access provides cyber-bullies with a perfect means by which to engage in ongoing, persistent threatening and harassing behaviour. The home was traditionally one of the few places where an individual could seek refuge from the outside world. However, given the integration between the public and private spheres through technological innovation, a cyber-bully can easily penetrate the walls of even the victim's most sacred spaces, including the home and the bedroom, to continually harass and threaten the target. While some young people are able to shrug-off instances of being bullied, many other children have experienced extremely serious repercussions, including depression, eating disorders, chronic illness, and, in some extremely tragic cases, even suicide.

It is easy for some people to shrug this off as simply a phase or even a normal part of life. However, even though victims might not necessarily be getting physically hurt, they are suffering emotionally. One such example is the case of David Knight, a boy from Ontario, who was bullied through elementary and high school by the same classmates.[7] In high school, the bullying moved online as his classmates set up a website where they targetted David and his family members. They attacked him for being gay (which he wasn't) as well as a drug trafficker and a pedophile (which were also untrue). The website reportedly received millions of visitors who were invited by the website's creators to contribute to the insults by posting lewd and hurtful comments.

---

[7] See Joan Leishman, "Cyber-Bullying," CBC News Online, March 2005, available online at: http://www.cbc.ca/news/background/bullying/cyber_bullying.html and Shariff and Hoff, *supra*, note 1 at 85.

Fortunately, David was able to withstand these attacks and he successfully graduated from high school. However, many other Canadian children who have been victims of bullying have not been able to cope with the painful ridicule directed against them. For example, in 2005, a 16-year-old boy hanged himself in Roblin, Manitoba, after being bullied at the Goose Lake high school. The teenager was taunted for being gay. In 2004, 16-year-old Travis Sleeve shot himself after two-and-a-half months of harassment and vandalism, which included students throwing rocks at his car. In 2000, 14-year-old Dawn-Marie Wesley of Mission, British Columbia, hanged herself and left behind a suicide note in which she admitted she was being bullied at school.[8] These tragic incidents speak to the endemic nature of cyber-bullying and stress that it is an extremely serious problem that must be dealt with by the Canadian government.

THE LAW IN CANADA

While the *Criminal Code*[9] contains provisions targetting threatening and harassment, traditional legal responses are inadequate to deal with cyber-bullying because of the fact that it can be perpetrated anonymously in cyberspace by such a large pool of participants. Moreover, when parents and victims turn to the courts for help, their claims are often delayed or settled out of court due to the lack of clarity surrounding freedom of expression and privacy issues in cyberspace.[10] Internet bullying is also tough for law enforcement officials to investigate unless it crosses the line to involve death threats or other criminal offences.

There is no offence in the *Criminal Code* targeting bullying and nothing that allows police to investigate and obtain records and identify the person setting up the site. As for schools, their hands are often tied as well because the bullying takes place on computers away from school. ISPs (Internet Service Providers) are also not responsible for deciding what material should or should not be allowed on the Internet; as such, they are not responsible for censoring or screening the material they host online. This means that while Canadian ISPs can make reports to the police and remove illegal content from their servers, there is no legal requirement for them to do so except in the limited case of child pornography, where a judicial order is required. For example, under s. 164.1 of the *Criminal Code*, if a judge is satisfied by "information on oath" that child pornography is stored on or made available through a computer, he or she can order the "custodian" of the system, such as an ISP, to give an electronic copy of it to the court; provide the information necessary to identify and locate the poster of the material; and ensure that the material is no longer stored, or made available, through the computer. The judge can also order the custodian of the system to

---

[8] Another case in Canada of a teenager committing suicide as a result of being bullied is: Hamad Natosh, 14, who jumped off the Pattullo Bridge between New Westminster and Surrey, British Columbia. He left behind a note that stated he was being bullied.

[9] R.S.C. 1985, c. C-46.

[10] Shariff and Hoff, *supra,* note 1 at 86.

delete the child pornography,[11] and in cases where the court has an electronic copy of the material, the judge can order that it be deleted by the court.[12]

Cyber-Bullying and Freedom of Expression

As I discussed in Chapter 4, s. 2(b) of the *Charter*[13] guarantees everyone the fundamental freedoms of thought, belief, opinion and expression, including freedom of the press and other media of communication. The Supreme Court of Canada has interpreted the s. 2(b) guarantee of freedom of expression broadly to mean that if the activity conveys or attempts to convey a meaning, it has expressive content and *prima facie* falls within the scope of the guarantee.[14] The exception to this general definition is that s. 2(b) does not protect activity that conveys a meaning in a violent form.[15] If the activity in question falls within the protected sphere of conduct, meaning that it conveys or attempts to convey a meaning in a non-violent form, it is normally safeguarded by the Canadian courts.

The reason that this is relevant in the context of cyber-bullying is that many cases of online harassment and cyber-bullying have, because they involve young people, turned on the question of whether or not school officials have a right to suspend, expel or otherwise sanction the cyber-bully for his or her conduct. Since s. 2(b) of the *Charter* protects us from government interference with our right to express ourselves freely, and many schools are government institutions, the question arises as to whether or not the school's interference with the s. 2(b) rights of its students is permissible or not. There have been no cases brought before the Canadian courts on this issue; however, a number of cases have been brought forward in the United States challenging the right of school officials to limit students' speech (posted online about other students or school employees). The courts in these cases have typically adopted a hands-off policy when it comes to school policies dealing with cyber-bullying.[16] For those on the other end of the spectrum claiming that a school did not intervene and deal with the problem of cyber-bullying, victims can also turn to the law of torts and negligence for compensation.

The Civil and Criminal Response to Cyber-Bullying

Cyber-bulling can be addressed either under the civil or criminal law in Canada. Civil law deals with property rights, personal dignity and freedom from harm. Under the civil law, the victim can sue the bully for defamation. When the bully harms someone's reputation by spreading false information about them, it

---

[11] Section 164.1(5).

[12] Section 164.1 (6).

[13] *Canadian Charter of Rights and Freedoms,* Part I of the *Constitution Act, 1982,* being Schedule B to the *Charter Act 1982* (U.K.), 1982, c. 11.

[14] *R. v. Sharpe,* [2001] 1 S.C.R. 45 at para.41.

[15] *Ibid* at para.147.

[16] See, for example, *J.S. v. Bethlehem Area School Dist.,* 807 A.2d 847 at 850 (Pa. 2002), where a student created a website targetting a teacher, called "Teacher Sux," in which graphic pictures of severed heads, along with a statement to "send $20.00 to help pay for a hit man," was sufficient for the judge to uphold the expulsion of the student.

is called slander. When the defamation is recorded permanently, for example in a book or on a website, it is called libel. To be libelous, a statement must harm a person's reputation; have a clear and obvious target; and be seen by other people. The perpetrator may have to pay damages (i.e., financial compensation) to the victim if found liable for libel or slander. Defamatory liable is a crime under the *Criminal Code*. It is most often used if the libelous statement is directed against a person in authority and could seriously harm his or her reputation.

A bully can also be punished for creating an unsafe environment by making the target feel that he or she cannot go to school without facing threats and harassment. Schools are required to provide a safe environment for their students; thus, a school might punish a student for online behaviour that makes it difficult for other students to learn. For instance, in 2007, Ontario amended the *Education Act* to include online bullying. Students can now be suspended for cyber-bullying, even if it occurs outside the school.[17]

Criminal harassment occurs when someone says or does something to make a person fear for his or her own safety, or the safety of others. Section 264 of the *Code* sets out the offence of criminal harassment:

> 264 (1) No person shall, without lawful authority and knowing that another person is harassed or recklessly as to whether the other person is harassed, engage in conduct referred to in subsection (2) that causes that other person reasonably, in all the circumstances, to fear for their safety or the safety of anyone known to them.
>
> (2) The conduct mentioned in subsection (1) consists of
>
> . . .
>
> (b) repeatedly communicating with, either directly or indirectly, the other person or anyone known to them;
>
> . . .
>
> (d) engaging in threatening conduct directed at the other person or any member of their family.

Case law has established the test to be met:

1. the accused has engaged in one of the specified forms of conduct;
2. the complainant was harassed;
3. the accused knew that the complainant was harassed or was reckless or willfully blind as to whether the complainant was harassed;
4. the conduct caused the complainant to fear for his or her safety or the safety of anyone known to them; and

---

[17] *Education Amendment Act*, S.O. 2007, c. 14. "Bullying" is now added to the list of behaviours for which students can be suspended. "Bullying" is defined in the Ministry's Policy/Program Memorandum No. 144 as "repeated, persistent, and aggressive behaviour directed at an individual or individuals that is intended to cause (or should be known to cause) fear and distress and/or harm to another person's body, feelings, self-esteem, or reputation." Bullying is further defined as taking different forms: physical, verbal, or social. The Ministry definition also recognizes cyber-bullying. The definition states bullying "may also occur through the use of technology" such as email, cell phones, text messaging, Internet websites, or other technology.

5.   the complainants fear in all of the circumstances was reasonable.[18]

Being harassed has further been defined as feeling tormented, troubled, worried continually or chronically plagued, bedeviled and badgered.[19]

The offence of threatening death or bodily harm is set out in s. 264.1(1)(a) of the *Code*, which reads:

> 264.1(1) Every one commits an offence who, in any manner, knowingly utters, conveys or causes any person to receive a threat
>   (a)   to cause death or bodily harm to any person;

Bodily harm is defined in s. 2:

> "bodily harm" means any hurt or injury to a person that interferes with the health or comfort of the person and that is more than merely transient or trifling in nature.

Note that bodily harm includes psychological hurt, as well as physical injury.[20] The threat does not have to be directed at a particular person, but simply an ascertainable or identifiable group.[21] Conditional and future threats are also included.[22] Moreover, the offence does not require that the person uttering the threats have any intention to carry them out or act on them.

When do school yard taunts cross over the line to become a criminal offence of harassment? These questions were recently considered in the case of *R. v. W. (D.)*,[23] which concerned the threats uttered by several grade 9 students toward Dawn-Marie Wesley in Mission, British Columbia. At the age of 14, Wesley tragically committed suicide the evening of November 10, 2000. Following her death, DW was tried for two counts of uttering threats to cause death or bodily harm and one count of criminal harassment.

DW and Wesley were students together in grade 9. DW confronted Wesley at school and told her to stop talking about her or she would beat her up. DW also told Wesley's best friend that she was going to get people to beat Wesley up. Wesley was frightened, spoke to the school counselor on a daily basis, and ensured that she did not walk home alone. During lunch, the group of girls approached Wesley's group, and DW threatened Wesley again. Wesley was crying. During a telephone conversation with Wesley the next evening, D.W. yelled into the phone, "You are fu—ing dead." Wesley committed suicide on the same day as the telephone call.

DW was convicted for criminal harassment. The court found that there was no doubt that DW intended her words to intimidate or be taken seriously, or that a reasonable person would consider them a threat. It was not necessary that DW

---

[18]   *R. v. Sillipp* (1997), 120 C.C.C. (3d) 384 (Alta. C.A.), leave to appeal refused (1998), , 123 C.C.C. (3d) vi (S.C.C.).

[19]   *R. v. Kosikar* (1999), 138 C.C.C. (3d) 217 (Ont. C.A.), leave to appeal refused (2000), 142 C.C.C. (3d) vi (S.C.C.).

[20]   *R. v. McCraw* (1991), 66 C.C.C. (3d) 517 (S.C.C.).

[21]   *R. v. Rémy-Mercier* (1993) 82 C.C.C. (3d) 176 (Que. C.A.), leave to appeal refused (1993), 84 C.C.C. (3d) vi (S.C.C.); and *R. v. Deneault* (2002), 2002 CarswellBC 500, [2002] B.C.J. No. 517 (B.C. C.A.).

[22]   *R. v. Ross* (1986), 26 C.C.C. (3d) 413 (Ont. C.A.).

[23]   (2002), 2002 CarswellBC 641, [2002] B.C.J. No. 627 (B.C. Prov. Ct.).

actually intend to harm Wesley. In a related case, DH was convicted with uttering a threat to Wesley, contrary to s. 264.1(1)(a) of the *Criminal Code*. DH was 15 and also in grade 9 with Wesley; however, the two were not friends. Wesley had heard SW was spreading lies about her and she confronted SW and told her to stop. DH heard from SW about this and believed that Wesley was trying to bully SW.

DH and four of her friends confronted Wesley, who was with three of her friends. She used aggressive words and body language. She told Wesley to leave SW alone or she would kick her and beat her up. Wesley was scared and started to cry. Following this, Wesley and her friends tried to avoid DH and her friends. However, Wesley committed suicide shortly after the incident. The court found that in the context of the surrounding circumstances, it was clear that DH intended her words to be a threat to cause bodily harm to Wesley, that she intended that the words be taken seriously and that the words caused fear to her. It was irrelevant that the words were spoken between high school students. More importantly, Provincial Court Judge Maltby stressed that if the court ignored the law and excused DH's conduct, it would send a message that it is permissible for children to intimidate and threaten other young people. As a result, DH was sentenced to 15 months probation and 20 hours of community service. The terms of probation included that DH reside at a facility directed by her youth worker, attend school or maintain employment and that she attend anger management and drug and alcohol counselling. As well, she was not permitted to communicate with any of the other individual young people involved in these incidents.

A bully can also be found to be in violation of the *Canadian Human Rights Act* if he or she spreads hateful or discriminatory messages about another person based on race, national or ethnic origin, colour, religion, age, sex, sexual orientation, and so on.[24] It is important to keep in mind, however, that freedom of expression is central to a democracy. As such, although racist and hateful comments are offensive to the vast majority of Canadians, they are not necessarily illegal. Section 13 of the *Canadian Human Rights Act* prohibits the communication by means of telecommunication (including the Internet) of messages that are likely to expose a person to hatred or contempt on the basis of race, national or ethnic origin, colour, religion, age, sex, sexual orientation, marital status, family status, disability or conviction for which a pardon has been granted.[25]

In the case of *North Vancouver School District No. 44 v. Jubran*,[26] a teenager was repeatedly subjected to insults and harassment of a homophobic nature during the 5 years he was in high school. Before graduating, he filed a complaint under the *British Columbia Human Rights Code*,[27] against the School Board. The Human

---

[24] *Canadian Human Rights Act*, R.S.C. 1985, c. H-6.

[25] For example, in January 2002, the Canadian Human Rights Tribunal ordered Ernst Zundel to cease and desist from publishing hate messages on the *Zundelsite* because his writings violate s. 13.

[26] (2005), 2005 CarswellBC 788, [2005] B.C.J. No. 733 (S.C.C.), leave to appeal refused (2005), [2005] S.C.C.A. No. 260, 2005 CarswellBC 2475 (S.C.C.).

[27] R.S.B.C. 1996, c. 210.

Rights Tribunal concluded that Jubran was discriminated against on the basis of sexual orientation. It further found that it was irrelevant what Jurban's sexual orientation truly was, or whether or not his harassers believed he was, homosexual. He was subjected to a course of conduct that constituted harassment on a prohibited ground of discrimination (i.e., sexual orientation). Moreover, the Board of School Trustees was responsible for the discrimination as it failed to provide an educational environment that was free from discriminatory harassment and did not respond effectively to the discriminatory conduct.

However, the School Board's application for judicial review of this decision was granted by the British Columbia Supreme Court. The judge decided that Jubran was not a victim of discrimination pursuant to s. 8 of the *Human Rights Code* because he was not homosexual and the students who attacked him did not believe he was a homosexual.

Fortunately for Jurban, the British Columbia Court of Appeal overturned that ruling and reinstated the tribunal decision. The Court held that for the purpose of discrimination based on sexual orientation, s. 8 does not require that the complainant identify himself as a homosexual or that his harassers believe he is a homosexual.

Schools often maintain that they are not responsible for cyber-bullying incidents because they take place off campus, in cyberspace, outside of regular school hours. However, based on the cases that have been brought forward in the United States, this argument is not likely to hold much weight if the cyber-bullying actions cause substantial disruption to the school learning environment.[28] Many Canadian school boards now have anti-bullying programs that include training for both teachers and students.

CANADIAN LAW AND HATE SPEECH ON THE INTERNET

Sections 318 and 319 of the *Criminal Code* make it an offence to advocate genocide, publicly incite hatred or willfully promote hatred against an "identifiable group." For example, "advocating genocide" includes publicly arguing that members of an identifiable group should be killed. An identifiable group is defined as any section of the public distinguished by colour, race, religion, ethnic origin and sexual orientation.

In summary, these *Criminal Code* provisions are intended to prohibit the public distribution of hate propaganda. Inciting hatred is only prohibited if statements are communicated in a public place. Online communications that advocate genocide or willfully promote or incite hatred are likely to fall within the provisions because the Internet is a public network. Under s. 320.1 of the *Code*, a judge has the authority to order the removal of hate propaganda from a computer system that is available to the public.[29] This authority extends to all computer systems located within Canada.

---

[28] Sharif and Hoff, *supra*, note 1 at 100.

[29] Note that this is similar to the *Criminal Code* provision that can be used to require ISPs to remove child pornography materials from their networks, taking them out of circulation. See discussion of s. 164.1 of the *Code*, *supra*, note 11.

In 1990, the Supreme Court of Canada considered whether s. 319(2) of the *Code* violated freedom of expression.[30] James Keegstra was an Alberta high-school teacher who taught his students that the Holocaust did not occur and that it was part of a Jewish conspiracy. He was charged under s. 319(2) of the *Code* with wilfully promoting hatred against an identifiable group by communicating anti-semitic statements to his students. However, Keegstra argued that s. 319(2) violated freedom of expression, as protected by s. 2(b) of the *Charter*. The Supreme Court of Canada held that, although s. 319(2) necessarily limits free expression, it is a reasonable limit consistent with s. 1 of the *Charter*, and is therefore constitutional.

As mentioned earlier in this chapter, a communication in a non-violent form is considered expressive and therefore falls under the s. 2(b) guarantee. Also bear in mind that s. 2(b) does not only protect good or positive forms of expression. While it may seem obvious that this form of speech contributes little or nothing positive to society, experience demonstrates that in other cases it can be difficult to draw the line between speech that has value and that which does not. And, while it is imperative to curb hate-mongering, creativity and the free exchange of ideas must be also promoted. As such, the majority of the Supreme Court of Canada found that communications that wilfully promote hatred against an identifiable group are protected by s. 2(b) of the *Charter*.

However, after considering whether the law satisfies the Oakes Test and is justified under s. 1 of the *Charter*, the Court found that s. 319 of the *Code* was a reasonable limit upon freedom of expression. Hate propaganda was said to be only tenuously connected with the values underlying freedom of expression, including the quest for truth, the promotion of individual self-development, and the protection and fostering of a vibrant democracy where the participation of all individuals is encouraged. Further, Parliament's objective of preventing the harm caused by hate propaganda was of sufficient importance to warrant overriding the guarantee, particularly considering our historical knowledge about the devastating effects of the promotion of hatred against identifiable groups. Canada's commitment to the values of equality and multiculturalism, enshrined in ss. 15 and 27 of the *Charter*, also strongly supports this objective.

The exclusion of private communications from the scope of s. 319(2), as well as the need for the promotion of hatred to focus upon an identifiable group in order for it to be subjected to state scrutiny, further supports the view that the offence set out in s. 319(2) is narrowly confined. While other modes of combatting hate propaganda clearly exist, the Court concluded that it is better to use a variety of legislative tools to prevent the spread of racist expression. Indeed, s. 319(2) was said to send a strong message of condemnation and deter those who would otherwise harm individuals, as well as society at large, by communicating hate propaganda.

---

[30] *R. v. Keegstra*, [1990] 3 S.C.R. 697 (S.C.C.).

THE AMERICAN LEGAL FRAMEWORK

It might come as a surprise to some readers to learn that American law protects telecommunication service providers at the expense of victims of cyber-bullying and harassment. Pursuant to the *Communications Decency Act (CDA)*,[31] Congress granted broad immunity for ISPs. In other words, ISPs will not be treated as the publisher or speaker of content posted by third parties. Further, s. 230(c)(2) gives ISPs immunity from civil liability for attempting to restrict objectionable material posted by third parties. It mandates that any good faith action taken by ISPs to remove or restrict availability to objectionable content posted by third parties is not actionable against the ISP.

The case of *Zeran v. America Online Inc.*,[32] is the general precedent used by the American courts regarding Internet abuse. The case involved a series of anonymous postings on AOL message boards following the Oklahoma City bombing in April 1995. The postings claimed to advertise "Naughty Oklahoma" tee-shirts, with captions that included "Visit Oklahoma. . .it's a blast!!!." The individual posting the messages claimed to be Zeran and provided his phone number. As a result, he received abusive phone calls and even death threats. When new messages continued originating on AOL, Zeran sued AOL for failing to stop the harassing threats. However, the court ruled that s. 230 of CDA provided absolute immunity to AOL regardless of its knowledge of the defamatory material. The judge focused on the ISP's role as distributor rather than publisher. Publishers, such as the publishers of this book, are responsible for statements made by third parties using their services; however, mere distributors are not.

Another well-known cyber-bullying case in the United States further illustrates the challenge of prosecuting cyber-bullies and holding them accountable for their actions under American law. In October of 2007, Josh Evans sent a message to 13-year-old Megan Meier that said, "You're a sh—-y person and the world would be a better place without you in it." A few hours later, Megan committed suicide. After her death, police investigators discovered that Josh Evans was not a real person but a fictional character created on MySpace by Lori Drew, the mother of one of Megan's classmates. Lori Drew apparenly created this fictional character to find out what Megan was saying about her daughter. Under the guise of Josh Evans, Lori befriended Megan and then, after a few months, began to harass and torment her. Following Megan's death, Lori Drew was charged under the *Computer Fraud and Abuse Act* for one count of conspiracy and three counts of accessing a computer without permission. On December 4, 2008, she was convicted of unauthorized access; however, she was merely found guilty of violating the MySpace regulations stating that a profile cannot be created to impersonate another person. This case illustrates the difficulty of targetting cyber-bullying, particularly when there is no national law against it.[33]

---

[31] Communications Decency Act, enacted by the U.S. Congress on February 1, 1996. Also known as the Telecommunications Act of 1996.

[32] 129 F.3d 327 (C.A.4 (Va.),1997)

[33] *United States v. Lori Drew*, 08-CR-582 (C.D. Cal. 2008). Note that Drew was subsequently acquitted on August 28, 2009.

CYBER-HARASSMENT AND CYBER-STALKING

As I discussed above, cyber-bullying is when a person under the age of 18 is tormented, harassed, embarrassed, humiliated or otherwise targetted by another young person under the age of 18. The person who is doing the bullying, as well as the victim, must be a minor for the harassment to constitute bullying. If adults are targetting each other in this way, it is called cyber-harassment or **cyber-stalking** and not cyber-bullying.

Stalking can be defined as continued communication or interaction with someone with the goal of intimidating, upsetting or otherwise emotionally affecting the target. This includes causing the victim to reasonably fear for his or her safety, whether that is physical, emotional or psychological. It includes following a person, appearing at a person's home or place of business, making harassing phone calls, leaving messages or gifts and vandalizing the person's property. Often the person communicating the message implies that he or she will cause injury or harm to the victim.

Not surprisingly, cyber-stalking is an old crime, rather than the development of a new offence. Stalkers have long used technology to perpetrate their crimes; in fact, obscene telephone calls are still made today. However, digital technology has increased the capacity of those who would like to direct unwelcome communications against a target.

From this perspective, cyber-stalking can be characterized as threatening behaviour or unwanted advances directed at another using the Internet and other forms of online computer communications, including search engines; online forums; chat-rooms; social networking sites; bulletin and discussion boards; electronic viruses or unsolicited emails; and unwanted text-messages sent from cell phones or other electronic communication devices.

Cyber-stalkers can conceal their true identities by using different screen names or anonymous remailers that make it difficult to determine the true identity or source of an email message. Digital technology can also be mobilized to recruit others and involve them in negative activities against the victim. Email allows a perpetrator to transfer threatening pictures, video or audio to a victim's electronic mailbox. In a newsgroup, a cyber-stalker can post negative comments about the victim. On an Internet site, a person can post information designed to intimidate or harass the target. This can include advertisements for sexual services using the victim's name, address or phone number.

Most cyber-stalking cases involve former intimate partners, although stranger stalking occurs in the real world as well as in cyberspace. Stalkers are generally motivated by the desire to control their victims. Cyber-stalkers often engage in a pattern of both online and offline conduct that is designed to annoy and harass their victims, including repeated telephone calls, driving by their place of residence, following them and communicating with them by email, instant messaging, social networking sites and in chat-rooms.[34] Cyber-stalkers have also

---

[34] See *R. v. Owens* (2007), 2007 CarswellOnt 2088, [2007] O.J. No. 1350 (Ont. C.J.).

been known to create websites that are designed to harass, annoy, intimidate and embarrass their victims.

In the first successful prosecution under California's cyber-stalking law, prosecutors in Los Angeles obtained a guilty plea from a 50-year-old former security guard, Gary Dellapenta, who used the Internet to solicit the rape of a woman who rejected his romantic advances.[35] He posted invitations on the Internet under the name of a 28-year-old woman, the would-be object of his affections. He said that she had fantasies of rape and gang rape. He then communicated via email with men who replied to the solicitations and gave out personal information about the woman, including her address, her phone number, details of her physical appearance and instructions on how to bypass her home security system.

Strange men turned up at her residence on six different occasions, sometimes in the middle of the night, and she received a number of obscene phone calls. While she was not physically harmed, she was afraid to leave her home, would not answer her phone and lost her job. Dellapenta pleaded guilty in April of 1999 to one count of stalking and three counts of solicitation of sexual assault. He was convicted and sentenced to 6 years in a California state prison.[36] The conviction was a victory for law enforcement officials, but one that required a colossal amount of manpower.

Another example, which is also taken from the American context, is *U.S. v. Murphy*. On June 29, 2004, 38-year-old James Robert Murphy of Columbia, South Carolina, pleaded guilty in the United States District Court for the Western District of Washington to two counts of use of a telecommunications device (i.e., the Internet) with intent to annoy, abuse, threaten or harass.[37] Murphy had a sporadic romantic relationship with Joelle Ligon from 1984 until 1990. In May of 2002, Murphy began sending dozens of harassing emails and fax messages to Ligon and her coworkers. Murphy created the Anti Joelle Fan Club and repeatedly sent threatening emails from this alleged group, including false information about Ligon's background to her coworkers.

The harassment worsened over time with Murphy making it appear that Ligon was sending pornographic material to her coworkers in the City of Seattle. Even after Ligon was able to get a court order barring Murphy from contact, he violated the order by sending an email denying he was the harasser. Eventually, Murphy was sentenced to 5 years probation, 500 hours of community service and a $12,297.23 fine. Ligon successfully lobbied Washington state lawmakers to sponsor a bill to outlaw cyber-stalking and testified about her experience.

In Canada, individuals who commit cyber-stalking can be charged under s. 264(1) of the *Criminal Code*. A recent illustration is *R. v. Weavers*. In that case, Weavers was charged with criminally harassing Mandi Perkins contrary to s.

---

[35] Doug Simpson, "Feds Find Dangerous Cyber Stalking Hard to Prevent," CNN.com, June 12, 2000, available online at: http://www.cnn.com/2000/TECH/computing/06/12/cyberstalkers.idg/index.html.

[36] Tom Zeller, Jr., "Despite Laws, Stalkers Roam On the Internet" *NY Times*, April 17, 2006.

[37] *United States v. Murphy*, United States District Court for the Western District of Washington. D.C. No. CR-04-00163-TSZ.

264(1)(2)(d) of the *Code*. Perkins is a Canadian living in Los Angeles, California. She produced an independent record that she promoted on a MySpace website. Fans could request that they be added as friends of Perkins and they would be automatically added to reflect the rising increase in her popularity. Eventually, Perkins had over a hundred thousand friends connected to her MySpace account.

However, in October 2007, Weavers began sending emails on an increasingly frequent basis in which he professed his love for Perkins and stated that he wanted to be with her. Perkins was not a friend of Weavers and she did not know who he was. Weavers' own MySpace account was completely devoted to Perkins with her pictures, mp3s of her songs, lyrics from her songs and writings, which suggested that Weavers and Perkins were married. After Weavers was blocked from having access to Perkins' MySpace account, he continued to request that he be added as a friend and because of the automatic adding of friends on MySpace, he would be added and would continue to post comments.

The court convicted Weavers of criminal harassment and observed that there was no doubt that the emails sent by Weavers established that he engaged in repeated communications, both directly and indirectly, with Perkins, contrary to s. 264(2)(b). Furthermore, the tone and nature of the emails' content and Weavers' persistence in sending them despite being aware that they were unwanted clearly established that he was engaged in threatening conduct. Weavers was aware that his conduct was unwanted and he knew his conduct was harassing Perkins.

The court also noted that when one read the over 100 emails sent by Weavers to Perkins, a reasonable person would be fearful for their safety. The frequency of the emails increased despite measures taken to advise him to cease and desist in contacting Perkins and to block Weavers' access to Perkins' MySpace website. Further, from reviewing Weavers' emails it was apparent that as time passed, they were becoming more bizarre, more alarming and more aggressive in their tone and content. Perkins was clearly in fear for her safety as a result of Weavers' conduct.

Unfortunately, as with a number of other types of cybercrime, a lack of sufficient reporting and statistics on this type of criminal activity makes it hard to arrive at an accurate number of incidents. Cyber-stalking is under-reported to police because many victims feel that nothing can be done to help them. And, in fact, many police agencies are also reluctant or ill-equipped to deal with the problem.

As the *Weavers* case suggests, one of the difficulties facing law enforcement officials is the fact that cyber-stalkers can target victims in multiple jurisdictions. The challenge of investigating and prosecuting cybercrime when it occurs in one's own jurisdiction is daunting enough. However, when a cybercrime originates in another country, the problem is compounded. In order to conceal their location, cybercriminals physically present in one jurisdiction may "loop" or "weave" their attacks through a number of jurisdictions on the way to their target. Even in the absence of deliberate intent to conceal one's location, the nature of Internet traffic is such that criminal communications may cross jurisdictional boundaries as a matter of course.

Once it is determined that a computer crime originated from a foreign jurisdiction, one must seek the cooperation of authorities in that jurisdiction to identify the suspect. This may be difficult as authorities in the other country may lack the capacity to assist. They might not have laws prohibiting the conduct. They may not have officers with sufficient training in computer forensics or they may lack interest; their priorities may lie elsewhere. These issues will be further explored in Chapter 9.

Proving Cyber-Stalking

Notwithstanding these difficulties, there are a number of important things that victims can do to protect themselves against cyber-stalkers and assist the police with their investigations. Most important, the victim must make the stalker aware that the behaviour is unwelcome. Either the victim or a law enforcement officer should tell the stalker to stop. The stalker can also be reported to the ISP as well as to local law enforcement. The victim should also keep copies of all threatening emails, messages, texts and the like.

INTERNET DEFAMATION

When an individual publishes false statements on the Internet and/or emails these statements to others regarding the victim, he or she can be tried for defamatory liable. Canadian courts have recognized the increased potential for harm associated with the publication of defamatory material on the Internet, particularly given the broad reach of these statements.[38] The law of defamation protects a person's reputation from defamatory falsehoods. Pursuant to this law, a "publication" is the communication of a defamatory statement to a third party; in fact, publication to a wide audience is not required. This can take place through a variety of media, including through the Internet.

In Canada, the law of defamation (outside Quebec) is based on the common law and typically requires the plaintiff to establish three things:

1. the offending statement was communicated or published to a third party;
2. the offending statement refers to the plaintiff; and
3. the offending statement is defamatory in that it is false and discredits the plaintiff.[39]

The threshold inquiry is whether the words that are published are reasonably capable of a defamatory meaning.[40] The essence of a defamatory statement is its

---

[38] The Ontario Court of Appeal in *Barrick Gold Corp. v. Lopehandia* (2004), 2004 CarswellOnt 2258, 187 O.A.C. 238 (Ont. C.A.), stated at para. 34: "The mode and extent of publication is therefore a particularly significant consideration in assessing damages in Internet defamation cases."

[39] A. Gahtan, M. Kratz, J.F. Mann, *Internet Law: A Practical Guide for Legal and Business Professionals* (Scarborough: Carswell, 1998) at 278.

[40] R.E. Brown, *The Law of Defamation in Canada*, 2nd ed., (Toronto: Carswell, 1994) at vol. 1, at pp. 5-4 and 5-5:

In determining whether a publication is capable of conveying a defamatory meaning, the court will be guided by the test of reasonableness. "Whether a publication is defamatory depends on the circumstances of publication and will vary with time and place." [Per

tendency to injure a person's reputation. A statement is defamatory if it tends to lower the reputation of the victim in his or her community in the estimation of reasonable persons.[41]

Monetary damages are intended to compensate a victim for the injury suffered as a result of the defamatory publication and also to provide for vindication of reputation.[42] The following factors are considered in an assessment of general damages for defamation: the plaintiff's conduct, position and standing; the nature of the defamation; the mode and extent of publication; the absence of any retraction or apology; and the whole of the defendant's conduct from the time of publication to the end of trial. This is well-illustrated by the recent case of *Newman v. Halstead*.[43]

In that case, Halstead was a parent of children who were at schools in British Columbia, at which some of the plaintiff teachers taught. She posted negative information about a number of teachers and a school trustee on chat-rooms, bulletin boards and a website, all of which she created. On the website she placed some of the teachers' names in close association with teachers who had been convicted of crimes, such as pedophilia. She also posted pictures of the teachers and if she did not have a picture of the teacher she used a picture of an apple with a worm. She referred to the teachers as "British Columbia's Least Wanted." She also claimed that the teachers were violent towards students, unprofessional, incompetent and the type of people who associated with pedophiles. She further indicated that the school trustee was corrupt, a bully and unprofessional.

She also wrote a large number of emails to people, including District staff, trustees, principals and vice-principals, media outlets, and politicians, including the Minister of Education, regarding the plaintiffs. In addition, she submitted written complaints to various officials, including members of the Human Rights Tribunal, the College of Teachers, the Workers Compensation Board, the Information and Privacy Commissioner and the Superintendent of Schools, which she copied widely to other individuals.

The court found that statements made by Halstead were defamatory and untrue. It was also defamatory to place bad apples as pictures for some of the teachers. It was further defamatory to place these teachers in a rogue gallery on the same website near teachers who had been convicted of criminal offences. Referring to the teachers as bullies was defamatory and these statements and pictures lowered the plaintiffs in the eyes of a reasonable observer. The damages

---

Eichelbaum J. in *Short v. Kirkpatrick*, [1982] 2 N.Z.L.R. 358 at 366 (H.C.)] The test is objective. It may be defamatory by virtue of the ordinary meaning of the words or because of extrinsic facts and circumstances known to the listener or reader that give it a meaning different from that in which it would ordinarily be understood. [See *Botiuk v. Toronto Free Press Publications Ltd.* (1995), 126 D.L.R. (4th) 609 (S.C.C.)].

[41] *Botiuk, ibid* at 24.

[42] *Brown v. Cole* (1998), 61 B.C.L.R. (3d) 1, [1998] B.C.J. No. 2464 (B.C. C..A.) at para. 107, leave to appeal refused (1999), [1998] S.C.C.A. No. 614, 243 N.R. 400 (note) (S.C.C.).

[43] (2006), 2006 CarswellBC 52, [2006] B.C.J. No. 59 (B.C. S.C.). See also *Campbell v. Cartmell* (1999), 1999 CarswellOnt 2967, [1999] O.J. No. 3553 (Ont. S.C.J.), additional reasons at (2000), [2000] O.J. No. 840, 2000 CarswellOnt 784 (Ont. S.C.J.).

awarded ranged from $150,000 for the most egregious defamation to $15,000 for the less serious defamation. Halstead was also ordered to pay $50,000 in punitive damages. An injunction was also awarded preventing Halstead from making further defamatory statements.

CONCLUSION

The Internet has been hailed as a groundbreaking interactive marketplace of ideas, in which anyone can promote their ideas and viewpoints. But the downside of this unparalleled information exchange is that cyberspace also offers a wealth of offensive materials – including hate materials, defamatory speech and cyber-bullying – that encourage people to act out against certain people or groups of people. This chapter explored the ways in which these individuals use the Internet to promote their agenda, and provided an overview of relevant legislation.

In the next section, we turn to an examination of the technical and legal issues surrounding new electronic crimes. Unlike the crimes explored in this section, those explored in the next section did not exist prior to the Internet. For example, Chapter 7 introduces you to hacking and denial of service attacks. You will learn about the various motivations of hackers and the kinds of nefarious activities that are being perpetrated on the Internet. You will learn that Canada has fallen behind other Western industrialized nations in enacting legislation to deal with these threats. You will also learn about the obstacles associated with investigating and prosecuting online offenders, including the need for international cooperation and user education.

QUESTIONS FOR FURTHER THINKING AND DISCUSSION

1. How is technology used in cyber-bullying? How is this different from bullying in real space?
2. Who are cyber-bullies and their victims?
3. How can we lessen or prevent cyber-bullying? Is the current legal framework adequate?
4. What forms of discipline are most appropriate for cyber-bullying cases? Should all cases be reported to law enforcement authorities?
5. When and how are schools responsible for cyber-bullying cases?
6. How should rights like freedom of expression, guaranteed under the *Charter*, be balanced in cyber-stalking and cyber-bullying cases?
7. Does anonymity make perpetrators more or less responsible in cyber-bullying and cyber-stalking cases?
8. What does criminal harassment involve? Is there a difference if things are said in public or private?
9. What is defamation and how does it relate to cyber-stalking?
10. What is the difference between libel and slander?
12. Should Canadian ISPs be held liable for cyber-stalking, cyber-bullying and other online transgressions?
12. What is the difference between cyber-stalking and cyber-bullying and the dissemination of hate propaganda?

13. Why does the *Criminal Code* prohibition against both hate propaganda and child pornography contain an exception for (some forms of) private speech?
14. Is it possible to limit some forms of non-violent expression and still promote the vigorous and open debate essential to a democratic society, which s. 2(b) is designed to safeguard and advance?

PART THREE

COMPUTER MISUSE CRIMES

6

Viruses and Other Malicious Programs

KEY TERMS AND CONCEPTS		
• Bot	• Payload	• Trojan horse
• Fake codec	• Rogue security software	• Virus
• I Love You Virus	• Rootkit	• Web attack
• Internet Relay Chat	• Self-replicating	• Worm
• Malware	• Slave	• Zeus botnet
• Morris worm	• SQL injection attack	• Zombie

INTRODUCTION

The term **malware** is simply another means of saying malicious software. It includes any file or program harmful to a computer user, such as computer viruses, worms, Trojan horses and spyware. Malware is typically spread by social engineering or through the exploitation of security vulnerabilities. For example, a social engineering attack might try to convince a user to open an email attachment or download a file from a website. Often, malware is propagated using viruses and worms. For instance, a virus or worm might be used to install keystroke-logging software on a user's computer. Alternatively, an attacker can make malware available on a website by exploiting a security flaw or weakness. An attacker might also lure unsuspecting users to a malicious website through a social engineering technique, such as a message that promises some new anti-virus software program. These attacks frequently span multiple jurisdictions and are often perpetrated by highly sophisticated organized criminals.

It used to be that the authors of malicious software or malware were primarily interested in fame and notoriety. However, as I discussed in Chapter 1, the cybercriminal is now increasingly motivated by the desire to earn money. With more and more people conducting financial and other sorts of business-related transactions online, attacks are proliferating at an alarming rate. Furthermore, there is now an elaborate underground economy in fraud-related goods and services, including malicious software. These programs can be used to perpetrate attacks and gather information about unsuspecting users.

This chapter contains information about the online threat landscape as well as how to deal with harmful software that performs malicious activities on a user's computer. Keep in mind that many of the malware threats discussed in this chapter overlap with one another. For example, a spam email message might be designed to trick the victim into downloading a virus, which could be used to install a keystroke-logging software program on his or her computer. This information can then be transmitted back to the attacker through an otherwise legitimate server than has been compromised.

WHAT IS A VIRUS?

The computer **virus** is the most widely recognized malware term. It is sometimes misused by the media as a catch-all phrase designed to refer to any form of malicious software or computer misuse. This is both erroneous and unhelpful because it fails to capture the wide range of malicious programs being used to cause damage to computer systems. As such, you should define the term virus as narrowly as possible to distinguish it from other types of malware.

A computer virus is a program that aims to cause harm to a computer. Generally speaking, a virus is a self-reproducing or self-replicating program or malicious code that can "infect" or compromise other programs by modifying them or their environment. In order for a virus to spread, it must attach itself to some form of host, such as a file, and replicate between different systems. Note that viruses are typically concealed within materials that the user will readily accept or open, such as an email attachment, pirated copies of software or shareware/public domain programs. There are three primary ways that a user can trigger the infection of his or her system:

1. booting a PC from an infected medium (e.g., a CD);
2. executing an infected program; or
3. opening an infected file.

For example, a virus can be distributed as an email or instant message attachment. The user is tricked into opening the infected file because it appears to have some value or come from a trusted source. Viruses are also distributed through peer-to-peer (P2P) file sharing programs, which I discussed in Chapter 1.[1] Another method of distribution is through pop-ups advertising protection against viruses and other forms of malware. These applications are often termed rogue security software programs, and they are discussed in further detail below.

---

[1] Minaxi Gupta, Markus Jakobsson, Andrew Kalafut and Sid Stamm, "Crimeware in Peer-to-Peer Networks" in Markus Jakobsson and Zulfikar Ramzan, *Crimeware: Understanding New Attacks and Defenses* (Upper Saddle River, NJ: Pearson Education, 2008).

A virus will typically activate a **payload** element that causes unexpected and potentially harmful activity when it is executed. This can range from the relatively harmless display of messages on the screen to the destruction and manipulation of data. When a computer virus first enters the computer, it copies the virus program and a launch program to the hard disk.[2] If the computer is running Windows, it then modifies the startup file so that the launch program is activated whenever the computer starts up. This is why shutting off and restarting the computer won't get rid of the virus because the launch program is automatically run as part of the startup procedure.[3]

One of the key problems with the distribution of viruses through the Internet is the fact that cyberspace has no geographic boundaries — virus authors can sit back and watch their viruses quickly replicate and spread around the world. What can be done about this problem? Countries must work together and respond quickly by sharing information and coordinating resources. As I discuss in Chapter 9, the Council of Europe's Convention on Cybercrime can facilitate international cooperation.[4]

The problem is that if many countries are not combatting computer crime, this creates a large number of safe havens for criminals to exploit. The I Love You virus provides a useful illustration of this point. Onel de Guzman, a 24-year-old, computer-knowledgeable Filipino man, admitted to creating the I Love You virus that plagued computers globally and caused an estimated $10 billion (USD) worth of damage.

There were no Philippine laws against virus writing at the time that the I Love You virus was disseminated. Subsequently, the government of the Philippines passed legislation to deal with the problem of computer viruses on June 14, 2000. Under the law, those who spread computer viruses or otherwise engage in cybercrime can be fined a minimum of 100,000 pesos (about USD $2,000), and imprisoned for 6 months to 3 years. However, De Guzman could not be charged under this law because it was not in effect at the time that he disseminated his virus. Consequently, he has never been prosecuted for his crimes.

This story illustrates that countries must implement laws to enable law enforcement officials to obtain data from ISP (Internet Service Provider) networks for use in criminal investigations. Countries also need to assist each other with criminal investigations and prosecution, which includes establishing effective mutual assistance treaties (obligating countries to help each other and preserve and share data in cross-border investigations) as well as extradition treaties (enabling the surrender of fugitives between countries upon request). These issues will be further explored in Chapter 9.

---

[2] Jim Keogh, *The Essential Guide to Computer Hardware* (Upper Saddle River, NJ: Prentice Hall, 2002) at 55.

[3] *Ibid.*

[4] Article 4 of the Cybercrime Convention states that "each Party shall adopt such legislative and other measures as may be necessary to establish under its domestic law, when committed intentionally, the damaging, deletion, deterioration, alteration or suppression of computer data without right."

WHAT IS A WORM?

A **worm** is a self-contained program or set of programs capable of spreading copies or segments of itself to other computers without intervention by the user. As its name suggests, it "worms" its way through a computer system. Unlike a virus, a worm does not need to be clicked on and executed to carry out any number of functions ranging from the purely frustrating to the extremely destructive. For example, some worms replicate themselves by sending emailed copies of themselves to all of the contacts in the victim's address book. Worms also consume a significant amount of computer memory and network resources, making them especially destructive. They also frequently install a backdoor on an infected computer that allows the attacker to install other forms of malware, including keystroke loggers and redirectors. Computers infected with worms can also be enlisted into a botnet that is controlled by the attacker, which is subsequently used to attack another target or to distribute spam.

It is interesting that a new worm was discovered in 2008.[5] Previously, Symantec reported that network worm attacks had declined as a result of changes in security measures (following a number of highly successful worm attacks that prompted these changes). The inclusion of personal firewall applications in operating systems, which are automatically turned on, is an example of the kinds of measures that have helped protect users from worm threats. However, in late 2008, it was discovered that remote communication is allowed through the Windows firewall when file and print sharing is turned on. This led rogue attackers to create a new worm (called Downandup or Conficker) to exploit this vulnerability. By the end of 2008, over a million computers were infected with this worm, which downloads updated versions of itself or installs other malicious code into the infected computer.

The Morris Worm

It might surprise you to learn that the first computer worm was disseminated back in 1988. At that time, Robert T. Morris was a graduate student in computer science at Cornell University in Ithaca, New York. He became intrigued with the idea of creating a computer program that would exploit the holes he had found in the Unix operating system. On November 2, 1988, he released a computer worm into a national computer network that links government, corporate and university computers. To disguise his authorship of the program, Morris logged onto the system through his computer account at Massachusetts Institute of Technology (MIT) and released the worm from there. Morris intended the worm to spread slowly across the network, so as not to draw attention to itself. However, the self-replication feature turned out to be a fatal programming flaw and Morris had severely underestimated the speed at which it would replicate. The worm quickly clogged computers, causing many systems to crash or become catatonic.

---

[5] Symantec, "The Downandup Codex: A Comprehensive Guide to the Threat's Mechanics" March, 2009, available online at: http://www.symantec.com/content/en/us/enterprise/media/security_response/whitepapers/the_downadup_codex_ed1.pdf.

Morris and his friend from Harvard tried to send a message over the network with instructions about how to destroy the worm. However, because the network was already jammed up from the worm that Morris disseminated, the message, or "antidote," never reached its intended audience. In fact, Morris' worm was benign — it did not cause any permanent damage to hardware, or compromise or destroy computer files — but it still caused significant damage through the loss of valuable research time and hours spent fighting and killing it. One estimate put the cost as high as $186 million!

As a result, Morris was indicted under ss. 1030(a)(3) and (5) of the *Computer Fraud and Abuse Act*. He was convicted of violating s. 1030(a)(5), which covers anyone who

> *[I]ntentionally* accesses a Federal interest computer without authorization and. . .alters, damages, or destroys information. . .or prevents authorized use of any such computer or information and (A) causes loss to one or more others of a value aggregating $5,000 or more during any one year period.

On appeal, Morris argued that he had authorization to access the network and to access the *send mail* and *finger demon* programs, two of the programs he used to launch his worm. As such, he argued he did not fall within the unauthorized access requirement of the statute. However, the Court of Appeal (2nd Circ.) found that Morris exceeded the scope of his authorization. Clearly, his use went beyond sending or reading mail; instead, he found holes in the system that permitted him a special and unauthorized access route into other computers. Morris was sentenced to 3 years probation, 400 hours of community service, a fine of $10,050 plus the costs of his probation. He is now an associate professor of computing science at MIT.[6]

WHAT IS A TROJAN HORSE?

Just as their name suggests, **Trojan horses** are programs that appear to perform a useful or harmless function, but also contain hidden functionality. The hidden functionality typically causes unwanted and damaging effects for the user. The most common use of these programs is to operate in stealth, so as not to be noticed by the user. Trojans differ from viruses and worms in a couple of important respects. First, the process of replication is not automated, as it is with respect to worms. Instead, the spread of the program relies upon manual download and distribution. Secondly, they are most likely to be introduced into a system with the user's consent, such as when the user is tricked into downloading a file with an attractive name.

Trojans are often used to infiltrate targetted computers and allow someone else to control the computer, monitor usage and gain confidential information, such as passwords. They are most commonly used to create backdoors into the network for later exploitation. For example, a backdoor program is a specific type

---

[6] *U.S. v. Morris*, 928 F.2d 504 (2nd Cir. 1991).

of Trojan that enables infected machines to be accessed remotely, by incorporating both client and server components within the software.

A backdoor simply opens up a means for the remote control of the victim's computer, usually through a TCP/IP (Trasmission Control Protocol/Internet Protocol) port on which the backdoor listens for instructions from the attacker.[7] Downloader Trojans are designed to install other malware programs. They are a quick and seamless way of infecting a system while opening the computer up for the surreptitious installation of more complex malware, such as a bot. The primary goal for a downloader Trojan is to remain hidden; in other words, it must be able to burrow deep into the system without being detected. There are also spammer Trojans that infect systems and distribute spam from the infected computer.

Trojan authors, who may not be attackers themselves, often sell their wares on the underground crime market, discussed in Chapter 3, or they might use the program themselves.[8] Trojans can also be used to steal entire identities, which later can be used by organized criminals to commit more serious crimes. Those who use Trojans to steal information not only include cybercriminals, but also governments, the military and business organizations who use them to gather intelligence about their adversaries by infecting their computer systems. As such, it is not surprising that malware authors design special programs to steal information, get out unnoticed and cover their tracks. The average price for developing information-stealing Trojans is reported to be somewhere in the low-thousands of dollars, making it a potentially very lucrative business if someone can secure a number of different contracts.[9] Some of these specialized malware authors advertise their services on the black market, whereas others are employed by the government to develop tools that can be used against enemy states.

WHAT IS A ROOTKIT?

A **rootkit** is a component that uses stealth to maintain a persistent and undetectable presence on the machine. Rootkits are typically installed along with malicious programs, such as backdoors or Trojans, without the knowledge or consent of the victim. To avoid detection, a rootkit is used to hide the presence of the malicious program on the victim machine (e.g., it can be used to hide processes and files that the attacker has installed, along with the presence of the rootkit). A rootkit typically uses sophisticated techniques to conceal memory and disk space in an effort to hide the presence of the malware and avoid user detection.[10] The rootkit can also hide the malicious program itself and avoid detection by anti-virus software running on the victim's computer.

---

[7] Jakobsson and Ramzan, *supra*, note 1 at 29.
[8] *Ibid* at 367.
[9] *Ibid* at 372.
[10] *Ibid* at Chapter 8, Rootkits.

HOW IS A MALWARE ATTACK CARRIED OUT?

The steps in executing a malware attack are brief, once the damaging program has been created.

1. Malware is distributed. Malware can be distributed through social engineering (through the sending of spam email, for example) or through the exploit of a vulnerability in security in a particular software program (such as a worm that exploits a particular vulnerability in a Web browser's security).
2. The computer is infected. For example, a virus executes a payload or a keystroke logging program is installed on the victim's machine.
3. Confidential data is provided by the user or this data is retrieved from the machine. For example, a keystroke logger can be used to record the victim's keystrokes or the malware might scan the victim's hard drive for confidential information.
4. The legitimate (compromised) server receives the confidential data for the attacker.

Note that keystroke logging software can be installed on a user's machine to steal confidential data, such as passwords, account numbers and credit card information. For example, a user's activities can be monitored by a keystroke logger or a malicious browser component.

Web Attacks

An attacker can send spam email messages that advertise links to malicious Web pages; however, the user must open the email and click on the embedded link. This means that the attacker will only be able to target a small number of victims because he or she must rely on the spam message not being intercepted by a spam filter. As well, there is a great likelihood that the user will not be tricked into opening the spam email message and clicking on the harmful link. As a result, this is not necessarily the most advantageous way for an attacker to perpetrate his or her attack against a pool of potential targets.

Alternatively, adversaries can use the Web to serve malicious content that is capable of compromising a user's computer and running arbitrary code on it. This has been facilitated by increased complexity of Web browsers and vulnerabilities that come with complex software. In most applications, when you visit a Web page, the page pulls content from many different providers (e.g., advertisements, maps, online videos, etc.). These features augment the complexity of the Web browser's components and lead to an increase in the number of remotely exploitable vulnerabilities. This way, an attacker doesn't need to trick or socially engineer anyone into opening an email and clicking on an attachment or link. Instead, he or she can simply wait for an unsuspecting user to visit the compromised site and fall victim to his or her exploits. The stages of a Web attack are generally carried out in the manner outlined below.

1. An attacker breaks into a legitimate website and posts malware. Many websites act as hosts to serve up malware to unsuspecting users. This is also

known as content injection, which refers to the process of injecting malicious or harmful content into a legitimate website.

2. The end-user machine is attacked. Malware is downloaded onto a user's machine or the user is redirected to another malicious website controlled by the attacker.

3. The end-user machine is leveraged for malicious activity (e.g., theft of passwords).

As I discussed in Chapter 3, during phishing attacks, cybercriminals often steal user credentials by directing them to spoofed Web pages, which trick them into entering their personal information, or by installing key logging software that records their confidential information and transmits it back to the attacker. On the other hand, an attacker can modify a legitimate website and point the victim to the attacker's own website that mimics the legitimate one (such as a banking website). The victim will not realize that he or she is entering credentials, such as usernames, passwords, credit card and bank account numbers, into the attacker's own website. This type of attack can easily lead to the user's personal information being compromised and his or her identity stolen.

SQL Injection Attacks

A poorly validated input field in a Web input form (e.g., a login form) can allow an attacker to insert (or inject) additional Structured Query Language (SQL) instructions into a legitimate Web server. This technique provides attackers with the layout of the database and a means to bypass login or administrative access and gain unauthorized access to the server. The attacker can then add his or her own malicious content directly into the server running behind the Web page, which is later accessed by the unsuspecting user. For example, the attacker can embed malicious content that will be transmitted to the victim or he or she can imbed hidden links to malicious websites that serve malware to the user.

In what is commonly referred to as a drive-by-download, any visitor to a compromised website becomes a target (i.e., the browser will automatically download and execute the payload or the malicious code carried by the exploit to the target computer). In other words, a successful **SQL injection** exploit can be used to cause malware to be delivered and executed on a user's machine without his or her knowledge or consent. The malicious code can be used to steal the user's personal information and send it back to the attacker. This is one of the most common forms of malware infection today.

Malicious Advertisements

Many websites display advertisements hosted by third-party advertising sites. Malicious ad content can be inadvertently hosted on legitimate websites using social engineering techniques. The rogue ads can then redirect a user to a malicious Web page hosting Web attacks. Given the volume of online advertisements published every day, these rogue ads are extremely difficult to detect and eradicate.

Fake Codec

There are dozens of multimedia file formats on the Web, and many require special software to view or listen to them. Web users sometimes need to download and install a new media player or browser plug-in module to view content. A **codec** (otherwise known as a coder-decoder) is a piece of software that decodes a binary file and reconstitutes a version of the original audio or video. Malware authors play on this by establishing websites that host tempting content, then prompting users to install new codec to gain access; however, the executable content is really a piece of malware downloaded and installed on the computer.

Rogue Security Software

A rogue security software program is a type of misleading application that pretends to be legitimate security software (such as an anti-virus program), but which actually provides the user with no protection and also facilitates the installation of malicious code that it claims to protect against. Frequently, these rogue programs use legitimate-sounding names, such as VirusRemoved2008, to trick the user into thinking that they are genuinely helpful. Most rogue security software programs also have websites that include the ability to download and purchase the software.

How is rogue security software installed on a user's computer? To fool potential victims, rogue security software programs deliver specially crafted notification alerts, such as "Antivirus 2008 Web Scanner detected dangerous spyware on your system!" The security warnings mimic those created by legitimate security software vendors and can even display fake virus scanning dialogues, along with the infections presumably found on the computer.[11] They indicate that the user needs to purchase a fake security product in order to remove the reported threats and clean the computer. Attackers also market rogue security software with claims that the programs can remove unwanted applications, such as spyware or adware. Not only are these scams designed to cheat users out of money by charging for these fake security products (e.g., costs range from $30 to $100 (USD)), in some cases, the personal and credit card information that users provide is used for fraudulent schemes.

Rogue security applications also install additional threats onto the compromised computer, while reporting back to the user that it is clean. In other words, these programs deliberately misrepresent the computer's security status or performance through the display of phony or exaggerated security threats and reports. Sometimes these programs also instruct the user to lower existing security settings or switch off firewalls and legitimate anti-virus software programs. This step allows the attacker to compromise the computer with additional threats, including the installation of keystroke loggers or backdoor functionality, allowing access to personal information that can be used to commit fraud and/or identity theft.

---

[11] *Symantec Report on Rogue Security Software: July 2008 – June 2009*, available online at: http://eval.symantec.com/mktginfo/enterprise/white_papers/bsymc_report_on_rogue_security_software_WP_20100385.en-us.pdf.

Bot Networks

A bot is a remote control computer program designed for a single purpose, such as spamming, a **Distributed Denial-of-Service (DDoS) attack** or for multiple purposes, including distributing malware and stealing confidential information. The key is the remote control mechanism that allows them to be networked into botnets — groups or networks of infected computers — that offer considerable computer power to attackers. Botnets are an emerging threat with a wide range of harmful uses, including the distribution of spam, phishing, denial of service attacks, data harvesting, the dissemination of viruses, among others.

Generally speaking, a bot is an end-user machine that contains malware that allows it to be remotely controlled by an attacker using a command and control network, frequently from a central server.[12] The attacker sends commands to the bot from the central server without the knowledge and consent of the owner of the bot computer. The attacker may have tricked the user into installing the bot software through the use of social engineering, such as by convincing him or her to open an email attachment or click on a pop-up advertisement.

Once infected with the bot software, a bot computer may lay dormant and not do anything out of the ordinary until it receives instructions from the attacker. Once it receives the command, it will blindly follow the attacker's instructions. For this reason, bot computers are also referred to as **zombies** or slaves. Once a host has been infected, an attacker will often scan for new victims, simply by looking for improperly protected computers, such as Windows PCs that are missing patches and do not have a security suite installed that would detect and block the bot (which is distributed using spam, downloader Trojans, or other means).[13] Once a substantial network of infected computers is created, which is known as a botnet (or simply a network of bots), the botnet will either be used by the attacker or rented through the black market to others.[14]

In many cases, the person whose machine is infected is completely unaware that he or she is part of a botnet. And, of course, the bot computers do not need to be located within the same jurisdiction in order to launch an attack. For example, an attacker in Russia can harvest bots in Australia, China, Canada and France and use them to launch a coordinated attack against a Web server in Mexico. As such, botnets provide attackers with a considerable amount of anonymity and stealth. They are also very difficult to track because thousands of zombie computers can be used to perpetrate an attack across international borders. The most common types of attacks perpetrated using botnets include DDoS attacks, identity theft, spam, phishing and spyware distribution.[15]

Frequently, a bot communicates with the attacker using Internet Relay Chat (IRC).[16] IRC is a protocol that enables users to chat on the Internet. If the attacker

---

[12] James Hoagland and Zulfikar Ramzan, "Bot Networks" in Jakobsson and Ramzan, *supra*, note 1 at 183.

[13] Jakobsson and Ramzan, *supra*, note 1 at 378.

[14] *Ibid.*

[15] *Ibid* at 379.

[16] *Ibid* at 193.

installs an IRC client in the compromised computer, along with the bot software, the client will connect to an IRC server, whereby the attacker can instruct the bots within his or her network to carry out malicious activities. As such, IRC enables bot writers to build in a mechanism for the attacker to communicate with the bot from the command and control server. Alternatively, bots can use HTTP (Hypertext Transfer Protocol), through which most communication occurs between a Web browser and server.[17]

In addition to a communication component, that enables the attacker to control and issue commands to the bots in the network, most bots are capable of propagating (i.e., they find other vulnerable hosts on the network and infect them) and updating themselves. Some bots also contain a rootkit component, which enables it to avoid detection on the host machine, as well as the ability to disable anti-virus or security software running on the victim's machine. Many bots also contain malicious applications, such as keystroke loggers, which can enable the attacker to gather personal information about the victim. A bot can monitor network traffic to and from the victim's machine and steal information residing on the machine itself.

For example, **Zeus** is a bot package that has existed since 2007 and can readily be purchased in the underground economy for as low as $700 USD.[18] It is also freely traded and it likely originates in Russia or another Russian-speaking country as initial help files were written in Russian. It is distributed worldwide and the primary methods of infection include drive-by-downloads and spam. The Zeus bot is used widely and is highly prevalent on the Internet, allowing even the most novice attackers to compromise unprotected computers.

The main purpose of Zeus is to steal online credentials. It gathers system information, steals passwords and online credentials and then connects with the command and control server for additional instructions. In its report (which it stores in the computer as a text file and sends to the command and control server using HTTP), Zeus transmits the information it collects, including stolen bank credentials, files, screenshots and all information typed using the keyboard. This information, which is encrypted, can be used by the attacker or sold through the underground economy, as discussed in Chapter 3.

Many different entities contribute to the botnet problem. The most obvious targets are the individuals who create and disseminate malware, as well as those who hire others to perpetrate botnet attacks. The criminal law can be used to deal with these individuals; however, by itself this is clearly not an effective mechanism to deal with the problem of botnets. The end-users who fail to secure their computers are also responsible for the creation of botnets because they are effectively supplying the computers that become infected. In addition, software manufacturers are responsible for security vulnerabilities that can lead to the infection of user computers, as well as for the delay between the discovery of a

---

[17] *Ibid.*

[18] Nicolas Falliere and Eric Chien, "Zeus: King of the Bots" (Symantec Security Response, 2009), available online at: http://www.symantec.com/content/en/us/enterprise/media/security_response/whitepapers/zeus_king_of_bots.pdf.

vulnerability or the creation of a patch or anti-virus update. It can also be argued that ISPs have a responsibility to filter or better monitor traffic on their networks. However, firewalls alone cannot safeguard against infections delivered via email or through a user unwittingly browsing a website infected with malicious code.

POLICY RESPONSES TO MALWARE

Clearly, there are a number of non-legal solutions that can be employed to deal with the problem of malware. Spam filters, for example, can prevent the delivery of harmful email messages that can contain viruses or harmful links. Automated patching can also make systems less vulnerable. Network monitoring is also important for businesses and network administrators must be on the lookout for malicious traffic. For example, if a large number of machines appear to be connecting to IRC channels all of a sudden or exhibit unusual DNS (Domain Name Server) query patterns, or if traffic on the network is unusually high, this might indicate the presence of a botnet.[19]

Packet sniffers can also be used by network administrators to determine if their networks have a botnet problem. ISPs can also monitor their networks for patterns associated with spam, scanning and other kinds of malicious software or denial of service attacks. Once a bot or bot network is detected, the best thing to do is to quarantine the infected computers and block traffic to and from them until the machine can be cleaned using anti-virus software.[20] Another important measure is for law enforcement officials to try to identify the command-and-control server behind the infected computers and take them offline.

An ounce of prevention is worth a pound of cure when it comes to computer crime. Having a comprehensive security software package, which includes anti-virus software, a personal firewall and other such tools is critical. **Anti-virus software** can be used to respond to a variety of malware threats discussed in this chapter; however, these programs are not always able to respond to new threats, or to rootkits that can hide malware. Thus, it is important to ensure that this software is kept up to date, as new versions of malicious code are constantly emerging on the Internet. Encryption can also help protect against transmitting confidential data to an attacker through the use of a keylogger or packet sniffing program. Important data should also be backed up regularly in case the computer is infected and files are not able to be accessed because of the malicious program.

Finally, the most important countermeasure is to raise users' awareness of the threat posed by malware. Through increased awareness, individuals will engage in less risky online behaviour, and, thus, be less likely to have their computers become infected with malware. Another important thing to note is the fact that a great deal of malware is spread through social engineering techniques. Internet users also need to become aware of these methods of attack and learn to be less responsive and trusting in their online interactions, especially when using

---

[19] Jakobsson and Ramzan, *supra*, note 1 at 225.
[20] *Ibid* at 226.

P2P file sharing networks, which are ideal for surreptitiously sharing malicious content.

I previously discussed the fact that the *Criminal Code*[21] was amended in 1985 to include s. 342.1 (unauthorized use of a computer). Similarly, the 1985 amendments to the *Code* also included s. 430, which is also directed at computer crime, and which reads as follows:

(1.1) Every one commits mischief who wilfully
  (a) destroys or alters data;
  (b) renders data meaningless, useless or ineffective;
  (c) obstructs, interrupts or interferes with the lawful use of data; or
  (d) obstructs, interrupts or interferes with any person in the lawful use of data or denies access to data to any person who is entitled to access thereto.

. . .

(8) In this section, "data" has the same meaning as in section 342.1.

This provision can be used to prosecute individuals for malware attacks. However, there have not been any cases reported in Canada of this section of the *Code* being used to target the perpetrators of computer misuse crimes.

CONCLUSION

This chapter provided an overview of the malware threat. Malware represents a serious security threat for everyone. There are also many ways through which malware might advance in sophistication and present an even greater threat to our infrastructure. The problem has already reached significant proportions and shows little sign of improving. Moreover, given the increased reliance upon networked communications in our society, malware poses a significant threat to more than just electronic commerce. As you turn to the next chapter, keep in mind what you learned here and ask yourself whether Canada is equipped to deal with the malicious activities carried out as part of professional organized crime. If the problem continues to get worse, with more serious and coordinated attacks spanning multiple countries, will Parliament need to enact new legislation and/ or amend the *Criminal Code*?

QUESTIONS FOR FURTHER THINKING AND DISCUSSION

1. Is the financial penalty awarded against Robert Morris consistent with the staggering monetary loss attributed to his crime?
2. Did a sentence that did not involve any jail time serve as a sufficient deterrent to others?
3. Is the sentence fair, given that Morris did not act with malicious intent to cause damage?
4. What is the difference between a virus and a worm?

---

[21] R.S.C. 1985, c. C-46.

5. What is a trojan horse and how is it relevant to cybercrime?
6. What is spyware? How is it distributed and what risks does it pose?
7. Is it appropriate for large corporations to use malware to gather information about their staff and other companies?
8. Should those who produce malware and sell it to third parties, for example on the black market, be treated the same as those who actually use these programs for nefarious purposes?
9. Is Canada equipped to deal with the cyber-threats discussed in this chapter?

7

Hacking and Denial of Service Attacks

KEY TERMS AND CONCEPTS

- Black hat
- Black hat hackers
- Bots
- Cyberpunks
- DEFCON
- Denial of Service (DoS)
- Denial of Service Attacks
- Distributed Denial of Service (DDoS)
- Firewall
- Grey hat hackers
- Hacker ethic
- Hackers/crackers

- Hacking
- Hacktivist
- Kevin Mitnick
- Legion of Doom
- Malware
- Organized criminals
- Packet sniffing
- Password cracking
- Phone phreakers
- Phreaking
- Port scanning
- Red box
- Rogue security software

- Scareware
- Script kiddies
- Second life
- Slaves
- Social engineering
- Spyware
- Telecommunications fraud
- War dialing
- War driving
- White hat hackers
- Zombies

INTRODUCTION

It might surprise you to learn that the term **hacking** was introduced at the Massachusetts Institute of Technology (MIT) back in the 1960s.[1] In those early days, most hackers were primarily interested in thrill-seeking and notoriety. In the 1990s, we witnessed the emergence of hacking websites and the introduction of commercially available security products. From the early part of the present decade until now, we have seen **denial of service (DoS) attacks** launched by

---

[1] Marjie T. Britz, *Computer Forensics and Cyber Crime – An Introduction*, 2nd ed. (Upper Saddle River, NJ: Prentice Hall, 2009) at 60.

various websites, including Yahoo!, eBay and Microsoft. Organizations of sophisticated cybercriminals have emerged and information has become the leading commodity for criminals.

Cybercriminals have become more sophisticated and realized that they can make significant money from their attacks. With more and more people conducting business and financial transactions online, it also became apparent that there is a large pool of potential victims to target. This trend has given rise to increasingly sophisticated scams that have moved away from being mischievous to being significantly harmful.

PHONE PHREAKING: THE PRECURSOR TO HACKING

The origins of hacking can be traced back to phone phreaking during the 1960s and 1970s. **Phreaking** involves the manipulation of telecommunication carriers to gain knowledge and/or theft of services. It has also been defined as telecommunications fraud because it involves the illegal use or manipulation of access codes, access tones or switches in order to avoid connection charges and route one's own calls.[2] What is interesting to note is that the majority of phone phreakers didn't necessarily have an interest in talking to anyone *per se*, the goal was simply to see whether they could manipulate and control the telephone networks.[3]

Although these exploits might be considered harmless pranks, the telephone companies sought to crack down on them because they were being deprived of valuable revenue, especially when phreaking was used to make international calls for free. Fortunately, the advent of digital telephone switches and improvements to telephone security systems have largely prevented this crime from continuing. However, phone phreaking is closely related to hacking and illustrates how emerging technologies have enabled criminals to carry out increasingly more sophisticated attacks.

The most elementary form of phreaking is the theft of telephone access codes, which can be accomplished simply by shoulder surfing or stealing the code from an unsuspecting individual while he or she is dialing it. A more sophisticated method is called **war dialing** that involves using random number generators, which produce and test numerous codes, until one proves successful. The successful codes are compiled into a database and then used to obtain free phone service.

Another method of phreaking involves the use of tone dialers and other tools easily assembled from inexpensive goods commonly sold at electronic stores.[4] For example, a **Red Box** can be created and used to mimic the tones of pay phones, which can be played after depositing a few coins. By playing back these tones, it

---

[2] *Ibid* at Chapter Three.

[3] Steven Furnell, *Cybercrime: Vandalizing the Information Society* (Boston: Addison Wesley, 2002) at 45.

[4] Britz, *supra*, note 1 at 59; Samuel C. McQuade, *Understanding and Managing Cybercrime* (New York: Pearson, 2006) at 82.

is possible to make phone calls without depositing any additional money into the pay phone. Similarly, phone phreakers also used a device called a Blue Box, which is a tone dialer used to create pairs of tones, as well as a single 2600 Hz tone, to control the telephone network. These kinds of devices were widely used by university students living in dorms.

THE DEFINITION OF HACKING — A FORM OF SPYING AND INTRUSION

Hacking generally refers to the development of novel techniques to identify computer shortcuts. The use of the term has changed over the years and today it typically refers to individuals who deliberately gain (or attempt to gain) unauthorized access to computer systems.[5] The term "hacking" is actually derived from the metaphor of hacking away at an object until it gives way.

Hackers are persons who access other people's computer systems without authorization, and who can be classified according to their level of skill and expertise, or according to the final goal or objective of their hacking. They come from all walks of life and include disgruntled employees, fraud perpetrators, political activists, juveniles and career criminals. Since hacking is a global phenomenon, hackers can also be located in virtually any country in the world.

From a technical standpoint, hacking primarily relates to illegally gaining access to computer systems after exploiting vulnerabilities in security or overcoming security barriers. Hacking computer systems typically involves committing a number of computer crimes, including illegitimate packet sniffing, port scanning and running spyware. Doing these things, in addition to socially engineering people into giving up confidential information, such as passwords, are common methods of computer hacking. Thus, it should be apparent that hacking is not a single activity or event but rather a complex process that often involves multiple steps and parties. It is also important to keep in mind that most attacks are propagated through social engineering techniques rather than through exploiting technical weaknesses or vulnerabilities in the computer or network.[6]

On the most basic level, hacking can include entering into a system as a form of entertainment or thrill-seeking. On the other end of the spectrum, hacking can be perpetrated by those with serious destruction or financial gain in mind. It can include gaining knowledge of security obstacles and a system or programming; gaining unauthorized access; manipulating information or launching a coordinated attack; monitoring the activities of users and harvesting information; or creating backdoors that can be used for subsequent access.

Hacking thus refers to trespassing and exploring computer systems as a form of thrill-seeking to extremely harmful attacks involving the manipulation, destruction or theft of information. The concept of what a hacker is has been

---

[5] S.M. Furnell and M.J. Warren, "Computer Hacking and Cyber Terrorism: The Real Threats in the New Millennium?" (1999) 18(1) Computers & Security 28.

[6] Markus Jakobsson and Zulfikar Ramzan, *Crimeware: Understanding New Attacks and Defenses* (Upper Saddle River, NJ: Pearson Education, 2008) at 29.

constantly evolving from those initial stages in which hackers were simply considered to be people with advanced computer knowledge who were fighting for a cause justified by ethical principles. With the rapid expansion of access to computers and the Internet in the 1990s, hacking was demystified and was no longer something that could only be done by those with advanced computer knowledge. Thus, the concept of hacking has been broadened to include a wide range of activities in which computer technology is used as a tool or medium, as well as those in which computers are the target of hackers.

METHODS OF HACKING — DIGITAL SPYING AND INTRUSIONS EXPLAINED

Password Cracking

Password cracking is a means of computer trespass that involves figuring out passwords required to access computers or computer systems or networks. Computer criminals attempt to figure out passwords in order to gain illegal access to computers to steal, manipulate, damage or destroy data. The easiest and most basic form of password cracking is simple guesswork. Many people foolishly derive their passwords from simple criteria, such as the name of their child, their birth date or something else of obvious importance. This makes it extremely easy for another person to crack the password and gain access to the individual's computer.

A more sophisticated form of password cracking involves the use of password cracking or recovery tools. Some of these software tools are extremely robust and can generate millions of passwords in a very short time period. The fact that cybercriminals now have such powerful tools at their disposal underscores the importance of changing passwords regularly and ensuring that a password consists of multiple upper and lower case letters and numbers. It is also important to keep in mind that a password should not contain any reference to information that another person could know or easily find out about you.

Packet Sniffing and War Driving

Packet sniffing involves capturing and deciphering network traffic. To fully understand packet sniffing, you need to understand how the Internet works. As discussed in Chapter 1, the Internet is a super-network of computers. When a computer sends information to another computer across the network, it breaks it up into a number of pieces called packets. To commit the act of sniffing Web packets, one only needs to use one of the free packet analyzer software tools that are available online, such as Wireshark. With the help of these special software tools, an individual can monitor network traffic and read the data in an understandable format.

Packet sniffers are typically only able to read information travelling over the network they are being used on. This method is quite effective if the attacker is in a coffee shop or airport terminal and his or her victims are connected through a wireless network and all within close proximity. In the case of wireless networking, a packet sniffer can intercept all of the traffic on the wireless network.

If the network is not encrypted and a large number of users are connected, this makes it all the more useful for launching a packet sniffing attack. In a similar vein, **war driving** involves using a computer equipped with a wireless connection to seek out open wireless networks. This can enable an individual to acquire free wireless service or, more ominously, capture and read traffic data. This can lead to the theft of passwords and other kinds of sensitive information that can be used to target the victim.

Port Scanning

Port scanning involves using a network connection to determine what types of services a computer has running at any given time. The means of accomplishing this task are relatively simple. When a computer provides a network function, such as hosting a website, the computer assigns a port number to the software application providing the service. When traffic is sent to the computer with a specific port number, the recipient computer knows which application to send the data to and the computer typically sends an acknowledgement back to the sender. As such, an attacker can send messages to all open ports on a network and wait for a reply, thereby obtaining information about all of the applications running on the various computers on the network.

Why might such information be useful to a cybercriminal? Well, it gives him or her valuable knowledge about how to best launch an attack. For example, by knowing which applications are running on a targetted computer, the cybercriminal can figure out which attacks are likely to be the most effective. Note, however, that not all programs and devices are necessarily vulnerable to attack. We will examine this in further detail later on. Keep in mind, though, that simply knowing the number and type of applications running on a system helps an attacker plan his or her attack but does not necessarily render them vulnerable to being exploited or compromised.

Scareware

A **rogue security software** program is a type of misleading application (otherwise known as scareware) that pretends to be legitimate security software, such as an anti-virus program, but which actually provides no protection and, in some cases, facilitates the installation of malicious code.[7] There are two central ways that rogue security software can be installed on a user's computer: it can be downloaded and installed manually by a user after he or she has been tricked into believing that the software is legitimate; or it is unknowingly installed onto a user's computer, such as when a user visits a website designed to automatically

---

[7] *Symantec Report on Rogue Security Software: July 2008 – June 2009,* available online at: http://eval.symantec.com/mktginfo/enterprise/white_papers/bsymc_report_on_rogue_security_software_WP_20100385.en-us.pdf.

download and install malicious applications. These methods of attack are further discussed in this chapter as well as in Chapter 6.

Spyware and Keystroke Loggers

Spyware is designed to monitor and record the activities of an individual user, including Web activity. **Key loggers**, or **keystroke logger programs**, are designed to monitor and record an individual user's keystrokes. Software key loggers typically install themselves into a Web browser or as a device driver and transmit data back to a remote server. They often contain screen capture capabilities, which attackers can use to acquire screenshot images of the victim's computer. Hardware key loggers are small devices that can easily be installed and removed from the victim's computer. For example, a device such as this can be plugged into the USB port on the target's computer and used to record the victim's keystrokes.

Through these methods, a cybercriminal can gain knowledge of a user's passwords, account numbers and other personal information that can be used to victimize the individual. Keystroke logging software can also be programmed to periodically transmit the information derived from the user's computer back to the cybercriminal. Unfortunately, these kinds of programs are widely available for purchase on the Internet. This means that even those with minimal technological training and background can secretly install these harmful and malicious programs onto the computers of other individuals.

Once installed, these programs quickly go to work monitoring and logging the keystrokes of the targetted individual whenever the computer is in use and may also automatically transmit this information back to the attacker, without the knowledge of the targetted individual. Typically, the information is transmitted back to the attacker in the form of a log report or by giving the attacker direct access into the target's computer so that the cybercriminal can monitor what the user is doing at any given time.

SOCIAL ENGINEERING — THE ART OF THE CON

Social engineering is the act of getting access to or information from people or places that the social engineer should not be able to access. It involves conning, manipulating or tricking people into doing things that helps the attacker to achieve his or her goal. The social engineer knows that human beings are a company's weakest security link and that much of the seemingly useless information in a company's possession is actually important because it can play an essential role in the con artist's attempt to cloak him- or herself in a believable disguise.[8] Social engineering is not only employed to victimize individuals in the corporate sphere, however; in fact, it is an essential part of many different forms of cybercrime that

---

[8] Kevin D. Mitnick and William L. Simon, *The Art of Deception: Controlling the Human Element of Security* (Toronto: John Wiley and Sons, 2003) at 16.

involve getting a victim to reveal confidential personal, financial or security information.

Social engineering can occur either in person or online. A typical online social engineering attack might involve posing as a vendor or systems manufacturer and sending free software or a patch for the victim to install, or sending a virus as an email attachment and convincing the user to open the file because it promises some alluring content, such as a pornography image. This kind of attack can be contrasted with the distribution of malware by exploiting a security vulnerability in the software. Common offline methods of social engineering include posing as an employee or someone in authority, leaving a CD around with malicious software on it and using insider lingo and terminology to gain trust.[9] The difference between online and offline attacks of this sort is that cyberspace attacks often span multiple jurisdictions and are commonly executed by sophisticated organized criminals with financial gain as their primary motive.

One of the most notorious of the early computer criminals is a Californian named Kevin Mitnick, who was once considered America's Most Wanted computer criminal. He began his criminal career as a phone phreaker in the 1970s, whereby he obtained unauthorized access to a telephone system in Los Angeles. For this, he was sentenced to 3 months in a juvenile detention centre, followed by a year's probation. Undeterred, Mitnick was arrested again in 1983 by campus police at the University of Southern California for gaining illegal access to the fledgling ARPANET (Advanced Research Projects Agency Network), discussed in Chapter 1. For this, he was sent to juvenile prison for 6 months in California.

In 1989, Mitnick was sentenced to 1 year in prison and 6 months counselling for computer addiction following repeated unauthorized entries into systems at Digital Equipment Corporation's Palo Alto Research Lab. The company claimed he stole several million dollars worth of software and cost them $2,000 in efforts to keep him out. In 1992, Mitnick violated his probation and went underground. He continued offending, stealing software from Motorola, Nokia and Sun. After a nationwide search and more than 2 years on the run, Mitnick was arrested in 1995 and in 1999 he was sentenced to 68 months in federal prison with 3 years of supervised release. The cost of his final hacking exploits was approximately $291 million. He was released in 2000, after serving 59 months in prison. He is now the principal of an information security consulting firm and has written two books about his exploits.

Over the course of many years, Mitnick perfected various social engineering techniques in order to deceive people and steal information. His book, *The Art of Deception*, describes how he carried out many cybercrimes, often simply by conning or manipulating people without the help of computers or technology. His primary message is that humans are the weakest security link in any organization. Using one or more of the social engineering methods that he describes in his book, people can be conned into helping a sophisticated cybercriminal carry out his crime. Indeed, most of us are socialized to be friendly, compliant and helpful

---

[9] *Ibid.*

toward others. This makes us particularly vulnerable to being victims of the social engineer.

One popular class of social engineering attacks includes images that resemble popular video players, with a false warning that a newer version of the video player plug-in is required to view it. Instead, the provided link is for downloading a Trojan horse that gives the attacker control of the user's computer! Alternatively, a specially crafted website can display fake virus scanning dialogues, along with the infections presumably found on the computer. Symantec has reported that between July 1, 2008, and June 30, 2009, it detected over 250 distinct rogue software security programs. The top reported rogue software security products, in order of prevalence, include:

- Spyware Guard 2008
- AntiVirus 2008
- AntiVirus 2009
- Spyware Secure
- XPAntivirus
- WinFixer
- SafeStrip
- Error Repair
- Internet Antivirus
- DriveCleaner

Of the servers hosting rogue security software that Symantec located, 53% were in the United States. Germany ranked second, accounting for 11% of the total servers hosting rogue security software identified by Symantec, followed by the Ukraine (5%), Canada (5%), the United Kingdom (3%) and China (3%).

Attackers often rely on fear tactics and other social engineering techniques that are distributed through spam, pop-up and banner advertisements on websites and instant messaging programs. They indicate that the user needs to purchase a fake security product in order to remove the reported threats and clean the computer. For example, these advertisements often display messages with bogus claims such as, "If this ad is flashing, your computer may be at risk or infected," and urge users to follow a link that will provide the software to remove the threat. All warnings are false and meant to scare the user into believing their machine is infected. Attackers also market rogue security software with claims that the programs can remove unwanted applications such as spyware or adware. Not only are these scams designed to cheat users out of money by charging for these fake security products (costs range from $30 to $100 (USD)), in some cases, the personal and credit card information that users provide is used for fraudulent schemes. These issues are further discussed in Chapter 6.

Once installed on a user's computer, rogue security applications often misrepresent the computer's security status or performance. Some rogue security applications even install additional threats onto the compromised computer while reporting back to the user that it is clean. Some rogue security software programs also instruct the user to lower existing security settings, such as switching off firewall settings and/or disabling existing (and legitimate) anti-virus programs.

Also, once installed, the rogue program may prevent the computer from accessing legitimate security vendor websites.

Most rogue security programs also have websites that allow users to download and purchase fake security software, with some actually using legitimate online payment services to process credit card transactions. Some scams return an email message to the victim with a receipt for purchase that includes a serial number and a valid, functioning customer service phone number. As the graphic in Figure 7.1 illustrates, the advertisements, pop-up windows and icons used for these scams are designed to mimic legitimate antivirus software programs.

Figure 7.1: Sample Rogue Security Program Warning

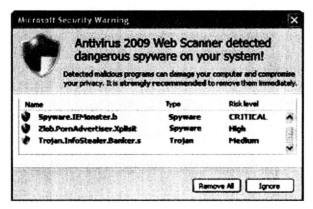

Source: Symantec

Once adversaries have control over a user's machine, they usually try to turn their work into profit. For example, some versions of rogue security software install spyware, keystroke loggers and backdoors that allow the adversary access to the machine and stored information on the user's computer or for harvesting passwords and banking information. It is also possible for a computer compromised with rogue security software to be used in a larger botnet that transmits personal information, such as passwords and banking information, back to the attackers. This form of malicious activity is also discussed in Chapter 6.

HACKER SUBCULTURE AND HACKER ETHICS

Hacker Typologies and Hacker Motivations

Clearly, hackers are not a homogeneous group and these individuals differ widely depending on their motivations, skill set, level of expertise and targets, among other things. Based on these differences, various hacker typologies have emerged, each with their own categories and subcategories. For example, a hacker can be classified as an "internal," forming part of a group of disgruntled employees or former employees that hack into computer systems belonging to their current or former employers. These hackers take advantage of their inside knowledge about the employer's computer system and sometimes misuse the access privileges they were granted through their position of employment. In other cases, hacking occurs as part of an addiction or obsession with computing. Many of these hackers are motivated by thrill-seeking or by their ability to control or gain power over computer systems and the individuals behind them. Alternatively, some merely hack out of curiosity about what they might find on the Internet or on other people's computers. Note that these typologies are not mutually exclusive and a hacker can belong to more than one category at a time, or in succession, as his or her career progresses.

Within the hacker nomenclature, individuals who commit hacking offences may be classified according to which hat they wear. **White hat hackers** are those individuals who identify system vulnerabilities in the interest of promoting security. They may be employed as research or computer security personnel. They generally disclose security holes responsibly, work with vendors to resolve problems and cooperate with law enforcement. In contrast, **black hat hackers** are those individuals who identify and exploit system vulnerabilities for harmful purposes, including destruction and theft. **Grey hat hackers** are individuals who gain unauthorized access to the computer systems of other parties for the purpose of enhancing their security systems and reporting or patching existing security flaws. What differentiates them from white hat hackers is that they have not been hired by a company for the purpose of increasing security. In other words, they are acting without authorization. Thus, although their objective might be the same, they are not acting legitimately. Notwithstanding the noble intentions of grey hat hackers, they represent a danger to corporations and individuals who are exposed to these unauthorized intrusions.

In summary, there are many different motivations for hacking, including opportunity, revenge, greed, challenge or boredom. (See Figure 7.2 for a list of typologies.) In the case of hacktivism, the hacker engages in ecological, political or religious activism online and the Internet is used as a vehicle through which their cause can reach a large pool of potential targets. Alternatively, a hacker might engage in industrial espionage, extortion, fraud or information warfare, if their goal is to steal information solely for nefarious purposes.

Figure 7.2: A Hierarchy of Cybercriminals

Script Kiddies	Inexperienced hackers who employ scripts or other programs authored by others to exploit security vulnerabilities in a system. Not capable of writing own programs and often don't understand programs they execute. Are often frowned upon by the hacker community because they make hackers look bad.

Cyberpunks	Those who use vandalism, destructive programs (viruses/worms) and mischief for no economic gain. They intentionally engage in malicious acts of defacing Web pages and disseminating viruses. Have more technical skills than script kiddies and can often write their own software programs.
Hackers/Crackers	Sophisticated computer criminals who can program/write code and breach complex systems. Can target data to further criminal activity in real space or cyberspace. Commonly perform openly malicious or harmful activities, such as deleting files, modifying data and stealing information.
Hactivists	Hackers who break into computer systems in order to advance or draw attention to an activist agenda. Examples include the defacement of websites to promote some political or social cause.
Organized Criminals	Groups of criminally minded individuals who use the Internet to communicate, collaborate and facilitate cybercrime. Motivations are political extremism or economic gain. Have a high degree of sophistication and expertise. These criminal enterprises are highly productive and staffed by dedicated individuals.

The Culture of Hacking

Traditionally, hackers were united by a code of ethics and a desire to understand technology. The early **hacker ethic** was characterized by anti-establishment rhetoric; however, contemporary hacker communities have lost this ideological bent. In the early 1980s, Steven Levy introduced the world to a set of norms internalized by early hackers, who regarded technology as a means of liberation rather than a tool for destruction. The hacker ethic included principles such as "access to computers should be unlimited and total" and "information should be free."[10] The Ethic is described in detail by Levy; however, the essential principles are outlined below.

1. Access to computers should be unlimited.
2. All information should be free.
3. Mistrust authority — never use your real name or personal information and be careful who you share information with.
4. Do not hack government computers.

---

[10] Steven Levy, *Hackers: The Heroes of the Computer Revolution* (New York: Anchor Press/ Doubleday, 1984).

5. Only hack for good reason.[11]

According to the hacker ethic, hackers do not necessarily consider unauthorized access to a company computer system without malicious intent to be unethical. In fact, many hackers believe hacking to serve a useful purpose by uncovering security flaws and vulnerabilities. Moreover, activities such as unauthorized access and password cracking are seen as a means of safeguarding their liberty and promoting the freedom of information. Along these same lines, the term "hacker" has been viewed internally within the hacking subculture as a badge of respect that should not be used to refer to those who vandalize and misuse computer technology. However, for members of the general public, the practice of hacking was generally considered to involve unauthorized access and damage to computer systems.[12]

One of the earliest and most notable hacking groups was the Legion of Doom (LoD). This group derived its name from the Superman comic book villains and, in fact, was founded by a hacker who referred to himself as Lex Luthor (the arch-rival of Superman).[13] The members of the LoD began as phone phreakers, but their members quickly expanded their activities into the realm of hacking as technology progressed. They also boasted about their exploits on a variety of online bulletin boards; however, many of the LoD members claimed that they were benevolent hackers, merely trying to point out security flaws in institutional networks so that repairs could be made. Indeed, in 1986, a hacker who operated under the alias "The Mentor" and was also one of the members of the LoD, drafted a text entitled *The Conscience of a Hacker*, which is widely referred to as the Hacker Manifesto.[14] The final portion of the text, which is still widely available on the Internet nearly 15 years after it was written, reads as follows:

> Yes, I am a criminal. My crime is that of curiosity. My crime is that of judging people by what they say and think, not what they look like. My crime is that of outsmarting you, something that you will never forgive me for.
>
> I am a hacker, and this is my manifesto. You may stop this individual, but you can't stop us all. . .after all, we're all alike.

The LoD eventually disbanded in 1990 as a result of a crackdown on hackers by the United States government. Some of its members were arrested and others went on to establish a security firm known a ComSec, which later became LoD Communications Inc.[15]

The emergence of the term hacking in the popular media, combined with the proliferation of computer technology dramatically increased the number of individuals engaging in this form of illicit activity. For years, the members of hacking communities were widely regarded as young, socially awkward males

---

[11] "The Mentor, A Novice's Guide to Hacking – 1989 Edition" (Dec. 1988), available online at http://www.undergroundnews.com/files/texts/underground/hacking/guide.htm.

[12] Furnell, *supra,* note 3 at 43.

[13] *Ibid* at 70.

[14] Available online at: http://records.viu.ca/~soules/media_112/hacker.htm.

[15] Furnell, *supra,* note 3 at 71. Note that there are a number of other hacking groups discussed by Furnell in this chapter of his book.

who were fascinated with technology and highly computer proficient.[16] Indeed, the commonly held view of the hacker was a teenage, mostly male, kid with anti-social tendencies and an addiction to science fiction.

This stereotype was reinforced through Hollywood films during the 1980s and 1990s that featured hacking as a central element of the storyline. The first of these was *War Games* (1983), a highly improbable tale in which a high-school student and computer geek turned hacker gains access to NORAD and almost starts another world war. The most infamous hacker movie was, of course, the 1995 film *Hackers* in which a group of young hackers finds evidence of illegal activity on a corporate server and must use hacking techniques to secure justice and avert disaster. It is interesting to note that segments of the *Hacker Manifesto* were quoted in the *Hackers* film.[17] In contrast with *War Games*, *Hackers* attempted to portray hackers as attractive and sophisticated masters of technology, who are the benevolent heroes in the battle against corporate corruption and greed. This artificial theme has been re-worked into many other films in recent years, most notably in *The Matrix*, which also served to glorify the mystique that surrounds the hacker community.

Another feature of the hacker culture celebrated in these films is that all of the hackers have aliases. This is something that can be legitimately recognized as being part of the hacker subculture, since many of the most notorious cybercriminals use handles instead of their real names.[18] For example, "Mafiaboy" was a 15-year-old Canadian high-school student who brought the websites of CNN, eBay and Yahoo, among others, to a halt for several hours in early 2000. He was later apprehended by the FBI and RCMP and pleaded guilty to 56 charges. After serving his sentence, he co-wrote a book about his exploits.[19]

While the majority of today's hackers are not members of a cohesive community bound by ethical guidelines, remnants of the hacker ethic remain. For example, there are a multitude of hacking competitions sponsored by security firms each year and some hackers have made careers out of working for the same institutions that they formerly victimized.[20] Each year, hackers and cyber-security professionals meet together for the notorious security conference know as Black Hat, as well as DEFCON, the hackers' convention that is held annually in Las Vegas, attracting participants from around the world. The goal of these events is to showcase hacker tools, talents and techniques. Furthermore, each year the United States Department of Defense sponsors the Dc3 Digital Forensics Challenge as a means of pioneering new investigative techniques, tools and methodologies and to excite students about the study and choice of digital forensics as a rich and rewarding career path. In addition, some security companies sponsor hacking contests as a means of advertising their products and endorsing them with rigorous scrutiny. These contests are extremely popular among hackers

---

[16] Britz, *supra*, note 1 at 60.
[17] Furnell, *supra*, note 3 at 61.
[18] *Ibid* at 48.
[19] Craig Silverman and Michael Calce, *Mafiaboy* (Toronto: Penguin Group Canada, 2008).
[20] Britz, *supra*, note 1 at 54.

because they recognize the importance of bragging rights and appeal to hackers' competitive spirit, as well as the need for ego validation and challenge.

Today, however, hacker motivations are far more complex. The more sophisticated hackers are primarily motivated by the prospect of significant economic gain. At the other end of the spectrum are those who are merely curious and not necessarily malicious. These hackers are able to bypass security protocols to identify problems and provide solutions for them. Ethically speaking, they often believe that their efforts are more efficient and effective than following established rules.

PREVENTING AND MANAGING HACKING — REGULATORY AND NON-REGULATORY MEASURES

In Chapter 6, we examined some of the ways that cybercriminals can misuse computers or other IT devices to cause harm, launch attacks and steal information. Similarly, computer misuse crimes include the creation and distribution of malicious computer programs, including viruses, worms and other kinds of malware. The threats to information systems examined in this chapter pose a real threat to individuals, organizations and society in general. At the most basic level, hacking can lead to lost or stolen data. If an individual is victimized, his or her personal information may be stolen and used to steal money from bank accounts, make charges to one or more credit cards, or take out loans and/or make major purchases. These problems are explored in Chapter 3.

If a private or public organization is victimized, this can result in the loss of work product (i.e., in terms of the time and resources spent responding to and fixing the problems). It can also lead to negative publicity for the victimized company, which can translate into a loss of their existing and future customer base, a decline in profits or general revenue, as well as a decline in their share price. For small companies, especially those that conduct a majority of their business online, these effects can be so devastating that they can lead to financial ruin and even bankruptcy. It's no wonder, then, that companies tend to handle cyber-security breaches internally and are generally reluctant to report being victimized by cybercriminals!

On a broader level, cyber-attacks are harmful to society because they decrease our overall confidence in the virtual marketplace. This is important given the fact that our society has become increasingly dependent upon the safety and security of online networks. Indeed, many of our daily interactions and activities, from paying bills on time to booking flights and filing our income taxes, are carried out online. Thus, the loss of confidence in the safety and security of the online marketplace has important implications for everyone. More importantly, cyber-attackers can cause major disruptions in critical services including telephone, power and air traffic control. It's not hard to see, then, that cyber-attacks can have profound effects upon individuals and organizations, causing widespread catastrophic loss and significant threats to the safety and well-being of individuals.

Many new software flaws and vulnerabilities are discovered each year. Inevitably, computer hackers and other cybercriminals exploit these vulnerabilities by gaining control of, or causing damage to, a system, or stealing information. As I discussed in the previous chapter, it can take a considerable amount of time, money and resources before software engineers develop a patch to fix the problem. In the best case scenario, they are able to create a new version of the software that corrects all vulnerabilities and prevents future attacks. However, another problem is that many users are not in the habit of routinely updating their software applications and virus definitions.

There are a number of measures that can be employed by individuals and organizations to deal with the threats posed by malicious hackers and other cybercriminals. Clearly, individuals and network administrators should update anti-virus definitions regularly and ensure that all desktop, laptop and server computers are updated with all necessary security patches from their operating system vendor. Automated patching can also help to make systems less vulnerable to security threats. In addition, computers should use the latest protection from spyware and other security risks, such as Norton Internet Security. Spam filters can also prevent the delivery of harmful and deceptive messages, as I explain in the next chapter.

Organizations must also perform filtering on all network traffic, as well as screening out potentially malicious email attachments. Network administrators should also monitor all network-connected computers for signs of malicious activity and deploy anti-virus software as well as firewalls. However, given that most attacks are perpetrated through social engineering means, one critical yet often overlooked countermeasure is to encourage users to engage in less risky behaviour online. Organizations must also educate their users about the latest scams and how to avoid falling victim to them, as well as provide a means to report suspected malicious activity. Both private and public organizations also need to educate users to be cautious about visiting unknown or un-trusted websites and viewing or following links in unsolicited emails. Users should also be cautioned that pop-up displays and banner advertisements can mimic legitimate displays or promote rogue security products. Also, users should only purchase security software from reputable and trusted sources and only download applications directly from the vendor's website.

Aside from education and technical solutions, legal action can be taken against those who perpetrate malicious schemes online. For example, in 2006, the Attorney General for Washington State obtained a $1-million settlement from a New York-based company through a combination of the state's 2005 *Computer Spyware Act*, federal and state spam laws and the *Consumer Protection Act*. The company was fined for marketing and distributing a rogue security software program. These kinds of legal measures have been effectively used in many American states that have robust legislation to combat the threats posed by cybercriminals. Unfortunately, though, Canada does not have a sophisticated network of laws in place to deal with these threats.

Section 184(1) of the *Criminal Code*[21] can be used to target packet sniffing. It applies to anyone who "willfully intercepts a private communication" (other than for law enforcement purposes, pursuant to the *Code*) and provides that a person convicted under this section "is guilty of an indictable offence and liable to imprisonment for a term not exceeding five years."

Canada's *Criminal Code* also contains ss. 342.1 and 342.2, which I previously discussed in Chapter 3. These provisions deal with the unauthorized use of devices to obtain computer services and the unauthorized use of computers. Section 342.1 can be used to prosecute an individual who commits one of the hacking offences described above and s. 342.2 can also be used to prosecute those who produce and/or distribute or use any one of the hacking tools described above, including rogue security software. In addition to these actions, ISPs (Internet Service Provider) can also take action against rogue security software distributors and hosts. Those who host or distribute these products can simply be taken offline and denied service. Similarly, s. 430(1.1) of the *Code*, which I also discussed in Chapter 3, can be used to prosecute those who commit the various hacking offences discussed in this chapter.

Another more controversial approach involves fighting fire with fire. In March 2004, a company called Symbiot Inc. based in Austin, Texas, announced its development of the first IT security solution that can repel hostile attacks and identify malicious attackers to plan and execute appropriate countermeasures. The company has stated that its product can enable users to "reflect" electronic intrusions back on their originators to disable, destroy or seize control of the attacking assets or launch counterstrikes against the originators of network attacks. This unique tool was apparently designed to empower individuals and organizations to protect themselves from hostile attacks.

Dramatic countermeasures have also been used against those who perpetrate hacktivism (see Figure 7.2). For example, in 1998, a group of hackers calling themselves the Electronic Disturbance Theatre (EDT) attacked DefenseLink, the United States Department of Defense's (DOD) public information Internet site, to support the Mexican Zapatistas and denounce the government of the United States. With advanced knowledge of the attack, DOD officials fought back with a program that automatically shut down the Internet browsers of anyone logging onto the hackers' website to participate in the attack.

ATTACKS AGAINST SERVERS

Denial of Service Attacks

A **denial of service attack (DoS)** is an attack on a computer system or network that causes a loss of service to users by consuming the bandwidth of the network or overloading the resources of the system. It usually involves inundating the network with more requests than it can process, which has the effect of making a computer system unable to answer legitimate requests from its clients. Examples

---

[21] R.S.C. 1985, c. C-46.

of a DoS attack include flooding a network, preventing legitimate network traffic; disrupting connections between two machines, preventing access to a service; preventing a particular individual from accessing a service; and simply disrupting service to a system or person. The reasons for perpetrating this kind of attack are varied and include the desire to take down a business competitor's site, to cause mischief, for political protest, for revenge, malice or spite and for commercial blackmail.

A popular type of DoS attack involves extortion. For instance, an attacker can inform a business that it is subject to a DoS attack, and launch a relatively small-scale attack to prove that it has the capacity to attack the network.[22] An extortion demand is then made, backed by the threat of a larger scale attack, unless the attacker receives payment. Sometimes, increasingly large-scale attacks are launched against the business, in conjunction with demands for payment.

These kinds of attacks are particularly popular against off-shore casinos and online betting sites that only make money when they are capable of responding to user requests. For instance, if the attacker threatens to launch his or her attack on the day of the Super Bowl when a significant number of bets are placed (knowing that the business will get $20 million in revenue, for example, and asking for a $2 million payout in return for not crippling its network on the day of the big event), the business will stand to lose a significant percentage of its revenues and may simply pay the extortionist's fee rather than face a DoS attack that would cripple its network. One of the difficulties for law enforcement is that a typical DoS attack is accomplished by making a very large number of "legitimate" demands upon the target's computational resources. As such, it is difficult for law enforcement to distinguish between legitimate traffic (sending email, downloading a file) and illegitimate traffic (intended to bring down the system).

DoS Attacks in the Metaverse

Second Life is a three-dimensional virtual world[23] created by its inhabitants.[24] Many real-world businesses, government entities and figures have

---

[22] Jacobsson and Ramzen, *supra,* note 6 at 33.

[23] Richard A. Bartle, "Virtual Worldliness" in *State of Play*, Jack M. Balkin and Beth Simone Novak (eds.) (New York: New York University Press, 2006) 31 at 31. Bartle notes that virtual worlds are ". . .persistent, computer-mediated environments in which a plurality of players can interact with the world and each other. . .[they] have evolved to become major hubs of entertainment, education and community."

[24] The Terms of Service describe the terms upon which Linden Lab offers access to its services. Section 1.1 of this agreement describes Second Life in the following terms: "'Second Life' is the multi-user online service offered by Linden Lab, including the software provided to you by Linden Lab (collectively, the 'Linden Software') and the online environments that support the service, including without limitation: the server computation, software access, messaging and protocols that simulate the Second Life environment (the 'Servers'), the software that is provided by Linden Lab and installed on the local computer or other device you use to access the Servers and thereby view or otherwise access the Second Life environment (the 'Viewer'), application program interfaces provided by Linden Lab to you for use with Second Life (the 'APIs'), and access to the websites and services available from the domain and subdomains of http://secondlife.com (the

established a virtual-world presence in Second Life. This includes the Swedish embassy, a Virginia governor, members of the Dutch parliament and even President Obama and Secretary of State Hillary Clinton.[25] Some readers might also recall that in 2002, the Front National (FN) party earned 18% of the popular vote in France, which led to a runoff between the FN leader, Jean-Marie Le Pen, and then-president Jacques Chirac.[26] In the ensuing years, there was much political and social turmoil in France, as riots broke out with respect to France's Muslim immigrant community; and, this strengthened the FN's call to remove non-European immigrants from France.[27] These highly controversial issues spilled over into Second Life when the FN set up an official location in-world.

Before long, two anti-FN groups bought land next to the FN headquarters and displayed banners and signs in protest. This public outcry against extremism soon escalated into a full-scale attack, as an informal group of users declared war on the FN and bombarded their virtual headquarters with explosions and gunfire.[28] The battle slowed the server to the point that users were unable to use this portion of Second Life and, in some cases, could not gain access at all.[29] Of course, as landowners, the neighbours of FN could have used technology to deal with the presence of the headquarters in Second Life. For example, they could have built large structures to block FN from public view, or banned FN members from their territory.[30] Instead, they attempted to drive FN from the land using firefights and angry protest. The centrepiece of the conflict was political violence in order to achieve maximum publicity.

This raises the spectre of Second Life becoming a haven for radical ideologues, terrorists and other extremists to target their opponents. This is problematic when we consider the fact that, although it is only a virtual world, the users pay real money for the virtual land and other services available in Second Life. Furthermore, they have an ownership stake in their online content, which is protected by real-world intellectual property laws. And if we can characterize these cyber-attacks as interfering with the security and functioning of the community, as well as the network, in addition to inducing fear and causing damage to virtual property that has real-world value in order to further the ideological or political goals of a particular individual or group of individuals, they can be construed as a form of terrorism.

'websites'). The Servers, Viewer, APIs, websites and any other Linden Software collectively constitute the 'Service' as used in this Agreement." Available online at: http://secondlife.com/corporate/tos.php.

[25] Wagner James Au, *The Making of Second Life: Notes from a New World* (New York: HarperCollins, 2008) at 183.

[26] *Ibid* at 183-184.

[27] *Ibid*.

[28] *Ibid* at 184-185.

[29] *Ibid* at 185. Note that at 186 Au reports that shortly after this, the centre-left campaign of Segolene Royal, the Socialist party's candidate for president, had their Second Life headquarters attacked by right-wing protesters. Similarly, the Second Life headquarters of Spain's two leading political parties were attacked.

[30] *Ibid* at 187.

At the same time that these attacks were perpetrated, a number of individuals, who were rumoured to be members of a community of virtual miscreants known as the W-Hats[31] (generally speaking, participants who cause mischief are called "griefers" in Second Life) created self-replicating virtual bombs that shut down the servers altogether.[32] At first, the owners/operators of Second Life tried responding to the problem with a code-based solution: they developed a virtual barrier that confined the attacks to a specific area of Second Life.[33] But the attacks continued, making it impossible for Linden Lab to provide service to its customers and causing them to invest time and money to deal with the problem. The issue was not that the griefers were disseminating virtual bombs, *per se*; rather, their interference with Linden's servers caused actual harm to the company and its customers. The damage was the burden the virtual bombs caused to the system and the resources employed to deal with it.

Distributed Denial of Service (DDos) Attacks

The most famous type of DoS attack is a **distributed denial of service (DDoS)** attack. DDoS attacks work by using an army of remotely controlled computers to generate more requests of a device than it can serve. The remotely controlled computers are often directed without the knowledge and consent of their owners. As a result, the remotely controlled machines are commonly known as bots, slaves or zombies.

The bots or zombies are usually infected by being implanted with viruses or worms, which are discussed in Chapter 6. Once they are infected, zombie machines are remotely instructed to attack the target site simultaneously. Each zombie can generate a continuous flood of requests to a server, thereby making the server unable to handle legitimate requests from ordinary users. With the help of enough zombies, even the most secure sites or networks can be overwhelmed and incapacitated. The use of zombies makes the "master" (the criminal behind the attack) more difficult to locate. Zombies are also used to deliver spam email, as will be discussed in Chapter 8.

DDoS has been recognized as a major security and business concern since at least the year 2000 when the first major series of DDoS attacks occurred. In 2005, the FBI reported that 17% of all reported computer crime in that year involved DDoS. Note, however, that there are no reported cases involving Canadians prosecuted for DDoS attacks. As mentioned earlier, an attacker can also blackmail the owner of the server by threatening to debilitate the site unless payments are made.

---

[31] Tim Guest, *Second Lives: A Journey Through Virtual Worlds* (New York: Random House, 2007) at 100. Guest points out that the W-Hats were far more than just mischief-makers in Second Life; they were a self-appointed group of cyber-terrorists. They created a van that was painted red with a hammer and sickle and the slogan "W-Hats: Cyber Terrorists Since 2004." In addition, they disseminated swastikas and sexually-explicit imagery and they reenacted the 9/11 attacks, which included the virtual creation of the World Trade Center, with flames, a destroyed airplane and falling bodies.

[32] *Ibid* at 97-98.

[33] *Ibid* at 98.

CONCLUSION

This chapter has covered a wide range of issues relating to computer exploitation and abuse. We have also explored the nature of hacking, as well as who hackers are and why they engage in these exploits. What should be clear is that hackers are not a uniform group. There is no single hacker ethic or manifesto that all hackers ascribe to today and it is simply not possible to generalize and claim that all hackers follow the same set of goals or beliefs.

We have also examined a number of different kinds of attacks that hackers commonly use to target their victims. It is important to keep in mind that hacking attacks are not merely technical in nature; in fact, most attackers are likely to use social engineering techniques rather than exploit technical vulnerabilities in the systems themselves. This has important implications for how we, as a society, can best deal with these problems. Ideally, users must be educated about how to protect themselves online and what kinds of tricks and techniques to watch out for. Indeed, a hacker is only likely to be as successful as his target is vulnerable to exploitation.

QUESTIONS FOR FURTHER THINKING AND DISCUSSION

1. Are "hack-back" technologies appropriate? Are they legal? Should those who launch counterstrike measures be prosecuted?
2. Should it be legal for governments to launch counterstrikes against cyber-attacks directed against them? Should the government stick to strictly defensive means, such as blocking threats or slowing them down, rather than launching an offensive attack?
3. Is it appropriate for public and private organizations to hire notorious hackers as security consultants or employees to deal with cyber-security threats and programming issues?
4. What are the policy reasons in favour of prosecuting those who launch DDoS attacks different from those who launch DoS attacks?
5. Is the Canadian legal framework capable of dealing with the security threats discussed in this chapter? Why or why not?
6. Do the terms hacker, black/white hat hackers, script kiddies and cyber-punks have any real significance today?
7. Can you see any similarities between the Hacker Ethic and the early writings of cyber-scholars, such as John Perry Barlow, who penned the *Declaration of Cyberspace Independence*, discussed in Chapter 1? How are these works, and the principles they manifest, similar or different?
8. In making reference to hackers, the *Hacker Manifesto* frequently repeats the phrase: "They're all alike." Are hackers all alike in terms of their motivations and methods? Is there a difference between the hacker community at the time that the *Manifesto* was written and the hackers of today?
9. How do you think hackers are perceived by society? Are they viewed as college pranksters or sophisticated cybercriminals?

8

Spam in Cyberspace

```
KEY TERMS AND CONCEPTS

• 1267623 Ontario Inc. v.      • Filtering                    • Safe lists
  Nexx Online Inc.             • Flaming                      • Shunning
• Anti-Spam Action Plan        • Honeypot                     • Spam
  for Canada                   • Injunction                   • Spam Reporting
• Bandwidth                    • Intermeddling                  Centre
• Bill C-27                    • Mail-bombing                 • Spoofed email
• Blacklists                   • National Task Force on       • Spyware
• Bots                           Spam                         • Telemarketing
• Bulletin boards              • Netiquette                     restrictions
• CAN-SPAM Act                 • Newsgroups                   • Trespass to chattels
• Conversion rate              • Opt-in/Opt-out               • Zombies
• Dispossession                • PIPEDA
• Do Not Call Registry         • Re-mailing
```

INTRODUCTION

Direct marketing has a long history dating back to the distribution of the first mail-order catalogues in the 19th century.[1] As a result, the dissemination of spam email indiscriminately to multiple recipients constitutes the progression of an existing crime rather than the development of a new offence. The term "spam" is actually taken from an old Monty Python skit about a canned lunch-meat product. In the skit, a group of Vikings sing a chorus of "spam, spam, spam. . ." in increasing crescendo, drowning out other conversation.

---

[1] Chris Kanich, Christian Kreibich, Kirill Levchenko, Brandon Enright, Geoffrey M. Voelker, Vern Paxson and Stefan Savage, "Spamalytics: An Empirical Analysis of Spam Marketing Conversion," (2009) 52:9 Communications of the ACM 99 at 100.

WHAT IS SPAM?

The analogy is appropriate because unsolicited commercial email drowns out other discourse on the Internet. Not surprisingly, **spam** has emerged as one of the most persistent and popular marketing tools of the 21st century, as digital technologies enable individuals to send mass mailings quickly and inexpensively. As one commentator recently observed, "[s]pam is the price we pay for the Internet's principles of freedom and universal access."[2]

In fact, spam originated in Arizona in April 1994 when two Phoenix attorneys sent an advertisement over the Internet to about 8,000 newsgroups.[3] As an aside, it is noteworthy that **bulletin boards** and newsgroups are two of the oldest methods for online communications that involve posting information and exchanging electronic email. The attorneys' spam advertisement reached over 20 million people. This marketing technique quickly gained widespread popularity among companies trying to sell products, including pharmaceuticals, pornography and other money-making schemes.

Often, spammers will rent legitimate network services, frequently in an Eastern European country, and then disseminate a large amount of spam to an ISP's (Internet Service Provider) network.[4] The goal is to transmit as many messages as possible before the network's filtering software detects it. Using this method, hundreds of thousands of spam email messages are transmitted each day without detection. In addition, social networking sites are becoming more and more popular for the dissemination of spam. The reason is that it can't be filtered out by the social networking site's firewall since it appears to come from friends of the recipients.[5]

A federal judge in San Jose California recently ordered the convicted spammer Sanford Wallace to keep away from Facebook.[6] The social networking site sued Wallace and two other men in an attempt to combat spam and phishing attacks against its users. Facebook alleged that the three men gained access to legitimate Facebook accounts and then used those accounts to spam friends of the account holders. The judge awarded Facebook an astounding $873 million in damages after Wallace and his partners sent more than four million spam messages. Facebook says it doesn't expect the spammers to pay the fine; however, it hopes the judgment will serve as an important deterrent to other spammers.[7] In the previous year, Wallace was found guilty under the CAN-SPAM Act, discussed below, and ordered to pay $230 million for phishing and spamming the users of the social-networking site MySpace.

---

[2] Rebecca Bolin, "Opting Out of Spam: A Domain Level Do-Not-Spam Registry" (2006) 24 Yale Law and Policy Review 399 at 401.

[3] Elizabeth A. Alongi, "Has the U.S. Canned Spam?" (2004) 46 Arizona Law Review 263 at 263.

[4] Robert McMillan, "Spam Finds New Paths into Corporate Nets," *Computerworld* (May 25/June 1, 2009).

[5] *Ibid.*

[6] *MySpace v. Wallace*, 498 F.Supp. 2d 1293 (C.D. Cal. 2007). See also Robert McMillan, "Judge Kicks Notorious Spammer Off Facebook," *PCWorld*, May, 2009.

[7] McMillan, *ibid.*

Why Did Spam Proliferate?

Notwithstanding the fact that a few of the world's leading nations have enacted robust anti-spam regimes, we have witnessed a dramatic rise in the volume of these unsolicited bulk email messages in recent years.[8] This increase is reflected in various statistics. Six years ago, in 2003, an estimated 15 billion spam messages were sent over the Internet each day.[9] In 2008, the number of spam messages sent daily over the Internet grew more than ten-fold to an excess of 164 billion messages in August 2008. Almost 97% of email traffic in 2008 constituted spam, which cost ISPs and businesses in the United States an estimated \$42 billion (USD).[10]

According to Symantec, the most common type of spam detected in 2008 was related to Internet or computer-related goods and services (24% of all detected spam).[11] It also detected a 192% increase in spam on the Internet, from 119.6 billion messages in 2007 to 349.6 billion messages in 2008. These statistics demonstrate that spam is on the rise globally. Most of the world's spam originated in the United States in the year 2008 (15.9%), followed by Turkey (7.4%); Russia (7.2%); China (6.1%); Brazil (5.1%); the United Kingdom (3.4%); Korea (3.3%); and Poland (3.2%).[12]

In addition, bot networks, or botnets, were responsible for the distribution of about 90% of all spam email. As discussed in Chapters 6 and 7, the use of bots is a clever tool to evade IP-blocking systems. Typically, the spammer enlists so-called zombie or bot computers, owned by ordinary users, which have been infected with a virus or some other form of malware that gives the spammer control of the machine.[13] Often, the zombie attack is carried out by a specialist who infects a group of machines and then rents them out to spammers to use for the dissemination of email messages. Spammers typically prefer to use bot-infected computers because they can change the IP (Internet Protocol) address from which their spam is sent, making it harder to detect where the spam is being transmitted from.[14] This obscures the attacker and makes it more difficult for the source of the spam to be blacklisted.

Apparently, the number of spam messages containing dangerous attachments increased significantly from July through September 2008. During that period, a reported 1 in every 416 email messages received carried a dangerous attachment

[8] John Soma, Patrick Singer and Jeffrey Hurd, "Spam Still Pays: The Failure of the CAN-SPAM Act of 2003 and Proposed Legal Solutions," (2008) 45 Harvard Journal on Legislation 165 at 165.

[9] Carolyn Duffy Marsan, "CAN-SPAM What Went Wrong?" *Network World* (October 6, 2008).

[10] *Ibid.*

[11] Symantec, "Global Internet Security Threat Report Trends for 2008" Volume XIV, April 2009, available online at: http://www.symantec.com.

[12] Cisco, *Annual Security Report* (2008), available online at: http://www.cisco.com/en/us/prod/collateral/vpndevc/securityreview12-2.pdf.

[13] Joshua Goodman, Gordon V. Cormack, and David Heckerman, "Spam and the Ongoing Battle for the Inbox," (2007) 50:2 Communications of the ACM 25 at 29.

[14] Markus Jakobsson and Zulfikar Ramzan, *Crimeware: Understanding New Attacks and Defenses* (Upper Saddle River, NJ: Pearson Education, 2008) at 211.

designed to infect a computer with malicious software.[15] Other reports have suggested that in 2008, more than 83% of spam emails were trying to infect users with malicious software. Symantec reports that it observed a 192% increase in spam detected across the Internet, from 119.6 billion messages in 2007 to 349.6 billion in 2008, of which 29% originated in the United States.[16] It is also interesting to note that in 2008, bot networks were responsible for the distribution of approximately 90% of all spam email.[17]

Symantec further reports that spammers also took advantage of the global financial meltdown in 2008-2009. Spam reportedly spiked to as high as 79.5% of all email traffic at the beginning of February 2009 due, in part, to the ability of spammers to prey on the public's anxieties over the financial crisis.[18] Spammers sent out recession-driven messages, including "money is tight, times are hard," with links to well-known search engines. Similarly, phishers also exploited the public's vulnerability at that time of great financial stress by inundating users with fake messages from banks. These problems are further explored in Chapter 3.

Given the astounding proliferation of spam email, it is understandable that ISPs spend a considerable amount of time and resources on filtering out spam, which increases the costs of Internet services for consumers.[19] Spam emails also raise significant security issues.[20] They may contain spyware that tracks user activity or attempts to gain user information. Sometimes, software embedded in spam emails can harvest email addresses from the contact lists of spam recipients. They can also contain viruses, worms and other kinds of malicious software. Spam also provides opportunities for perpetrating fraudulent schemes. Spam emails are often used to deliver phishing scams, whereby perpetrators attempt to obtain sensitive personal information from Internet users. Technology also allows spammers to **spoof** their emails, hiding the originating source, and conceal their identities.

Since spammers do not incur additional costs for each message they send, the overhead cost to send one piece of spam is the same as sending thousands or millions. Many of the costs of spam are directly born by third parties, including consumers, ISPs and corporations. Spam recipients cannot refuse to accept spam and incur costs for the time spent reviewing and discarding this email. The massive increase in unwanted email traffic significantly detracts from the productivity of large organizations, whose employees spend a considerable portion of company time disposing of junk email. Consumers may also have to pay for extra storage

---

[15] Carrie-Ann Skinner, "Unsafe Spam Spikes with the Return of an Old Tactic," *PC World* (January 2009).

[16] "Symantec Global Internet Security Threat Report, Trends for 2008," available online at: http://eval.symatec.com/mktginfo/enterprise/white_papers/b-whitepaper_internet_security_threst_report_xiv_04-2009.en-us.pdf at 16.

[17] *Ibid.*

[18] Joan Goodchild, "Spammers Play on Current Economic Fears," *PC World* (May 2009).

[19] Alongi, *supra*, note 3 at 264.

[20] Perry Cheung, "The Need for Canadian Spam Legislation," (2007) 7 Asper Review of International Business and Trade Law 227 at 228-229.

space for their email accounts to deal with the volume of messages they receive and they may have to purchase filtering software.

ISPs are forced to upgrade their mail servers and hire staff to maintain them. ISPs must also either purchase or develop their own spam filtering systems. These efforts might even exacerbate the problem by filtering non-spam email. Companies also face lost productivity because filtering software is often ineffective at blocking all spam and employees must therefore waste time sifting through unwanted email. In addition, given that many filters over-block, employees must also double-check the work of their email filter. Thus, lost productivity in the workplace is one of the biggest costs of spam for the Canadian economy.

Although consumers and ISPs have been complaining about spam for more than a decade, attempts to control this global problem have proven to be extremely difficult. The Internet's popularity and use has skyrocketed in the last several years, vastly widening the pool of potential targets. But how many of those targetted actually end up making a purchase? Someone is clearly buying the products and services advertised through spam — but how often and how much?

In a recent study, a group of researchers assessed the **conversion rate** of spam (i.e., the probability that an unsolicited email message will ultimately result in a sale).[21] It's interesting to note that direct mail campaigns generally produce a response rate of 2.15%. This means that while it might cost $250,000 to send out a million direct mail solicitations, which might produce 21,500 responses, as long as profit revenues exceed the marketing cost, the campaign is profitable.

With this in mind, we can see how direct email marketing has become so popular. Since the cost to send out an email is virtually nil, an email-based marketing campaign can be extremely profitable even if the number of users who click-through to the site being advertised or actually complete a sale is extremely low. Indeed, the aforementioned research study found that out of 350 million email messages advertising male-enhancement products over a period of 26 days, only 28 sales resulted, which is a conversion rate of only 0.00001%.[22] However, the researchers extrapolated that if it were sent continuously at the same rate, pharmaceutical spam distributed through a peer-to-peer botnet could generate revenues of $3.5 million in one year. Other reports have suggested that only 1 consumer in 1,000,000 needs to respond for a spammer to earn a profit.[23] As such, the low marginal cost to spammers provides an incentive to increase volume.

---

[21] Kanich, et. al. *supra*, note 1 at 99.

[22] *Ibid* at 106.

[23] Kenneth C. Amaditz, "Canning 'Spam' in Virginia: Model Legislation to Control Junk E-Mail," (1999) 4 Virginia Journal of Law and Technology 4 at 18.

SPAM LAWS IN CANADA

Canadian Jurisprudence

The only Canadian case dealing with the problem of spam is *1267623 Ontario Inc. v. Nexx Online Inc.*[24] That case dealt with the question of whether the ISP Nexx Online was entitled to terminate service to the numbered company on the basis that it sent out unsolicited bulk email through the Internet at the rate of 200,000 emails per day. The numbered company had entered into a contract with the ISP to host their website. The contract provided that the plaintiffs agreed to follow generally accepted **Netiquette** when sending email messages.

It is noteworthy that in many Internet communities, participants have developed their own netiquette or rules to govern their online interactions, independently from ISPs. For example, some communities of Internet users have formulated their own normative standards and codes of conduct, such as:

- *Shunning*: users refusing to accept messages from a person,
- *Flaming:* sending insulting messages,
- *Spamming*: sending the same message to multiple recipients and
- *Mailbombing*: sending a large number of junk email messages, and
- *Banishment*: from online communities.

These examples illustrate that Internet users themselves can effectively develop their own internal systems of governance to regulate their online interactions.

In the *Nexx Online* case, the ISP warned the plaintiffs that if they did not cease sending the bulk email, the ISP would deactivate the website. When the plaintiffs continued sending out bulk email, the defendant carried out its threat. Subsequently, the court refused to grant the numbered company an **injunction** requiring that the ISP reactivate their website. The court held that sending unsolicited bulk commercial email is in breach of the emerging principles of netiquette. As the rules of netiquette governed the parties' contract, the plaintiff was clearly in breach of its terms, which justified the disconnection of service.

The lack of Canadian case law on the topic of spam is understandable, perhaps, when we consider that Canada has not yet enacted legislation to deal with the problem of spam. In fact, when Industry Canada released its first discussion paper on unsolicited email in 1997, it found that new legislative measures were not needed.[25] It concluded that spam could be controlled by the free market for ISP services, good business practices, privacy legislation, private civil actions and the existing *Criminal Code* provisions. However, given the proliferation of spam during the past decade, it is clear that these mechanisms have not succeeded in curbing spam.

---

[24] (1999), 1999 CarswellOnt 1850, [1999] O.J. No. 2246 (Ont. S.C.J.).
[25] Industry Canada, "Internet Bulk Unsolicited Electronic Mail (SPAM)" (July 1999).

Canadian Legislation

Indeed, there are a number of existing statutes, including the *Competition Act*,[26] the *Personal Information Protection and Electronic Documents Act* (PIPEDA)[27] and the *Criminal Code*[28] of Canada, which incorporate some of the measures that are commonly available in anti-spam legislation. The Competition Bureau can deal with spam that includes information that is false or misleading in a material respect. The Office of the Privacy Commissioner of Canada can address the use or collection of personal information without consent, as well as failure to adhere to opt-out requests. The *Criminal Code* can address spam involving fraud or other illegal activities,[29] and also includes provisions prohibiting the unauthorized use or abuse of computers.

An application can also be made to the Federal Court of Canada, either by the Office of the Privacy Commissioner of Canada or by complainants, for damages arising from a breach of PIPEDA. As I discussed in Chapter 3, this is the principle federal legislation related to e-commerce in Canada, which establishes rules for the collection, use and disclosure of personal information by private organizations involved in commercial activities.[30] It applies to federal works and undertakings, which include ISPs. PIPEDA is important because the distinction between the public and private sectors has become increasingly blurred. Private sector entities now have more resources and opportunities to collect information about individuals and public sector organizations often require that data to fulfill their obligations. By drafting privacy legislation targetted specifically at the private sector, Parliament was able to facilitate the exchange of valuable information with private organizations and ensure that the privacy rights of Canadians are protected in both the public and private spheres.[31]

The purpose of PIPEDA is to establish rules for the collection, use and disclosure of personal information in a manner that recognizes the privacy interests of individuals.[32] Personal information is defined in s. 2(1) as "information about an identifiable individual but does not include name, title, business address or telephone number of an employee of an organization." The definition of "personal information" is very broad and does not refer to the concept of the "biographical core" of information that arises from the *Charter* jurisprudence.[33] Thus, it can be said that a person's email address, including a business email

---

[26] R.S.C. 1985, c. C-34.

[27] S.C. 2000, c. 5.

[28] R.S.C. 1985, c. C-46.

[29] For example, s. 342.1 might be used to combat spammers who make unauthorized use of an ISP's server to transmit spam.

[30] PIPEDA, *supra*, note 27 at ss. 2(1) and 4(1).

[31] The passage of PIPEDA marked a significant milestone in the development of Canadian privacy law because previous laws only regulated the public sector.

[32] PIPEDA, *supra*, note 27 at s. 3.

[33] *R. v. Plant* (1993), [1993] S.C.J. No. 97, EYB 1993-66899, 1993 CarswellAlta 94 (S.C.C.); *R. v. Tessling* (2004), [2004] S.C.J. No. 63, 2004 CarswellOnt 4351 (S.C.C.).

address, is an individual's personal information for the purposes of the Act.[34] This will be further discussed in Chapter 10.

PIPEDA seeks to establish fair information collection and management practices in the private sector by ensuring that data is responsibly collected from individuals and then appropriately held, used or disclosed to a third party. One of the central principles behind PIPEDA is that consent must be obtained before information can be collected from an individual, and then used or disclosed. The standard of the "reasonable person" is used in that PIPEDA requires private organizations to collect, use and disclose personal information "for purposes that a reasonable person would consider appropriate in the circumstances," in compliance with ten broad privacy obligations specified in Schedule 1 of the Act.[35] Specifically, it requires commercial businesses that create or acquire lists of email addresses to ensure that their recipients have given consent to receive commercial solicitations. Email addresses can only be used for the purpose for which they are collected, and can only be put to secondary uses if the owners consent. Furthermore, PIPEDA requires that unsubscribe mechanisms be used and respected in these emails.

However, since PIPEDA only deals with the collection, use and disclosure of personal information about an identifiable individual, it does nothing to stop those who spam accounts by randomly generating combinations of names, numbers and words.[36] Therefore, under Canadian law, unless there is fraud or malicious conduct at issue, spammers who target consumers by randomly generating email addresses cannot be impeded. While the Office of the Privacy Commissioner in Canada and the Competition Bureau receive complaints from members of the public about spam, there is no all-embracing framework to deal with the problem of spam in Canada.

On May 11, 2004, the Government of Canada launched the **Anti-Spam Action Plan for Canada,** which established a private-sector task force chaired by Industry Canada to examine the issue of spam. By the end of 2004, spam had grown to comprise as much as 80% of all global email traffic.[37] The National Task Force on Spam held a round table of national stakeholders in December

---

[34] Office of the Privacy Commissioner of Canada, "Commissioner's Findings: PIPEDA Case Summary #297" (April 28, 2005).

[35] These include the following: collection limitation (the parties should limit how information is collected; collection must be with consent and knowledge that the information is being collected); data quality (the data must be accurate and relevant); purpose specification (the party must specify the purpose for which the information will be collected); use limitation (once information is collected for one purpose it cannot be used for another purpose unless the individual consents or this is authorized by law); security safeguards (the information must be secured from risk, e.g. from attacks by hackers); openness (transparency, i.e., the individual should know what is being done with his or her information); individual participation (the individual should have access to his or her information and be able to look at it and correct inaccuracies); and accountability (there must be an oversight mechanism).

[36] Cheung, *supra*, note 20 at 234.

[37] Alysia Davies, *Bill C-27: Electronic Commerce Protection Act,* Library of Parliament (Ottawa: May 27, 2009).

2004 and solicited feedback from Canadians. The task force issued its report in May 2005 and recommended that legislation specifically directed at combatting spam be enacted.[38] Moreover, it is clear that market forces, privacy legislation and existing civil and criminal penalties are insufficient to deal with the burgeoning problem of spam.[39]

Four years after the National Task Force on Spam unanimously suggested that the Canadian government introduce anti-spam legislation, the Canadian Government tabled anti-spam legislation in early 2009. Bill C-27, which is also known as *The Electronic Commerce Protection Act* (ECPA) addresses spam, and related threats from unsolicited email, including identity theft, phishing, counterfeit websites, viruses, botnets and spyware. It also grants an additional right of civil action to businesses and individuals targetted by those who perpetrate these harmful and malicious activities. However, this Bill did not become law before the second session of Parliament ended on December 30, 2009. Currently, Canada is the only G-8 country without specific anti-spam legislation and the prospect of becoming a safe-haven jurisdiction for spammers is an ever-increasing reality.

The ECPA addressed many of the shortcomings of the current Canadian legal framework, including the need for significant penalties, broad definitions of unsolicited commercial electronic messages (including text-message spam), targetted provisions against phishing and spyware, a private right of action for individual lawsuits against spammers, as well as greater government cooperation, a national coordinating body, and a **Spam Reporting Centre**. Many of these provisions were consistent with the recommendations of the Task Force and remain highly critical and relevant today. The ECPA also involved several important government agencies in the regulation of spam, including the Competition Bureau, the Office of the Privacy Commissioner and the Canadian Radio-television Telecommunications Commission (CRTC). The legislation would have given these agencies the power to share information and evidence with international agencies in order to deal with the problem of spam emanating from outside Canada.

It is also important to keep in mind that this legislation would likely not have eliminated spam entirely. The ECPA adopted a consent-based model whereby commercial email solicitations without consent were considered spam and subject to liability under the Act. There were exceptions to this rule, however, which included charities and political parties. Given the fact that there is now a major fissure in Canada's ability to combat spam, it is worth examining the approaches adopted in other jurisdictions to see whether they provide a more effective model for addressing this important problem.

---

[38] *Ibid.*
[39] Cheung, *supra*, note 20 at 233.

SPAM LAWS IN THE UNITED STATES

Trespass to Chattels

In the American courts, trespass to chattels has re-emerged as a cause of action in recent years in Internet advertising and emailing cases. Under s. 217 of the Restatement (Second) of Torts, a **trespass to chattels** occurs when one party intentionally dispossesses another person of the chattel, or uses or intermeddles with the chattel in the rightful possession of another person.[40] While the doctrine of trespass to chattels is clearly rooted in tort law, it is based on the notion of an underlying property right, which it seeks to foster and protect.[41] Thus, liability only arises if:

- the other person has in fact been dispossessed of the chattel;
- the intermeddling caused harm to the other's "materially valuable interest" in the physical condition, value or quality of the chattel;
- the possessor is deprived of the use of the chattel for a significant period of time; or
- bodily harm is caused to the possessor, or to some person or thing in which the possessor has a legally protected interest.[42]

A series of federal district court decisions, beginning with the 1997 case of the Southern District Court of Ohio in *CompuServe Inc. v. Cyber Promotions Inc.*,[43] have approved the use of trespass to chattels as a theory of liability for spam emails based upon evidence that the vast quantities of spam email overburdened the network and made it more difficult for the ISP's customers to use it. In that case, CompuServe brought an action against CyberPromotions for sending email solicitations to CompuServe customers, asserting trespass to chattels. The court maintained that a plaintiff can sustain an action for trespass to chattels based on "harm to personal property or diminution of its quality, condition or value." The electronic signals constituted intermeddling to CompuServe's computer system and, although no actual dispossession occurred, there was impairment to the value of the network. The value of CompuServe's computer equipment was said to be wholly derived from the extent to which it could serve its subscribers. Damage was found in the burden the spam caused to the computer system and the resources employed to deal with it. In the result, the court granted a preliminary injunction to the plaintiffs to stop CyberPromotions from continuing to transmit spam to CompuServe's customers.

The court relied on the case of *Thrifty-Tel, Inc. v. Bezenek*,[44] which was the first case to apply the doctrine of trespass to chattels to communications

---

[40] *Restatement (Second) of Torts* (1965).

[41] Shyamkrishna Balganesh, "Common Law Property Metaphors on the Internet: The Real Problems with the Doctrine of Cybertrespass," (2006) 12 Michigan Telecommunications and Technology Law Review 265 at 268. See also Andrea Slane, "Home is Where the Internet Connection Is: Law, Spam and the Protection of Personal Space," (2005) 2:2 UOLTJ 255.

[42] *Restatement of Torts, supra*, note 40 at s. 218.

[43] 962 F.Supp. 1015 (S.D. Ohio, 1997).

[44] 54 Cal.Rptr. 2d 468 (Cal. App. 4 Dist., 1996).

technology. In that case, the defendants' son used computer technology to find out the plaintiff company's telephone access and authorization codes, so he could use its network to place long-distance telephone calls for free. The court considered whether this gave rise to the doctrine of trespass to chattels and held that it did indeed arise from a mere interference or use, short of a dispossession. It is important to note that by allowing recovery where there was no physical damage to the chattel in question, this case opened the door to wider claims for cyber-trespass than was previously thought possible under traditional trespass rules.

In *AOL v. LCGM Inc.*,[45] LCGM, a well-known spammer for pornographic websites, sent millions of pieces of junk mail to AOL members. AOL sued, arguing that this constituted trespass to chattels. The court ordered LCGM to stop its transmission of junk mail to AOL customers. The court also noted that by employing methods and software designed to defeat AOL's spam filtering technologies, LCGM had committed fraud. Similar reasoning was also applied by the court in *eBay, Inc. v. Bidder's Edge, Inc.*,[46] in which the court issued a preliminary injunction to eBay, enjoining Bidder's Edge (BE) from using a software robot to access eBay's computer system without permission for the purpose of obtaining information regarding ongoing auctions at eBay, on the ground that this activity was likely to constitute trespass to chattels.

As you are probably aware, eBay operates a person-to-person trading website on which sellers can offer for sale various items to other users through an auction system. Currently, eBay is the largest consumer-driven online auction site on the Web. BE operated a website through which it offered online auction-buyers information concerning auctions being conducted on a number of different websites, including eBay. This information allowed prospective buyers to ascertain whether a single item was being offered for sale on one of numerous websites.

BE obtained information about eBay's auctions by causing its software robot to crawl eBay's site approximately 100,000 times per day. eBay maintained that this activity represented "between 1.11% and 1.53% of the total load" on its listing servers. In April 1999, eBay granted permission to BE to crawl its site for a period of 90 days. During this period, the parties attempted to enter into a formal licensing agreement; however, they were unable to reach a consensus. Following this, eBay requested that BE stop crawling its site and BE complied; however, before long, BE resumed its crawling activities again. eBay demanded that BE stop this activity immediately, and the parties attempted to negotiate a formal agreement once again; however, the process broke down a second time. At this point, eBay tried to block BE from continuing to access its site and, when this too failed, it moved for a preliminary injunction prohibiting BE from continuing to crawl its site without permission.

---

[45] *America Online v. LCGM, Inc.*, 46 F. Supp.2d 444, Civ. Act. No. 98-102-A (E.D. Va., Nov. 10, 1998).

[46] 100 F.Supp. 2d 1058 (N.D. Cal., 2000).

The court held that eBay had not established that BE's actions harmed or injured eBay or caused it to have to increase the capacity of its system, or slowed or diminished the use of its network. However, eBay demonstrated that there was a possibility that it would sustain irreparable injury because,

> [I]f BE's activity is allowed to continue unchecked, it would encourage other auction aggregators to engage in similar recursive searching of the eBay system such that eBay would suffer irreparable harm from reduced system performance, system unavailability or data loss.[47]

Note that this finding can be distinguished from the American cases on identity theft, such as *Bell v. Acxiom Corp.*,[48] discussed in Chapter 3. In those cases, the courts have refused to compensate plaintiffs for the increased risk of identity theft. Without some evidence of a tangible loss, such as the loss of money resulting from the misuse of the stolen information, plaintiffs have been unable to prove their claims in court. In *eBay, Inc. v. Bidder's Edge, Inc.*, in contrast, the court recognized that irreparable harm could be sustained from future misuse of the network. In other words, the court clearly recognized that the risk of future harm is important to take into account.

The court also found that eBay was likely to succeed on its trespass to chattels claim. It noted that,

> [I]n order to prevail on a claim for trespass based on accessing a computer system, the plaintiff must establish: (1) the defendant intentionally and without authorization interfered with the plaintiff's possessory interest in the computer system; and (2) the defendant's unauthorized use proximately resulted in damage to the plaintiff.[49]

The court held that BE's activities were unauthorized given that it continued to crawl eBay's site after eBay demanded that it discontinue to do so. In addition, BE's conduct interfered with eBay's possessory interest in its computer system. The court stressed that "intermeddling with or use of another's personal property is sufficient to establish a cause of action for trespass to chattels."

Note that the reasons for the courts' findings in these cases largely revolve around the commercial risks and realities of Internet-related businesses. In other words, in the United States cyber-trespass cases, the plaintiffs all suffered, or were worried they would suffer, significant financial or other losses if the defendant's activities were allowed to continue unchecked.[50] It can be argued that a website provider such as eBay should have legal recourse to exclude unwanted activity from its website when the activity is socially inappropriate or commercially unfair. This approach is also consistent with the notion that, as a private company, the ISP is under no obligation to provide service to everyone

---

[47] *Supra*, note 46 at 1066.

[48] No. 4:06CV00485-WRW (E.D. Ark., October 3, 2006).

[49] *Supra*, note 46 at 1070.

[50] Mary S.W. Wong, "Cyber-Trespass and 'Unauthorized Access' as Legal Mechanisms of Access Control: Lessons from the U.S. Experience," (2007) International Journal of Law and Information Technology 15(1) 90 at 97-98 and 109.

on equal terms and can exclude whomever it wants from using its network at any time.[51]

Note as well that where the plaintiff attempted to rely on self-help measures, such as technological filters in the case of *AOL v. LCGM*,[52] it turned to litigation only because these good-faith self-help measures failed. Thus, the development in the application of the doctrine of trespass to chattels to computer technology has taken place alongside a growing number of business-related resources for access to control in cyberspace.

Note that it is possible, under general contract formation rules, to limit a person's access to and use of a website, database and software or other information through the terms of service, which are frequently found within browse-wrap contracts where the user is required to click on a hyperlink, which is typically displayed at the bottom of the website homepage.[53] In this way, the owner and/ or operator of the Web page can expressly communicate the extent of the permission it grants to users of its site, which can help to determine, after the fact, whether the activities undertaken by the user were authorized.

In other words, by placing restrictions on its website, the owner can expressly withhold consent to do certain things. By disregarding or disobeying these restrictions, the user is either trespassing or acting without authorization.[54] At the same time, however, this begs the question of whether promoting and protecting the property-based rights of Internet businesses justifies the harm that can arise from these owners fencing off their portions of cyberspace.[55] Do you think that the claim of cyber-trespass promotes the idea of "cyberspace as place" discussed in Chapter 1?

The CAN-SPAM Act

In 2003, President Bush signed the Controlling the Assault of Non-Solicited Pornography and Marketing Act (the CAN-SPAM Act),[56] which took effect on January 1, 2004. It created a universal framework for the national regulation of spam, which is intended to override the state laws dealing with electronic mail.[57] The statute only applies to commercial email messages and it uses the phrase "commercial electronic message" throughout. It defines a commercial email message as "the primary purpose of which is the commercial advertisement or promotion of a commercial product or service (including content on an Internet

---

[51] *CyberPromotions, Inc. v. America Online, Inc.*, 948 F.Supp. 436 (E.D. Pa., 1996). In that case, the District Court for the Eastern District of Pennsylvania held that the plaintiff did not have a First Amendment right to send unsolicited email messages to AOL customers. Furthermore, as a private company, AOL is entitled to block attempts by CyberPromotions to solicit its customers.

[52] *Supra*, note 45.

[53] Wong, *supra*, note 50 at 113.

[54] *Ibid* at 114.

[55] *Ibid* at 99.

[56] The CAN-SPAM Act of 2003 (15 U.S.C. 7701, et seq., Public Law No. 108-187).

[57] John E. Brockhoeft, "Evaluating the CAN-SPAM Act of 2003," (2004) 4 Loyola Law and Technology Annual 1 at 2. Previously, 36 States had enacted anti-spam statutes. However, Congress found that the state regulations were inconsistent and unsuccessful at dealing with the problem of spam in the United States.

Website operated for a commercial purpose)."[58] The Act prohibits any person from sending a commercial email message without clearly identifying that the message is an advertisement or solicitation.

The Act was designed to apply to unsolicited messages only. Thus, it exempts "transactional or relationship messages," which include email messages that are designed "to facilitate, or confirm a commercial transaction that the recipient previously agreed to enter into with the sender," "to provide warranty information, product recall information, or safety or security information with respect to a commercial product or service used or purchased by the recipient" and "to provide notification concerning. . .account balance information. . ." It also exempts email messages that are designed to provide information directly related to an employment relationship or a benefit plan in which the recipient is participating or enrolled. Thus, a transactional or relationship message includes two kinds of unsolicited messages: those sent by a person with whom the recipient has conducted a commercial transaction and those sent within the employment context.

It also prohibits any person from using a computer to relay or retransmit "multiple commercial email messages." The statute defines multiple to mean "more than 100 email messages during a 24-hour period, more than 1,000 email messages during a 30-day period, and more than 10,000 email messages during a 1-year period." It also prohibits the use of deceptive subject lines or header information (To/From) in commercial email messages, and it prohibits any person from registering or using information that falsifies their identity for email accounts or domain names. It further prohibits the transmission of commercial email messages to email addresses obtained through "address harvesting."

The federal statute also restricts any person from sending a commercial email message that does not contain a clear return email address and make it clear that the recipient may use it to request to not receive future commercial email messages from the sender.[59] Once this request is received, the sender cannot transmit any further commercial email messages to the recipient more than 10 business days after receipt of the recipient's request.[60] This is what is known as an opt-out model, which allows spammers to email recipients until they are requested to stop. Note that this is different from an opt-in regime, currently in place in Europe, which provides that a spammer cannot target recipients unless it has secured their consent.[61] The disadvantage of this system is that it allows spammers to lawfully send spam messages to the recipient until the expiry of the 10-day window following the opt-out request. And since spammers can easily spoof their email address, or change email accounts, it allows them to send repeat emails from multiple sources.

---

[58] *Supra*, note 56, s. 3.
[59] *Supra*, note 56 at s. 7704.
[60] *Ibid* at s. 7704.
[61] Karen Ng, "Spam Legislation in Canada," (2005) 2 University of Ottawa Law and Technology Journal 447 at 466.

Law enforcement officials have prosecuted dozens of spammers under this legislation and won some high-profile cases. One of those cases addresses the question of whether the CAN-SPAM Act can be applied to messages sent entirely within the MySpace domain. In *MySpace, Inc. v. Wallace*,[62] the plaintiff asserted that Wallace had obtained some 342,000 MySpace.com members' usernames and passwords through his website that was designed to resemble a MySpace log-in page. After harvesting their log-in information, Wallace hijacked their accounts to send out 400,000 messages, including a group of 110,000 messages sent from 76,200 member accounts in a 48-hour period — in clear violation of the CAN-SPAM Act. The court granted MySpace a preliminary injunction against Wallace and enjoined him from the following: accessing or using any services by or through MySpace; establishing or maintaining MySpace profiles; referring to MySpace with respect to unsolicited commercial email communication; using any MySpace logo or graphic, interface or any other representation of MySpace's log-in page; and inducing MySpace members to provide identifying information.

It is noteworthy that private individuals have no private right of action under the CAN-SPAM Act. The Federal Trade Commission (FTC) bears primary responsibility for bringing enforcement actions against spammers and enforcement can also be sought by state Attorney Generals, or ISPs, in the courts. CAN-SPAM violators are also subject to fines, pursuant to FTC regulations. Spammers can receive fines of up to US $11,000 per violation (i.e., per spam).[63] Damages sought by state Attorney Generals and ISPs are limited to smaller violation amounts and have caps of between one and two million dollars.[64] Additional damages are available where spammers engage in willful or knowing violations or in certain aggravated activities.[65] CAN-SPAM also authorizes a criminal penalty of imprisonment of up to 5 years for certain spam-related activities.[66]

Notwithstanding the enactment of this ground-breaking anti-spam legislation and the fact that law enforcement officials have increased their prosecution of spammers within the United States, the volume of spam circulating on the Internet has increased and the content of those messages has become more harmful to users. Thus, it appears that the best tool available in North America for combatting spam has proven ineffective. Attackers have only become more sophisticated in their attacks and better at hiding their source. The Act has long been criticized for the fact that it was backed by lobbyists related to the mass mailing industry. Also, it specifically allows for spam as long as the sender follows the regulations (i.e., it simply outlines "rules" for those who send spam rather than trying to eliminate it). It also pre-empts state laws, some of which had more stringent requirements and heavier penalties.

---

[62] *Supra*, note 6.
[63] Federal Trade Commission, "The CAN-SPAM Act: Requirements for Commercial Emailers 2" (2004), available online at: http://www.ftc.gov.
[64] *Supra*, note 56 at s. 7706 (f) (3)-(g)(3).
[65] *Ibid* at s. (f)(3)(c)-(g)(3)(c).
[66] 18 U.S.C. 1037 (2000 & Supp. II).

Notwithstanding these criticisms, it's true that the Act has led to the arrest and conviction of more spammers. Thus, the CAN-SPAM Act has been effective in enabling law enforcement officials to take action against spammers. While it may not ever truly "can" spam, it has provided those within the justice system the ability to prosecute spammers. Another positive is that it promoted legitimate email senders to improve their marketing and it clarified the definition of spam.

The CAN-SPAM Act also contains provisions for the implementation of a Do-Not-Email Registry, which is similar to a Do-Not-Call Registry. A Do-Not-Call Registry is a list containing the telephone numbers of subscribers who have voluntarily indicated that they do not want to receive unsolicited calls from commercial telemarketers. The CAN-SPAM Act gave the FTC 6 months from its date of enactment to study the feasibility and effectiveness of establishing a Do-Not-Email Registry.[67] In June 2004, the FTC released a report setting out its findings and advised against implementing a Do-Not-Email Registry at that time.[68] The FTC considered several different types of Do-Not-Email Registries. A user could register an email address or a domain name and spammers would not be allowed to send to those addresses or domain names. Alternatively, a spammer could submit his or her distribution list to an FTC-approved third party forwarding service, which could cross-check the email addresses on the list against those on the Do-Not-Email Registry and forward the spam to those users not on the registry.

The proposal of a Do-Not-Email Registry has received popular support from the general public in the United States and some have suggested that the registry is critical to the success of the CAN-SPAM Act. Furthermore, for those who propose an opt-in regime rather than an opt-out regime, the registry would provide a *de facto* opt-in framework. Another benefit of this type of regime is that the consumer would only need to opt-in to the registry once, rather than having to opt-out of receiving spam from each individual solicitation. However, opponents counter that the registry would give spammers millions of valid email addresses to spam because this is like "trusting the fox to guard the hen house." If the legislation tasks the solicitor with maintaining a list of users who don't want to receive solicitations, how do we know that unscrupulous spammers won't simply use this list for their own spamming purposes? This is especially likely given the fact that spammers have been highly creative when it comes to finding new ways to avoid detection and circumvent the law. Furthermore, since spammers are difficult to track down and identify throughout the world, this kind of registry is not likely to decrease the volume of spam.

Another option is to implement a Do-Not-Spam List comprised of domains, such as @hotmail.ca or @sfu.ca addresses.[69] In this sense, the domain as a whole could opt out of receiving spam, or opt out by category of spam, such as pornography or prescription drugs. Since a Do-Not-Spam List of domains is far

---

[67] Grant C. Yang, Issue Brief, "Canning Spam: Consumer Protection or a Lid on Free Speech?" (2004) Duke L. & Tech. Rev. 16.

[68] *Ibid.*

[69] Bolin, *supra*, note 2 at 429.

less attractive and useful to spammers than a list of real addresses, this system would protect users' privacy and would be relatively inexpensive to administer, particularly if the domains were able to post notices of their preferences in a publicly accessible database.[70] However, identity-masking tools, including spoofing, proxies and open relays, as well as the use of zombie computers make this kind of list difficult to enforce. If spammers can render themselves untraceable, it will be difficult to hold them accountable for their actions, regardless of the existence of a robust Do-Not-Spam List.

Furthermore, ISPs can continue to implement filtering technologies to help enforce this regime. Since ISPs are already exerting enormous power over the communications their subscribers receive, by filtering email before it is even received by the user and articulating these values in their terms of service, creating a legally enforceable regime for the refusal of unsolicited email messages at the domain level might be a logical next step. In addition, the Do-Not-Spam List provides the added measure of notice and accountability that filtering cannot. Domains could be held accountable by their users for opting out of spam (or not) and users could choose service providers that enforce the views they share.

NON-LEGAL MEASURES TO COMBAT SPAM

Spam filtering devices and software tools now fill the vacuum that anti-spam legislation was meant to address.[71] Private email users and ISPs can use various forms of **filtering** technology to stop spam from reaching email inboxes (i.e., stopping spam at the point of entry). There are a number of technologically sophisticated filtering tools on the market today that are designed to distinguish spam and non-spam email. For example, learning algorithms can be used to find the characteristics of spam email versus good email.[72] Future messages can automatically be filtered to either the inbox or to a quarantine folder, which contains messages flagged as highly likely to be spam. To be effective, however, the programs need examples of spam and non-spam messages to train the system. And as spammers adapt and learn which words are likely to trigger the filter, the filters must be updated frequently. Hotmail currently uses a method by which it asks more than 100,000 volunteers per day to label messages sent to them as either "good" or "spam."[73] This helps to provide new messages to better improve the filters.

However, spammers have gotten more effective at hiding words. For example, they can break a word like "free" into multiple pieces, using an HTML comment (fr<!—><—>ee) that, when displayed, will appear as "free" to the user but cannot be read by the spam-filtering software.[74] Thus, when ISPs find new ways to combat the spammers, they quickly adapt their techniques. In fact,

---

[70] *Ibid.*

[71] Soma, Singer and Hurd, *supra*, note 8 at 168.

[72] Goodman, Cormack and Heckerman, *supra*, note 13 at 26-27.

[73] *Ibid.*

[74] *Ibid* at 27.

the marketplace is now rife with products that "protect" consumers from spam as well as those that facilitate the transmission of spam.[75]

Individuals can create safe lists, block senders, and set up new email accounts to avoid mailing lists. In addition, ISPs can hire employees to screen spam, terminate the email accounts of spammers and file lawsuits. However, spammers can respond by finding ways to circumvent filters. For instance, they can forge their email address so the recipient cannot find its origin (spoofing) or send anonymous email (re-mailing). Furthermore, when legitimate emails are accidentally filtered, important communications are lost. It is also noteworthy that email is not the only medium through which spam is currently being transmitted.[76] Instant messaging programs, chat-rooms and cellphone text messaging services all have their own forms of spam to contend with.

To deal with email spam, ISPs have been forced to expand their **bandwidth** capacity to accommodate the increase in volume of spam email traffic. A large number of ISPs also maintain address-based **blacklists** to reject email from hosts previously reported to disseminate spam.[77] Most blacklists are updated hourly, which has prompted some spammers to send out tens of millions of spam email messages in the first hour or so before the IP address is blocked.[78] This approach has a number of limitations, though, such as the ability of spammers to switch IP addresses. Blacklists can also create havoc when a good sender inherits a bad/blacklisted IP address from another user (IP addresses are randomly assigned to users for as long as they are using the network and then they are re-assigned for other users to make use of). Thus, blacklists do not offer a complete solution to the problem of dealing with spam.

An alternative approach is for ISPs to charge a minimal fee (e.g., one cent) for the assurance that a message will arrive at its destination inbox. This is effectively a "first class" email system to ensure that wanted email messages arrive at their destination and to certify that a received message is not spam. However, this would clearly not stop spam email as it only provides a way to authenticate good email. As such, this method, by itself, is not a workable solution to combat the problem of spam.

CONCLUSION

Aside from being a nuisance, spam has a significant economic impact on individuals and corporations. Spam is also a popular tool for perpetrating identity theft, fraud and other serious crimes. In response to these threats, a number of countries have adopted legislation aimed at combatting spam and diminishing its use. These laws vary significantly in terms of their effectiveness; however, ultimately, they have all failed to put an end to spam.

---

[75] Soma, Singer and Hurd, *supra*, note 8 at 170.

[76] *Ibid* at 33.

[77] Kanich, *et. al.*, *supra*, note 1 at 104.

[78] Goodman, Cormack and Heckerman, *supra*, note 13.

Given its ability to move across international boundaries, an international solution is required. Moreover, since law enforcement officials cannot be in all places at all times, they need to rely on the cooperation of third parties, such as ISPs, to target spammers. One method that has proven successful at combatting spam is the use of **honeypot** accounts to monitor spam activity.[79] Honeypot accounts are typically published in public places, such as a website or message board, and then harvested by spammers using specialized programs called spam bots.[80] These programs are able to quickly scan through Web pages looking for email addresses, which can then be sold to spammers.[81] When email is sent to the honeypot account address, the sender and associated sending servers can be linked to the harvesting IP address. Network administrators can then block the harvester's IP address or notify the ISP about the harvesting activities of its subscribers.[82] Of course, the ISP will not be under any legal requirement to deal with these problems unless the harvesting of email addresses is illegal under Canadian law. And, as I mentioned earlier, the harvesting of honeypot email addresses, as well as the spamming of these accounts, is not currently prohibited under PIPEDA.

It is noteworthy that telemarketing restrictions in both Canada and the United States limit the practice of telemarketing. The United States maintains a National Do Not Call Registry while Canada provides a less elaborate scheme whereby a telephone subscriber can place his or her number on a list maintained by individual marketers of people whom they are forbidden to call.[83] There has been some discussion in both the United States and Canada about creating a No-Spam List or a Do Not Spam Registry. The advantage of these registries is that they give people the right to decide whether or not they want to receive commercial email solicitations. And without assurance that this solution will actually decrease spam, it will be difficult to get ISPs and consumers to implement and pay for it.

It is also important to note that while individual and corporate lawsuits against spammers are helpful, they are likely to be costly and the anonymous nature of the Internet makes it difficult to identify spammers in order for these kinds of claims to be launched. Rather than rely on private enforcement, it might be easier for the Competition Bureau, or the federal or provincial Privacy Commissioner, to handle citizen complaints by initiating proceedings or forwarding the complaint to the sender's ISP.[84]

The question of international enforcement is also important given that spam is an issue of global concern. While it might be possible to create a large-scale multilateral spam treaty, this scheme is unlikely to work in practice. Although there appears to be great international impetus for dealing with the problem of

---

[79] Bolin, *supra,* note 2 at 420. Note that this method has been successfully used to deal with those who violate the CAN-SPAM Act in the United States.

[80] *Ibid.*

[81] *Ibid.*

[82] *Ibid.*

[83] In the United States, see the Federal Communications Commission National Do-Not-Call Registry Website at http://www.fcc.gov/cgb/donotcall/. In Canada, see the Telecommunications Act, 1993, c. 38.

[84] Slane, *supra*, note 41 at 284.

cybercrime throughout the world, there does seem to be a lack of willingness on the part of individual countries to update their local laws to conform to international standards. This is evidenced by the fact that out of the 43 signatory states that have currently signed the Council of Europe's International Cybercrime Treaty, which is discussed in Chapter 9, only a handful have ratified it. In addition, it is difficult to determine which international organization, such as the United Nations, the World Trade Organization or the Organization for Economic Cooperation and Development, would oversee the development and implementation of a global anti-spam agreement.[85]

QUESTIONS FOR FURTHER THINKING AND DISCUSSION

1. What specific problems or threats does spam pose for Canadians?
2. Should Canada enact legislation similar to the CAN-SPAM Act? Why or why not?
3. Is there a risk in encouraging Internet users to fence off their own corner of cyberspace? Is this similar to or different from the ways in which we have established boundaries to protect property ownership in the real, physical world?
4. Does the extension of trespass principles to cyberspace promote the idea of "cyberspace as a distinct place?" Keeping in mind what you learned in this chapter about cyber-trespass, what are the ramifications of this approach?
5. Is there a difference between a cyber-trespass and spam? Does spam pose a more serious threat in terms of server or network overloads and shutdowns?
6. Why do spammers use bot computers to disseminate spam? How is this different from the dissemination of other forms of spam?
7. Should Canadian courts be applying the doctrine of trespass to chattels to Internet-related cases? Why or why not?
8. What should Canada's anti-spam legislation look like? What kinds of activities should be prohibited? Who should be protected by the legislation and who should be held liable? What should the penalties be and who should enforce them?
9. Should Canada hold ISPs liable for spam that occurs within their networks?
10. Does s. 2(b) of the *Charter* protect the right of individuals and businesses to send spam email?
11. What are the costs of limiting or abridging the right to free expression in Canada? Are these costs outweighed by the benefits of regulating spam?
12. Should Canada implement a national Do-Not-Spam registry?
13. What kinds of international solutions might be effective at combatting spam?

---

[85] Cheung, *supra*, note 20 at 236.

PART FOUR

SPECIFIC PROBLEMS WITH THE REGULATION AND PROSECUTION OF CYBERCRIMINALS

9

International Jurisdiction and the Regulation of Cyberspace

INTRODUCTION

We have seen that computer crime is increasingly perpetrated across national boundaries. As a global network, the Internet allows for the instant exchange of information between individuals throughout the globe. The physical evidence needed to arrest and prosecute a cybercrime suspect can be located anywhere in the world and cybercriminals can set up their operations within countries that do not have laws criminalizing this conduct, or whose laws are very weak, making the investigation of the crime and extradition of the suspect extremely difficult.

Global interconnectivity is perhaps the most important feature of the Internet and it has facilitated the worldwide increase in cybercrime. Because the Internet enables the instant transmission of information worldwide, across national borders and between individuals from remote locations, our regulatory approach to this problem must be international in scope. International norms must be established and we must ensure that we coordinate our international law enforcement efforts to combat it.

Only recently have we begun to create harmonized standards at the international level on the question of how to combat computer crime. To be effective, these standards must be widely adopted and we must also implement law enforcement techniques that foster and promote inter-jurisdictional cooperation. This chapter will examine the measures that have been implemented to deal with the inter-jurisdictional nature of cybercrime offences. Recommendations are also made for how the problem of international cooperation can be better dealt with by the Canadian government and these issues are further explored in the next chapter.

SPECIFIC MEASURES FOR EFFECTIVE INTER-JURISDICTIONAL COOPERATION

The Importance of International Conventions

If many countries are failing to enforce and prosecute cybercrime offences, the problem cannot be effectively targetted. Without universal legal standards, a cybercriminal can move his or her website to a country where the laws are weaker and operate from there. The formulation of workable mutual assistance treaties is also necessary to facilitate cooperation between states in the prosecution of offenders. This includes providing for the swift and effective extradition of cybercrime offenders between countries. The **Council of Europe's Convention on Cybercrime**[1] was created in November 2001 by the Council of Europe and non-member states, including Canada, Japan, South Africa and the United States.[2] It is the best mechanism to achieve these goals on an international scale. It also requires signatory states to implement domestic measures that will assist in combatting computer crime more effectively in Canada.

The Cybercrime Convention, which establishes a framework for mutual assistance between jurisdictions, was specifically created to address hacking, child pornography and copyright offences, and the difficulties with investigating and prosecuting cybercrime offences across borders. The Convention entered into force on July 1, 2004. As of June 10, 2010, there were 46 signatory states, including Canada, and 30 countries have ratified it.[3]

The distinction between signing and ratifying a convention is critical to understand. When a country *signs* a convention, this indicates general support for the principles of the convention as well as its intention to be legally bound by it. However, the convention does not become legally binding until a country *ratifies* the convention by depositing an instrument of ratification with the relevant

---

[1] Budapest, 23.XI.2001.

[2] See Laura Huey and Richard S. Rosenberg, "Watching the Web: Thoughts on Expanding Police Surveillance Opportunities under the Cyber-Crime Convention," (2004) Canadian Journal of Criminology and Criminal Justice 597.

[3] US Department of State, Fact Sheet, Office of the Spokesman, Washington, DC, September 29, 2006, available online at: http://www.state.gov/.

international organization. Once a country ratifies a convention, the country is legally bound by its articles and must conform to its principles under international law. It is noteworthy that many countries sign but do not ratify treaties, including Canada, which has signed a number of international treaties but not ratified them.[4] Several amendments to the *Criminal Code* are needed in order for Canada to ratify the Cybercrime Convention, including enabling the interception of online communications, as well as various new search and seizure provisions, which are discussed in detail in Chapter 10.[5]

The Convention serves three major purposes.

1. It identifies a list of offences to be criminalized in signatory states.
2. It requires each signatory state to grant new search and seizure powers to its law enforcement officials.
3. It facilitates cooperation between signatory states.

The first principle is to identify a list of offences that each signatory state must criminalize under their domestic laws (Articles 2-11). The offences fall into four broad categories of computer-related crime: fraud and forgery; child pornography; copyright infringements; and security breaches, such as hacking, illegal data interception and system interferences that compromise network integrity and availability. Signatories must also enact laws establishing jurisdiction over such offenses committed on their territories or by their nationals abroad.

The Convention also requires each signatory state to grant new powers of search and seizure to its law enforcement officials, including the power to require an ISP (Internet Service Provider) to preserve a citizen's Internet activity records and the power to monitor user activity in real time (Articles 16-22). In other words, each signatory state must establish domestic procedures for detecting, investigating and prosecuting computer crimes, and collecting electronic evidence of any criminal offence.

Finally, it requires law enforcement officials in each signatory state to assist those in other participating states by cooperating with "mutual assistance requests" from police "to the widest extent possible" (Articles 23-35). Given that cybercrime offences often take place across international boundaries, mutual assistance provisions can be critical to investigating and gathering the necessary evidence to successfully prosecute a cybercriminal.

Much of the treaty deals with extradition and mutual assistance between nations in investigating and gathering evidence in cybercrime offences. The extradition provisions, contained in Article 24, supplement any formal extradition agreements or treaties that exist between the state parties. This Article is critical to the investigation and prosecution of online child pornography offences that can involve the apprehension of suspects in different countries than where they happen to be under investigation or charged. This might occur in the case where

---

[4] This is discussed by Professor Geist on his website at: www.michaelgeist.ca.

[5] See Department of Justice and Industry Canada and Solicitor General Canada, "Lawful Access Consultation Document," August 25, 2002, at 10.

an individual operates a website from one country and makes child pornography available in another country for a fee. It will help to address the fact that child pornographers can set up their operations within countries whose laws are weak and escape prosecution in the host country, as well as those to which they disseminate their illegal materials.

Similarly, the mutual assistance provisions obligate countries to help out other countries in cross-border investigations to the "widest extent possible." This can include drafting mutual assistance treaties with specific nations or responding to requests for mutual assistance from states with respect to specific investigations, in conformity with the requirements specified in the Convention. Specific requests for mutual assistance can include officials in one state asking those in another to access, seize, preserve and make available stored computer data. This is important because the physical evidence needed to arrest and prosecute a cybercrime suspect can be located anywhere in the world.

The Convention represents a significant step forward because it commits signatories to prosecute computer-related crimes forcefully, which many countries fail to do currently. However, some critics, such as the American Civil Liberties Union, maintain that the Convention lacks necessary privacy and civil liberties protections.[6] They are concerned that their country might be asked to hand over information about its citizens to other countries investigating actions that are illegal in the other country but perfectly legal within their territory. The result, they fear, is that law enforcement officials and ISPs might be forced to cooperate with foreign officials in conducting investigations on citizens in their country who have not committed a crime under their laws.

Yet nothing prevents a state from entering into mutual assistance treaties or other arrangements with states that only supply information with respect to conduct that is a criminal offence under its own laws.[7] Conversely, if a state does not wish to enter into specific mutual assistance treaties and prefers to follow the mutual assistance provisions set out in the Convention, it will have a number of safeguards at its disposal. Article 25, which sets out "general principles relating to mutual assistance," provides that in some cases the country being asked to provide information is allowed to make assistance conditional upon the existence of **dual criminality** (when a crime committed in the requesting state must also be recognized as a crime in the requested state) and refuse the request if the conduct underlying the offence for which the information is being sought is not a criminal offence under its laws. In other cases, such as under Articles 27, 29 and 30, a requested party can refuse, postpone or partially grant a request for mutual assistance, which means that it is not necessarily required to cooperate with foreign officials in investigations in all cases.

The issue of dual criminality illustrates the need for countries to establish uniform standards for the definition and prosecution of cybercrime offences. This is critical in order to ensure that relevant information can be gathered and shared

---

[6] Declan McCullagh, "Perspective: Fuzzy Logic Behind Bush's Cybercrime Treaty," November 28, 2005, available online at: http://news.com.com.

[7] Title 3 and 4 of the Council of Europe's Convention on Cybercrime address this possibility.

in cross-border investigations and offenders can be prosecuted. Ensuring that signatory states work together to establish uniform standards and comprehensive legislation will avoid the problem of dual criminality and further cooperation between nations.

The main thrust of the Convention is to require participating states to enact legislation granting broad search and seizure powers to law enforcement authorities, including the power to compel ISPs to intercept data transmissions to provide assistance to police in the storage and search of data transmissions, and to provide information about their individual customers to police. Article 16 requires signatories to adopt legislation to permit the preservation of computer data, including traffic data, for up to 90 days, if it is relevant to an investigation. Article 18 requires signatories to draft regulations that permit law enforcement officials to request computer data, as well as individual ISP service subscriber information. Article 20 requires that signatory states draft legislation to compel ISPs to permit law enforcement officials to monitor and collect the **traffic data** of their subscribers in real time. Article 21 requires signatories to draft legislation requiring ISPs to intercept and store data, or to assist law enforcement officials in doing so.

Together with the mutual assistance provisions discussed earlier, the Convention facilitates the collection, retention and dissemination of computer data not only within a single jurisdiction, but also between signatory states. It is useful for targeting a wide range of cybercrime offences committed inter-jurisdictionally, including hacking, identity theft and fraud, not just child pornography. However, critics maintain that the states that participated in the Convention's negotiations are not the problem countries in which cybercriminals operate relatively freely. For example, hackers frequently route cyber-attacks through portals in Yemen or North Korea, neither of which are part of the Convention. Notwithstanding these concerns, however, the Convention clearly removes or lessens the many procedural and jurisdictional obstacles that can delay or inhibit the international investigations and prosecutions of computer-related crimes.

Since 2002, Parliament has been considering how it should design and implement electronic surveillance rules, including production and preservation rules, requiring ISPs to collect and store traffic data and share it with law enforcement authorities. As yet, no workable data retention scheme has been enacted.[8] Canada has not yet ratified the Convention largely because it has not been able to draft workable data retention rules, including production and preservation orders, which the Convention requires signatory states to adopt. Furthermore, some business and consumer groups have expressed concern that these measures could increase costs to ISPs, impede the development of security technologies and negatively affect consumer confidence in e-commerce. However, many other countries, including the United States and all member states

---

[8] See the Canadian Internet Policy and Public Interest Clinic website, located online at: http://www.cippic.ca. These government proposals will be further discussed in a later section on "lawful access."

of the European Union, have already put these regulations in place. It is not a question of whether or not Canada will implement these measures, but how quickly and on what terms. These issues are further discussed in the next chapter.

International Law Enforcement Cooperation

As a global network, the Internet allows for the instant exchange of information between users throughout the world. Given that the Internet is a transnational medium, there is a palpable need for international law enforcement cooperation and, in fact, there has been increased international consensus around the importance of a global initiative to combat cybercrime. This is particularly important given that critical evidence, in the form of computer data, can be stored within almost any jurisdiction in the world. This means that law enforcement agents within the various countries must be required to preserve and facilitate access to computer data quickly, before it is modified or destroyed.

At the present time, computer crime investigators are using a cumbersome Mutual Legal Assistance Treaty (MLAT) process to obtain assistance from law enforcement officials in other jurisdictions. Due to the fact that MLAT investigations must be processed through official government channels in Canada and abroad, which can take between six months and a year, valuable evidence can be lost in cross-border investigations. Ideally, Canadian police should be given the necessary authority and resources to work with law enforcement officials on cross-border investigations. Specialist multi-jurisdictional law enforcement teams are an invaluable way to foster international cooperation on computer crime investigations. These units can apply their inter-jurisdictional expertise to investigations, operations, research and training in complex and time-sensitive computer crime cases.

In Chapter 4, I discussed the importance of resources aimed at enhancing international law enforcement cooperation, including the Virtual Global Taskforce (VGT) and the Child Exploitation Tracking System (CETS) tool. Through its **International Criminal Investigative Training Assistance Program** (ICITAP), the United States Department of Justice has played a key role in assisting countries, such as Indonesia, to implement CETS, by providing technical assistance in the form of training and education, equipment donations and renovations.[9] It has donated computer servers, and collaborated with Microsoft to develop a Computer Learning Laboratory that will enable Indonesian investigators to further develop the skills necessary to investigate instances of computer facilitated crimes such as child exploitation, identity theft and credit card fraud.[10] The laboratory will also serve as one of the training centres for CETS. Australia is further helping to deploy the software in police departments throughout Indonesia and the Canadian RCMP are working to train law

---

[9] See "Indonesian National Police Take Lead in Asia with Roll Out of Child Exploitation Tracking System," APAC Press Centre, June 28, 2006, available online at: http://www.microsoft.com/asia/pressCentre/default.aspx.

[10] *Ibid*.

enforcement officials from other countries on how to use this valuable investigative tool.

The potential for this system to operate as a global tracking and investigation method is enormous, particularly given the number of international child pornography investigations that have taken place in the past few years. Ideally, there could be one central database at Interpol (International Criminal Police Organization), or some other central police agency, and national versions could link into it. At present, we have separate image databases in various countries and none are linked, so what is needed is a large-scale initiative to combine the information into one database and coordinate it. We also need agencies to provide the necessary training, resources and technical support to keep the system running in a variety of countries throughout the world.

CONCLUSION

Our regulatory approach to the problem of cybercrime must be inter-jurisdictional. Implementing the Cybercrime Convention is a critical way to ensure that we achieve harmonization in our regulatory standards. As will be discussed in the next chapter, Canada must also implement measures to ensure that it is in compliance with this Convention, so as to facilitate the international effort to combat computer crimes.

We must also further assist other countries to implement the CETS program to ensure a unified and coordinated approach to the investigation of online child pornography and the apprehension of suspects.

QUESTIONS FOR FURTHER THINKING AND DISCUSSION

1. What are safe haven jurisdictions and why do we need to be concerned about them for the purpose of cybercrime investigations?
2. What are the essential aspects of the Council of Europe's Convention on Cybercrime?
3. Has Canada ratified the Council of Europe's Convention on Cybercrime – why or why not?
4. What are the advantages to using the CETS program in cybercrime investigations?

10

Searching and Seizing Evidence in Cyberspace

KEY TERMS AND CONCEPTS

- Bill C-74, *The Modernization of Investigative Techniques Act* (MITA)
- Biographical core
- Canadian Association of Police Chiefs
- *Charter*, s. 8
- *Charter*, s. 24(2)
- *Criminal Code*, Part VI
- *Criminal Code*, s. 164
- *Criminal Code*, s. 183
- *Criminal Code*, s. 487
- *Communications Assistance for Law Enforcement Act* (CALEA) – US

- Computer forensics
- Data preservation
- Data production
- Hash values
- *Hunter v. Southam*
- Intercept-capable networks
- Internet cache
- Lawful access
- Lawful Access Consultation Document
- Location data
- *Personal Information Protection and Electronic Documents Act* (PIPEDA)

- Privacy
- *R. v. Cole*
- *R. v. Duarte*
- *R. v. Plant*
- *R. v. Ward*
- *R. v. Wier*
- *R. v. Wong*
- Reasonable expectation of privacy
- *Regulation of Investigatory Powers Act* – UK
- Traffic data
- Wiretapping

INTRODUCTION

Few issues are as important to Canadians as the ability of law enforcement officials to invade our privacy without judicial authorization. However, life in the modern world creates competing expectations and demands. On the one hand, many Canadians are deeply concerned about their personal safety and security;

thus, they support giving law enforcement officials new investigative techniques to deal with the challenges brought about by emerging technologies.[1] On the other hand, Canadians also have an interest in protecting their privacy, particularly with respect to their personal information.

There is no specific constitutional right to privacy in the *Canadian Charter of Rights and Freedoms*.[2] However, s. 8 contains a robust constitutional protection against government intrusion into the private sphere of the individual. Building on the framework established by the common law, s. 8 creates certain areas of personal autonomy where government agents cannot intrude without judicial authorization. The common-law privacy protections are rooted in the law of trespass, whereby privacy was associated with private property and respect for the sanctity of the home against intruders. However, technological innovation has meant that physical intrusion into the home no longer begins and ends at the front door. For instance, wiretaps are easy to implement from a distance and information can be gathered about an individual through many other kinds of surreptitious electronic surveillance techniques. The challenge for the courts has been to protect the privacy interests of Canadians in the face of innovative electronic surveillance measures.

Section 8 of the *Charter* provides, "Everyone has the right to be secure against unreasonable search and seizure." The Supreme Court of Canada has stated that this provision protects the citizens' reasonable expectation of privacy in a free and democratic society.[3] Yet how do we know what our expectations of privacy are, much less whether or they are reasonable or unreasonable? In order to address these ambiguities, the Supreme Court of Canada has established a purposeful approach to s. 8 in which the protection of privacy is the overriding principle.[4] In other words, emphasis is placed on examining the totality of the circumstances, with regard to the reasonableness of one's subjective expectation of privacy.[5]

However, it is important to keep in mind that privacy is a protean concept with no single definition. Long ago, Samuel D. Warren and Louis D. Brandeis famously argued that privacy is based on the concept of an "inviolate personality" and the "right to be let alone."[6] Their well-known understanding of privacy protection is primarily based on individual freedom and moral autonomy, which means that it protects "people, not places,"[7] and it has been recognized as being essential to maintain the state's respect for the dignity of the individual.[8] Given

---

[1] For example, many Canadians were deeply concerned about the 9/11 attacks in which terrorists were able to hijack airplanes and effectively use them as guided missiles against the World Trade Centre towers. These events led to increased security measures being implemented in airports throughout North America and around the world.

[2] Part I of the *Constitution Act, 1982*, being Schedule B to the *Canada Act 1982* (UK), 1982, c. 11.

[3] *Canada (Director of Investigation & Research, Combines Investigation Branch) v. Southam Inc.*, [1984] 2 S.C.R. 145 (S.C.C.) at para. 24. ("*Southam*")

[4] *R. v. Tessling*, [2004] 3 S.C.R. 432 (S.C.C.), at para. 19.

[5] *R. v. Edwards*, [1996] 1 S.C.R. 128 (S.C.C.), at para. 45.

[6] Samuel D. Warren and Louis D. Brandeis, "The Right to Privacy," (1890) 4 Harv. L. Rev. 193.

[7] *Southam, supra*, note 3 at para. 23.

[8] *R. v. Dyment*, [1988] 2 S.C.R. 417 (S.C.C.) at para. 22.

its recognition of the relationship between privacy and intimate information about an individual, the "right to be let alone" concept of privacy underlies many of the laws developed in Canada to protect individual communications from state surveillance; however, this conception of privacy, by itself, is clearly insufficient in the modern world.[9]

Technological innovation has meant that the amount of personal information that can be recorded about us and shared with others is virtually limitless.[10] Parliament now has many methods by which it can collect information about us and conduct surveillance in previously unforeseen ways, including the sharing and cross-referencing of electronic records (medical, taxation, financial and business data about individuals), video, camera and satellite surveillance, as well as a range of electronic monitoring and interception techniques, including **wiretapping**. In addition, private actors (i.e., non-governmental) are now playing a vital role in the aggregation and dissemination of personal information and, as a result, individuals are demanding more state oversight and intervention on their behalf.[11]

The difficulty of balancing these competing expectations lies at the heart of s. 8 jurisprudence.[12] The Supreme Court of Canada has stressed that the guarantee against unreasonable search and seizure only protects a "reasonable expectation" of privacy when balanced against the other competing societal interests, including law enforcement.[13] This means that privacy rights can sometimes be limited when there is a reasonable and compelling state interest, in accordance with s. 1 of the *Charter*. The balance between the need to protect an individual's privacy from unjustified state intrusion and the interest in overriding the right can shift, depending on the nature of the privacy interest at stake.

The Supreme Court of Canada has stressed the need for even greater privacy protections to be accorded to the individual in light of new technological developments that enable more extensive encroachments upon our privacy and fundamental liberties. Thus, the Court has emphasized its need to carefully scrutinize the state's use of new technologies and has required compliance with the requirements for a "reasonable" search or seizure under s. 8, including the need to obtain judicial authorization, such as a valid search warrant. On the other hand, only those searches that are not authorized by reasonable law and carried out in a reasonable manner will offend s. 8 of the *Charter*.

---

[9] Lisa Austin, "Privacy and the Question of Technology," (2003) 22 Law and Philosophy 119. Austin maintains at 122 that "[t]he protected sphere of information defined by one's thoughts, emotions and sensations is too narrow."

[10] *Ibid* at 122-123.

[11] Richard B. Bruyer, "Privacy: A Review and Critique of the Literature," (2005) 43 Alta. L. Rev. 553 at 560. Bruyer notes that this phenomenon can help to explain the explosion in information privacy laws across Canada.

[12] *Ibid.*

[13] *Southam, supra,* note 3 at para. 25.

THE PRIVACY AND *CHARTER* IMPLICATIONS OF ELECTRONIC SURVEILLANCE

The restraints imposed on government to pry into the lives of its citizens are at the heart of the modern democratic state.[14] Early English common law protected an individual's home from unjustified intrusion by the sovereign, which was linked to personal property and the law against trespass.[15] Nevertheless, privacy protection in Canada is largely based on individual freedom and moral autonomy, rather than property *per se*, which, in the context of s. 8 means that it protects "people, not places,"[16] and it has been recognized as being essential to maintain the state's respect for the dignity and well-being of the individual.[17] This has led to special protection being accorded to bodily sanctity and personal information about the lifestyle or intimate personal choices of the individual.

The Supreme Court of Canada has established that privacy arises in three distinct domains:

1. spatial and territorial,
2. personal, and
3. informational.[18]

In the spatial or territorial realm, certain types of social interactions require a greater degree of privacy protection than others and this requires shielding certain types of social interactions from public scrutiny, such as those that occur within the sanctity of the home. In the personal domain, privacy has been linked with surveillance and the individual's right to maintain control over his or her own bodily movements,[19] as well as bodily sanctity, in the sense that an unlawful search can constitute an affront to human dignity.[20] The last zone of privacy identified by the Court requires respect for personal information. The retention of personal information about oneself has been said to be a fundamental right in the sense that it should be left up to the individual to determine under what conditions personal information is disclosed to others.[21]

The protection of individual privacy against state intrusion is particularly important, with respect to all three zones of privacy, concerning the state's power to monitor communications and conduct electronic surveillance. The Supreme Court of Canada has stressed the need for even greater privacy protections to be accorded to the individual in light of new technological developments that enable

---

[14] *R. v. Dyment, supra,* note 8 at para. 17.

[15] *Southam, supra,* note 3 at para. 21.

[16] *Ibid* at para. 23.

[17] *R. v. Dyment, supra,* note 8 at para. 22.

[18] *R. v. Dyment, supra,* note 8 at para. 19.

[19] *R. v. Wong,* [1990] 3 S.C.R. 36; see also *Dagg v. Canada (Minster of Finance),* [1997] 2 S.C.R. 403, where the Court found that government employees have a reasonable expectation that workplace sign-in logs that reveal information about their movements and location at work should not generally be made available to the public.

[20] This sense of privacy transcends the physical and provides protection against the indignity of a search, and its invasion of the person, in a moral sense (*R. v. Dyment, supra,* note 8 at para. 21).

[21] *R. v. Dyment, supra,* note 8 at para. 22.

more extensive encroachments on our personal privacy and fundamental liberties.[22] Thus, the Court has stressed its need to carefully scrutinize the state's use of new technologies and has required compliance with the requirements for a reasonable search or seizure under s. 8, including the need to obtain judicial authorization, such as a valid search warrant.

The Court's insistence on legal authority for searches and seizures involving new surveillance technologies is consistent with its goal of preventing unjustified searches before they happen. In the words of Dickson J., in *Hunter v. Southam*, "this can only be accomplished by a system of prior authorization, not one of subsequent validation." This approach has been consistently maintained by the Court and is reflected in many of the surveillance technology decisions dealing with the requirements for a reasonable search and seizure under s. 8. Generally speaking, these cases stand for the proposition that unauthorized surreptitious electronic surveillance will violate s. 8 where the target of the surveillance has a reasonable expectation of privacy.

In *R. v. Wong*, the Supreme Court of Canada considered whether surreptitious video surveillance by police of a hotel room without prior judicial authorization infringed s. 8 of the *Charter*. In that case, the police installed a video camera in a room registered to Wong in the course of their investigation into whether he was running a common gaming house. The Court found that the unauthorized video surveillance offended against the reasonable expectations of privacy of the occupants of the room and violated s. 8.[23]

The Court also refused to find authority for the issuance of surreptitious video surveillance warrants in the electronic surveillance provisions then contained in the *Code*.[24] At that time, there was no legislation specifically authorizing video surveillance and Justice LaForest, who wrote the decision for the majority of the Court, declined to "fill the lacunae" and read such authority into the *Code*, observing that the "common law powers of search were extremely narrow, and that the courts have left it to Parliament to extend them where need be."[25] In cautioning against the unfettered right of state agents to electronically eavesdrop on unsuspecting individuals without judicial authorization, LaForest J. observed that,

> George Orwell in his classic dystopian novel *1984* painted a grim picture of a society whose citizens had every reason to expect that their every movement was subject to electronic video surveillance. . .[t]he notion that the agencies of the state should be at liberty to train hidden cameras on members of society wherever and whenever they wished is fundamentally irreconcilable with what we perceive to be acceptable behaviour on the part of government.[26]

---

[22] Such as through hidden video surveillance (*R. v. Wong, supra*, note 19) and the use of a thermal heat imaging device to take "heat" pictures of an individual's home from overhead aircraft (*R. v. Tessling, supra*, note 4).

[23] *Supra*, note 19.

[24] *Criminal Code*, R.S.C. 1985, c. C-46.

[25] *R. v. Wong, supra*, note 19 at para. 34. Note that Parliament subsequently responded by amending the *Code* to enable video surveillance.

[26] *R. v. Wong, supra*, note 21 at para. 15.

Prior to this, in *R. v. Duarte*,[27] the Supreme Court of Canada found that the surreptitious audio recording of a private communication, without the consent of all parties, can only be reasonable where prior judicial authorization has been obtained. In that case, as part of an investigation into drug trafficking, the police rented an apartment for a police informant who was working with an undercover police officer. The apartment was equipped with audio-visual recording equipment embedded in a wall. Although the informant and the undercover officer consented to the interception of their communications, Duarte, who discussed a cocaine transaction there, and was later charged with conspiracy to import a narcotic, did not. The Court found that the interception of private communications by the state, even with the consent of the originator or the recipient, without prior judicial authorization, violated s. 8. Justice LaForest cautioned that:

> . . .the very efficacy of electronic surveillance is such that it has the potential, if left unregulated, to annihilate any expectation that our communications will remain private. A society which exposes us, at the whim of the state, to the risk of having a permanent electronic recording made of our words, every time we opened our mouths might be superbly equipped to fight crime but would be one in which privacy no longer had any meaning.[28]

These cases suggest that there is a strong connection between electronic surveillance and the infringement of one's reasonable expectation of privacy. However, these cases can be contrasted against *R. v. Tessling*[29] in which the police used an airplane equipped with a Forward Looking Infra-Red (FLIR) camera to record the thermal energy or heat radiating from Tessling's house. Based, in part, on the information gathered from this investigation, the police were able to obtain a search warrant for Tessling's home, where they found a large quantity of drugs and several guns. The question before the Supreme Court of Canada was whether the use of the FLIR technology without a warrant was a violation of Tessling's right to be secure against unreasonable search and seizure.

The Court found that the use of this technique without a warrant did not violate Tessling's s. 8 rights. The reason was that it did not intrude upon Tessling's reasonable expectation of privacy.[30] Binnie J., who wrote the decision for the majority, stressed that the FLIR technology was both non-intrusive and unsophisticated, in terms of the information it was capable of gathering, and did not see through the exterior surface of the house. This case raises the frightening spectre of the technological surveillance of our private residences, without prior judicial authorization, and it reminds us of the need to be vigilant against advances in technology that facilitate highly intrusive searches, such as those that are capable of disclosing intimate details of our private lives within our homes.

---

[27] *R. v. Duarte*, [1990] 1 S.C.R. 30.

[28] *Ibid* at para. 22.

[29] *Supra*, note 4.

[30] Note that this case can be contrasted against *Kyllo v. U.S.*, 533 U.S. 27 (U.S. Or., 2001) in which the United States Supreme Court reached the opposite decision in a case involving the use of FLIR technology to image the outside of the house. In that case, the Court primarily relied upon the notion of the "sanctity of the home."

If a search is found to be unreasonable under s. 8 of the *Charter*, such that the statutory requirements under the *Code* have not been met, the evidence can be excluded under s. 24(2) of the *Charter*, which provides that:

> Where, in proceedings under subsection (1), a court concludes that evidence was obtained in a manner that infringed or denied any rights or freedoms guaranteed by this Charter, the evidence shall be excluded if it is established that, having regard to all the circumstances, the admission of it in the proceedings would bring the administration of justice into disrepute.

The Supreme Court of Canada recently stressed that the purpose of s. 24(2) is to maintain the good repute of the administration of justice, in the sense of maintaining the integrity of and public confidence in the criminal justice system. In 2009, the court in *R. v. Grant*[31] enunciated a new test for determining whether the admission of evidence obtained by a *Charter* breach would bring the administration of justice into disrepute. When faced with an application for exclusion under s. 24(2), a court must assess and balance the effect of admitting the evidence on society's confidence in the justice system having regard to:

1.   the seriousness of the *Charter*-infringing state conduct (admission may send the message that the justice system condones serious state misconduct),
2.   the impact of the breach on the *Charter*-protected interests of the accused (admission may send the message that individual rights count for little), and
3.   society's interest in the adjudication of the case on its merits.

Prior to this, the governing test for the exclusion of evidence pursuant to s. 24(2) was set out in *R. v. Collins*.[32] It requires that three factors be considered. First, the court must determine whether the admission of the evidence will undermine the fairness of the trial. The second factor pertains to the seriousness of the *Charter* violation (e.g., whether it was committed in good faith, or was motivated by urgency, and whether the evidence could have been obtained without a *Charter* violation). Third, the court must look at the effect of excluding the evidence on the long-term repute of the administration of justice.

Recall that in Chapter 2 I discussed how third parties, such as ISPs (Internet Service Providers), have an essential role to play in the regulation of cyberspace. This raises the question of whether the recovery of electronic data by or from ISPs triggers the constitutional protections set out in s. 8 of the *Charter*. Unless ISPs are subject to the requirements of the *Charter*, they will not need to worry about the concerns that arise under s. 8. The actions of private parties are not

---

[31]   2009 SCC 32, [2009] 2 S.C.R. 353 (S.C.C.).

[32]   [1987] 1 S.C.R. 265 (S.C.C.). Note that the Court revisited this question in *R. v. Stillman*, [1997] S.C.J. No. 34. In that case, the majority held that evidence obtained in breach of the *Charter* should, at the outset of the s. 24(2) inquiry, be classified as "conscriptive" or "non-conscriptive." Evidence would be classified as conscriptive where "an accused, in violation of his *Charter* rights, is compelled to incriminate himself at the behest of the state by means of a statement, the use of the body or the production of bodily samples." Conscriptive evidence was also found to include real evidence discovered as a result of an unlawfully conscripted statement. *Stillman* held that conscriptive evidence is generally inadmissible – because of its presumed impact on trial fairness – unless it would have been independently discovered.

generally implicated by the *Charter*; however, if ISPs are required by Parliament to maintain interception capabilities and to play some role in data surveillance and search and seizure, the distinction between their role as private or public actors may become blurred and they may be characterized as "agents of the state."[33] This issue has been dealt with in only one Canadian case to date.

In *R. v. Weir*,[34] an ISP discovered attachments to an email message that appeared to contain child pornography while repairing Mr. Wier's electronic mailbox. The ISP opened the attachments and found that they contained child pornography. It informed the police of its findings and, upon request, forwarded a copy of the message to the police. The ISP also provided the police with Mr. Wier's billing address. Mr. Wier argued that the ISP was acting as an agent of the state, and that the opening of the message and the forwarding of the message to the police were both warrantless searches. The Alberta Court of Appeal agreed with him and held that the ISP was acting as an agent of the state when it forwarded a copy of the message to the police at the request of the police officer.[35] The Court classified the forwarding of the email as a "warrantless search," which is presumed unreasonable and in violation of s. 8.[36] This case establishes that if a third party is collecting data for law enforcement purposes, or carrying out some other type of surveillance function, the provisions guarding against unreasonable search and seizure may be engaged and the need for a valid search warrant may arise.

However, this case can be contrasted against *R. v. Cole*.[37] In that case, child pornography was found on the accused teacher's laptop computer, issued to him by the school. The illegal images were found by the school's information technologist, who forwarded it to police with the computer. No search warrant was issued because the police determined school authorities owned the computer. The accused challenged the legality of the search and seizure and on appeal the Ontario Superior Court of Justice held that the trial judge erred in excluding the child pornography evidence. While the accused had a subjective expectation of privacy in his workplace computer, this expectation was not objectively reasonable because he was informed that the school's computer use agreement applied to laptops and he knew his communications could be monitored by the school. In other words, the contract between the accused and his employer vitiated the reasonable expectation of privacy that the accused had in the materials stored on his computer.

---

[33] Dominique Valiquet, "Telecommunications and Lawful Access: II. The Legislative Situation in the United States, The United Kingdom and Australia." Law and Government Division, February 28, 2006; Library of Parliament, PRB 05-66E, at 8.

[34] (2001), 2001 CarswellAlta 1069, [2001] A.J. No. 869 (Alta. C.A.).

[35] *Ibid* at para. 11.

[36] *Southam, supra*, note 3; *R. v. Collins, supra,* note 32 at 278.

[37] (2009), 2009 CarswellOnt 2251, [2009] O.J. No. 1755 (Ont. S.C.J.).

INTRODUCTION TO COMPUTER FORENSIC INVESTIGATIONS

Now that you have a general understanding of search and seizure in Canadian law, it is time to look at the way that computer crime investigations are conducted. Throughout this text, we have examined the many ways that computer technology facilitates harmful and illegitimate conduct. It should not surprise you to learn that technology has also changed the nature of criminal investigations and led to the development of new forensic tools and techniques. In these investigations, the computer is often essential because it contains digital evidence and connects the suspect to the offence. However, computer forensic investigations must conform to the constitutional principles discussed in this chapter. This requires an understanding of what it means to search and seize computer data. More importantly, when can the search or seizure of computer data be considered constitutionally reasonable?

In order to answer those important questions, you must have an understanding of what makes the search of computers or other electronic storage devices so fundamentally different from other kinds of searches. Real spaces offer predictable, specific and discrete physical regions for searches. This involves physically entering into a space, and observing and moving items to expose them to visual observation. Physical space also tends to limit the amount of evidence because a room can only store so many items and a building can only contain so many rooms.

In contrast, the amount of data that a computer can store is extremely vast. For instance, if the average laptop computer hard drive sold today has a storage capacity of 160 gigabytes, this is roughly equivalent to 80 million pages of text – about the amount of information contained on two floors of an academic library! Electronic evidence is also extremely volatile – turning the computer on or off can change over 1,000 files (e.g., previously deleted files can be overwritten at any time). In addition, computer data is stored on hard drives, floppy disks, thumb drives and Zip disks, in strings of zeros and ones that a computer converts into letters, numbers and symbols.[38]

In technical terms, Professor Orin Kerr has explained that computer searches "require passing an electric current over rotating magnetic points, processing the data, and then sending it to a monitor or other output device."[39] As discussed in Chapter 1, the hard drive is made up of magnetized disks that contain as many as billions of tiny points, which in a magnetized state represent "1" or in a demagnetized state represent "0."[40] When a user enters a command requesting data to be retrieved or stored on the hard drive, the metal disks spin and the magnetized points generate an electrical current, which transmits the signal needed to either "input" or "output" (i.e., send and retrieve) the zeros and ones. The space on the hard drive is divided up into various parts, known as "clusters,"

---

[38] Orin Kerr, "Searches and Seizures in a Digital World," (2005) 119 Harvard Law Review 531 at 537.

[39] *Ibid* at 534.

[40] *Ibid* at 539.

which are used to store files in different locations on the hard drive. The operating system maintains a master list of where all the files are located on the hard drive, so when a user requests a certain file, the computer directs the magnetic heads to the location of the appropriate cluster.[41]

The process of retrieving data from a computer is known as **computer forensics**. This job is typically performed by highly trained government analysts at a special forensics laboratory pursuant to a search warrant.[42] The task of retrieving evidence can take days or weeks to complete because the analyst must use special software programs to locate specific sets of data. Professor Kerr has pointed out that "[t]he dynamics of computer searches turn out to be substantially different from the dynamics of home searches. . .[c]omputers replace the enter-and-take-away dynamic of home searches with something more like copy, scan, and copy."[43] In other words, a government official or analyst does not physically enter into a computer and move data nor does he or she observe the movement of the magnetic disks and the zeros and ones. Instead, the analyst simply enters commands that copy data stored on the hard drive. Furthermore, analysts typically use special software to create **bitstream copies** of the files on a suspect's computer, which are then saved as a read only file so that the information can be analyzed without the risk of deleting or altering it.[44] In a nutshell, the analysis of the data stored on a suspect's computer takes place on government technology rather than on the actual electronic storage device seized.

Using special forensic software, an analyst can retrieve vast amounts of information about the use of the computer and its contents. For example, he or she can recover deleted files and can also conduct extensive searches for all image files with particular extensions, such as ".jpg."[45] Comprehensive searches can also be done for text files, such as those that search the entire hard drive for a particular word or phrase associated with a particular type of evidence, such as the word "Lolita" in a child pornography case. Moreover, using a database of **hash values** maintained by the government, forensic analysts can look to see if there is a match between any of the files on the suspect's hard drive and those stored in the database, such as images of child pornography.[46] After searching through an enormous amount of data on the hard drive, on occasion the analyst will find no relevant evidence; and, in other cases, he or she will discover evidence relating to a different crime altogether.[47]

Web browsers such as Internet Explorer, Firefox or Safari can also provide valuable evidence. Google or other search engines can link a suspect with

---

[41] *Ibid* at 540.

[42] *Ibid* at 537.

[43] *Ibid* at 537.

[44] *Ibid* at 540.

[45] *Ibid* at 545. Note that in *U.S. v. Romm*, 455 F.3d 990 (9th Cir., 2006), government officials were able to recover deleted files through forensic analysis, which can also reveal when files or images are created, accessed or modified.

[46] *Ibid* at 546. Note that when the analyst locates a file with a matching hash value, he or she does not need to open it to record information about it and its location on the hard drive.

[47] *Ibid* at 538.

searching/downloading illegal files – this defeats the claim "I wasn't aware that the child pornography images were there" or "those files were sent to me by someone else." The Internet cache is also important, especially if files are deleted by the suspect (i.e., the Temporary Internet Files (cache) folder contains a record of files accessed or downloaded from the Web – it can make browsing the Web faster because your computer can call up some of the page's elements from the cache).[48] Forensic investigators can also determine what other computer use/ activity occurred at the relevant time period. Did the user name have a password? Did the email reference subscriptions to certain sites? Were external storage devices used? Note that the Windows Registry also contains information about when/how the computer was used and when files were opened or saved because manual actions are often recorded in the Registry.

To summarize, whenever government agents undertake an investigation that intrudes upon an individual's reasonable expectation of privacy, the law will require the search to satisfy the constitutional test of reasonableness. As I discussed earlier in this chapter, the *Charter* creates the presumption that the law requires law enforcement officials to obtain a warrant, or some other form of judicial authorization, unless some exception to the warrant requirement applies.[49] Section 487 of the *Criminal Code*[50] provides the most frequently used example of specific statutory authority to issue a warrant to search. However, a warrant under this section is only available to authorize certain kinds of investigative techniques and other provisions in the *Code* authorize other kinds of searches, such as the interception of communications.

Subsections 487(2.1) and (2.2) of the *Code* provide the specific authority to search a computer system for data.[51] Law enforcement officials can apply to obtain a warrant under this section when data stored on a computer is seized (e.g., an email stored in suspect's computer), when an electronic storage device is seized, such as a laptop computer, or when records stored by an ISP are seized. If law enforcement officials are seeking to intercept a suspect's communications in real time, then they should apply for a warrant under Part VI of the *Code*, as discussed below.

LAWFUL ACCESS – THE FUTURE OF SEARCH AND SEIZURE

Lawful access applies to the lawful interception of communications, as well as the search and seizure of information by law enforcement authorities, either with or without a judicial warrant. In 2002, after the federal departments of Justice,

---

[48] See *U.S. v. Romm, supra*, note 45, where the accused was charged with possession of child pornography after deleted images were found in his Internet cache.

[49] For example, consent.

[50] *Supra*, note 24.

[51] (2.1)(a) allows searches of data in computer system;
    (b) allows reproduction of data (printing/copying/extracting);
    (c) allows seizure of reproduced data for examination;
(2.2) ... requires person in possession/control of data to permit search and seizure on presentation of the warrant.

Industry and the Solicitor General conducted extensive consultation with members of the law enforcement community, the telecommunications industry and the public, Parliament tabled a Lawful Access Consultation Document,[52] that addressed the need to enact new regulations to enable law enforcement officials to lawfully intercept online communications and seize evidence from ISPs. Parliament maintains that lawful access provisions are necessary to provide law enforcement agencies with "modern and effective capabilities to support their investigative or intelligence gathering efforts" and to "bring the law into accordance with the current state of telecommunications technology."[53] One of the principle reasons behind this initiative was to ratify the Convention on Cybercrime,[54] as I discussed in Chapter 9, which requires Parliament to draft provisions for "production and preservation orders" and the lawful interception of online communications into the *Code.*

In 2005, Parliament tabled Bill C-74, or *The Modernization of Investigative Techniques Act* (MITA).[55] The purpose of the Act was "to ensure that telecommunications service providers have the capability to enable national security and law enforcement agencies to exercise their authority to intercept communications, and to require service providers to supply subscriber and other information, without unreasonably impairing the privacy of individuals, the provision of telecommunications services to Canadians or the competitiveness of the Canadian telecommunications industry."[56] The Bill passed first reading in November 2005, but died on the order paper when the 38th Parliament was dissolved at the end of that month.[57]

Strengthening investigatory capabilities through the implementation of lawful access measures would seem to be highly consistent with the "get tough on crime" agenda embraced by the Tories. However, the Harper Conservatives have not revived the MITA. It is noteworthy that a couple of the provisions contained in the Convention on Cybercrime, such as those relating to subscriber information and production orders, have already been implemented in Canada. However, the measures relating to the lawful interception of ISP networks and preservation orders have yet to be introduced as legislation.

The MITA would have required ISPs to have **intercept-capable networks**, which means that when an ISP introduced new technologies into its network, such as installing new equipment or software, it would have been obligated to include an interception capability.[58] This would have provided law enforcement officials with the ability to intercept and isolate information concerning a particular suspect, including the ability to simultaneously intercept communications of

---

[52] Canada, Department of Justice and Industry Canada and Solicitor General Canada, August 25, 2002.

[53] *Ibid* at 4.

[54] See Council of Europe's Convention on Cybercrime, located online at: http://conventions.coe.int/Treaty/EN/Treaties/Html/185.htm.

[55] 38th Parl., 1st Sess., 4 Oct. 2004-29 Nov. 2005.

[56] *Ibid*, s. 3.

[57] Valiquet, *supra*, note 33.

[58] *Ibid* at 2.

multiple users, and to provide the intercepted communication to law enforcement officials, and to remove, where possible, any measures taken to preserve the anonymity of a communication, such as encryption, compression or encoding.[59] The Act would also have required ISPs to disclose basic information about subscribers to law enforcement officials on demand, including an individual's name, address, and IP (Internet Protocol) address, without the need for a warrant or judicial order.[60] Other provisions contained in the Convention on Cybercrime, such as those relating to production and preservation orders, were not introduced as legislation; however, they were raised by the government in its extensive consultations on the issue of lawful access legislation.[61]

Given the challenges of combatting cybercrime offences, Parliament must establish an effective model for lawful access to data held by ISPs. Canada is in a good position to implement lawful access legislation because it has already undertaken an extensive consultation process and drafted legislation that could serve as a model for new regulatory initiatives.[62] In addition, lawful access legislation already exists in many other countries, including the United States and the United Kingdom, which provided the starting point for Bill C-74.[63] Given that other major western nations have already dealt with many of the difficult issues surrounding the implementation of a lawful access regime, including cost and competition concerns, which are discussed below, Canada has several excellent models from which it can develop its own workable legislative scheme.

The regulatory framework must be broader than the one set out in Bill C-74 because Parliament neglected to address all the provisions contained in the Convention on Cybercrime, including orders for the preservation and production of data, discussed below, which were proposed by Parliament in its Lawful Access Consultation Document but not included in Bill C-74. Implementing these measures will enable Canada to keep up with legislative developments in other nations and cooperate with our partners in combatting trans-border computer crime, as called for by the Convention on Cybercrime.

LAWFUL ACCESS PROVISIONS

Requirement to Ensure Intercept Capability

Law enforcement officials in Canada currently have powers under the *Code* to intercept private communications.[64] The *Code* authorizes the use of electronic

---

[59] *Supra*, note 55, s. 6(1).

[60] Valiquet, *supra*, note 33 at 2.

[61] See *Lawful Access Consultation Document, supra*, note 52.

[62] Valiquet, *supra*, note 33 at 2.

[63] *Ibid* at 12.

[64] Part VI of the *Criminal Code* sets out procedures for how to obtain judicial authorizations to conduct electronic surveillance in criminal investigations. An application must be accompanied by an affidavit sworn by a peace officer or public officer. The affidavit must include information such as the facts relied on to justify the need for an authorization, details about the offence and the names and addresses of the persons whose private communications is to be intercepted (s.

surveillance, yet there is no legal mechanism that can be used to require Canadian ISPs to ensure that they possess the technical capabilities to enable law enforcement officials to intercept communications on their networks.[65] Since 1995, the Canadian Association of Police Chiefs has urged Parliament to enact legislation to compel telecommunications service providers to maintain the technical capabilities to enable law enforcement officials to conduct lawful interceptions on their networks.[66] Under the current regime, ISPs are not required to have interception capabilities, so when a new technology or communication service is introduced, law enforcement agents must develop innovative methods to gain access to the networks.[67] Canadian police are frustrated because they have no standard means by which to intercept a suspect's online communications. This is why they are asking for legislation to compel ISPs to have a technical means to enable law enforcement officials to intercept communications built into their network technology from the outset.[68]

As discussed in Chapter 9, in 2001, Canada signed the Convention on Cybercrime, which requires all signatory states, including Canada, to adopt legislative measures compelling ISPs to permit the interception and seizure of both traffic and content data from their networks.[69] **Traffic data** is defined as including any computer data relating to a communication, indicating the communication's origin, destination, route, time, date, size, duration or type of underlying service.[70] This includes information about an email (including those that are located in a "draft" box, an "inbox," or are in transit), the sender, recipient, size, subject line, as well as the URLs visited, time spent online and requests to search engines for specific information and downloads. Content data is not defined in the Convention; however, it might include the content of Internet Web pages visited, as well as messages sent and received.[71] Article 20 provides that a service provider must be obligated to ensure the "real-time collection or recording of

---

185). Before authorization is issued, the judge hearing the application must be satisfied that it would be in the best interests of the administration of justice to authorize the electronic surveillance. Except in the case of certain specific offences, such as a terrorism offence, the judge must also be satisfied that other investigative procedures have been tried and failed, that other investigative procedures are unlikely to succeed or that there is an urgency such that other investigative procedures are impractical. The judge may impose terms and conditions on the authorization, including conditions to ensure that the privacy of individuals is respected as much as possible during the surveillance (s. 186). In addition to applying for authorization to intercept private communications under Part VI, law enforcement officials can apply for a general warrant under s. 487.01 of the *Code*. This section provides that a warrant can be issued for the use of any device or investigative technique, which would otherwise constitute an unreasonable search or seizure, and which is not contemplated elsewhere in the *Criminal Code* or any other Act of Parliament. Certain requirements must be met before a general warrant can be issued.

[65] *Lawful Access Consultation Document, supra*, note 52 at 8.

[66] Valiquet, *supra*, note 33.

[67] Paul Weinberg, "Wiretaps Could Raise the Cost of Web Access," *The Globe and Mail*, July 28, 2005, available online at: http://intperspectives.wordpress.com.

[68] *Ibid.*

[69] *Supra*, note 54, arts. 20 and 21.

[70] *Ibid,* art. 1.

[71] Valiquet, *supra*, note 33 at 3.

content data on specified communications in its territory," which is consistent with the interception of telecommunications, also known as wiretapping, already permissible pursuant to Part VI of the *Code*.

We need to expand these powers by updating the *Code*, making it clear that law enforcement officials can intercept new communications technologies. Interception is already permitted for a specific list of crimes in s. 183 of the *Code*, which includes serious offences, such as facilitating terrorism, child pornography and organized crime offences. This will simply expand traditional law enforcement methods for accessing information that can be vital to the successful investigation and prosecution of offenders for these crimes. The interception of ISP networks is particularly important for child pornography offences, perhaps more so than the other listed crimes, because the Internet is now the primary means by which these materials are disseminated and collected.

Judicial authorization can be required for all interceptions according to the standards already set out in the *Code* for other forms of communication, such as telecommunications. This will limit the potential for abuse of the new powers to intercept digital communications. An important question is whether we might want to implement different safeguards, such as requiring a different authorization threshold for different types of information. It may be that content data is considered more sensitive than tracking data and we might want to maintain a stronger requirement for judicial oversight and authorization concerning this type of information because the expectation of privacy is greater.

Part VI of the *Code* sets out the requirements that must be met to successfully apply for an authorization to intercept private communications. These requirements include: only the Minister of Public Safety and Emergency Preparedness, or persons specially designated by the Minister or the Deputy Minister of Public Safety and Emergency Preparedness, may make an application for an authorization with regard to offences that may be prosecuted by or on behalf of the Attorney General of Canada; an application must be accompanied by an affidavit sworn by a peace officer or public officer; and the affidavit must include information such as the facts relied on to justify the need for an authorization, details about the offence and the names and addresses of the persons whose private communications would be intercepted.[72]

Before an authorization is issued, the judge hearing the application must be satisfied that it would be in the best interests of the administration of justice to authorize the electronic surveillance. Except in the case of certain specific offences, such as a terrorism offence, the judge must also be satisfied that other investigative procedures have been tried and failed, that other investigative procedures are unlikely to succeed, or that there is an urgency such that other investigative procedures are impractical. The judge may impose terms and conditions on the authorization, including conditions to ensure that the privacy of individuals is respected as much as possible during the surveillance.[73]

---

[72] *Supra*, note 24, s. 185.
[73] *Ibid*, s. 186.

Authorizations are not issued for a period of time longer than 60 days.[74] However, designated persons may apply to a judge to have the authorization renewed, which extends the period of time during which police can lawfully conduct electronic surveillance. Before the judge may renew the authorization, he or she must be satisfied that the same circumstances that applied to the original application for authorization still apply.[75] Provisions also exist to obtain authorizations in emergency situations. Under s. 188 of the *Code*, a peace officer may apply to a judge for an authorization if the urgency of the situation requires interception of private communications, but there is not enough time to use the regular application process to obtain an authorization. In these circumstances, authorization may be issued for a period of up to 36 hours and the judge may impose terms and conditions upon it.

In addition to applying for an authorization to intercept private communications, law enforcement officials may apply to a judge for a general warrant under s. 487.01 of the *Code*. This section enables the issuance of a warrant for the use of any device or investigative technique that is not contemplated elsewhere in the *Criminal Code* or any other Act of Parliament. As with other judicial authorizations, certain requirements must be met before a warrant can be issued. In the case of warrants issued pursuant to s. 487.01, these requirements include: the judge must be satisfied by information provided under oath and in writing (i.e., a sworn affidavit) that there are reasonable grounds to believe that an offence has been or will be committed, and that information about the offence can be obtained by conducting video surveillance; the judge must be satisfied that it is in the best interests of the administration of justice to issue the warrant; and there must be no other provision in the *Criminal Code* or any other Act of Parliament that would provide for a warrant, authorization or order to allow the intended video surveillance to be carried out. The judge may also impose terms or conditions on the warrant, including conditions to ensure that the privacy of individuals is respected as much as possible during the surveillance.

As previously mentioned, the requirement to ensure lawful intercept capabilities has been implemented by other nations, including the United Kingdom, which enacted the Regulation of Investigatory Powers Act in 2000,[76] requiring telecommunications service providers to maintain a reasonable intercept capability, and similar legislation was also enacted in the United States. On October 25, 1994, Congress enacted the Communications Assistance for Law Enforcement Act (CALEA).[77] CALEA sets out the interception capability requirements that telecommunications carriers[78] must establish and maintain

---

[74] *Ibid*, s. 186(4)(*e*).

[75] *Ibid*, s. 186(6).

[76] Bill 64 of 1999-2000; in force October 2000.

[77] Pub L. No. 102-414, 108 Stat. 4279 (1994) (codified in 18 U.S.C. and 47 U.S.C.).

[78] Although the definition of "telecommunications carrier" in the Act, at 47 U.S.C. 1001, appears to only apply to telephone communications and not ISPs, the FCC issued a ruling in September 2005 to ensure that the Act would apply to ISPs and companies providing Internet telephone services, such as Voice Over Internet Protocol or VOIP. See FCC 05-153, First Report and Order, CC Docket No. 04-295, September 23, 2005.

within their networks to enable law enforcement officials to conduct electronic surveillance.[79] CALEA does not expand or modify law enforcement's authority to conduct electronic surveillance in the United States. It simply requires telecommunications carriers to modify and design their equipment, facilities and services to ensure that they have the necessary capabilities to assist law enforcement officials with electronic surveillance and the collection of both content and traffic data.[80] In this sense, it is similar to Bill C-74.

Telecommunications service providers were required to comply with CALEA by June 30, 2002.[81] Congress addressed the issue of financial expense by ensuring that a substantial portion of the costs of implementing CALEA would be born by taxpayers. Section 109 provides that the Attorney General may pay telecommunications carriers for all reasonable costs associated with updating their networks and Congress authorized a fund of $500 million to be set aside for this purpose.[82] This is similar to the legislation enacted in the United Kingdom which provides that the Secretary of State may make arrangements for contributions toward costs incurred by telecommunications service providers in maintaining intercept capability out of money provided by Parliament.[83]

The financial costs associated with the implementation of mandatory intercept capability requirements is an important issue for the Canadian Parliament because network upgrades could cost millions of dollars.[84] If Bill C-74 had become law, ISPs would have been required to face the costs associated with the implementation of new transmission apparatus or software into their networks, as well as with storing and deciphering data, and providing it to law enforcement upon request. This would have had a significant impact on their cost of doing business. For this reason, some members of the Canadian telecommunications industry expressed reservations about the costs of complying with the proposed regulations.[85]

ISPs would have most likely addressed the problem by passing the costs on to their subscribers, through service fees, resulting in an increased cost to consumers for Internet use in Canada. While the required costs may have been tolerable for large ISPs, smaller ISPs might have been put out of business and new providers may have been deterred from entering the marketplace altogether. A related concern is that this would significantly harm the telecommunications

---

[79] Department of Justice, Federal Bureau of Investigation, *CALEA Implementation Section, Flexible Deployment Assistance Guide*, 3rd edition, May 2002, available online at: http://www.askcalea.net/archives/docs/flexguide3.pdf.

[80] *Ibid* at 4.

[81] Federal Communications Commission FCC 02-108, CC Docket No. 97-213, April 11, 2002. *CALEA* also states that if a telecommunication service provider does not comply with the Act by the required date, it is liable to an enforcement action under s. 108 and fines of up to $10,000 per day. See 47 U.S.C. §1007; 18 U.S.C. §2522(c).

[82] Department of Justice, Federal Bureau of Investigation, *supra*, note 79 at 6.

[83] *Supra*, note 76, s. 14 and Gabrielle Garton Grimwood and Christopher Barclay, *The Regulation of Investigatory Powers Bill*, Research Paper 00/25, House of Commons Library, March 3, 2000.

[84] Wienberg, *supra*, note 67 at 2.

[85] See Selma M. Lussenburg, "Security and the Economy: The North American Computer and Communication Infrastructure," (2003) 29 Can-U.S. Law Journal 237 at 242.

industry in Canada by impairing the ability of ISPs to compete with those in other jurisdictions that do not impose similar requirements. However, this is no longer likely to be a significant obstacle because many other nations, including the United States, the United Kingdom, Germany, France, Australia, New Zealand and South Africa have now implemented legislation regarding the interception of communications transmitted using new technologies.[86]

Given that most other major industrialized nations have already enacted these measures into their domestic law, particularly since they are required by the Convention on Cybercrime, the question is not whether or not Canada will implement interception capability requirements but how quickly and on what terms. Canada's largest ISP, Bell Sympatico, recently opened the door for increased ISP interception capabilities through changes to its user agreement; although it emphatically denied that the modifications were related to the lawful access initiative.[87] Bell inserted a new clause into its user agreement, which took effect on June 15, 2006, informing customers that it had the right to "monitor or investigate content on your use of your service provider's networks and to disclose any information necessary to satisfy any laws, regulations or other governmental requests."[88] This change indicates that the ISP is willing to monitor network usage, including monitoring user content, and disclose subscriber information to law enforcement. This led to speculations that the change might have been in anticipation of legislative reform, as many have anticipated that the government will reintroduce lawful access legislation.

The implementation costs of reasonable interception capability and the impact of the proposed requirements on the competitiveness of the Canadian telecommunications industry remain important issues that will undoubtedly have an impact on how lawful access legislation is structured and implemented. Either ISPs (meaning their users) will have to pay for the costs or they will be imposed upon taxpayers. Parliament could commit to paying the costs by setting aside a substantial sum of money for that purpose, as was done in the United States. One group representing telecommunications service providers and members of the police in Canada recently proposed that a fund could be at least partially generated from the money seized from criminals.[89] Parliament could also make reimbursement for all discretionary costs, as is the case in the United Kingdom. Requiring ISPs to pay the full implementation costs is another option, although this might jeopardize Canada's ability to maintain a competitive and fair communications industry.

Parliament attempted to address the issues of cost and competitiveness by exempting telecommunication service providers with fewer than 100,000 subscribers from the requirements set out in Bill C-74 for a period of 3 years.[90]

---

[86] Valiquet, *supra*, note 33 at 10.

[87] Michael Geist, "Big Brother Bell," *Ottawa Citizen*, July 6, 2006, available online at: http://www.canada.com.ottawacitizen/news/technology/story.html.

[88] *Ibid.*

[89] Valiquet, *supra*, note 33 at 8.

[90] Bill C-74, *supra*, note 55, s. 12. This is what is known as a "sunset clause."

The Minister of Public Safety and Emergency Preparedness would also have been entitled to issue an order to suspend the obligation of a service provider to meet the operational requirements of implementing new apparatus or software.[91] The risks associated with this approach are that smaller ISPs, or those otherwise exempt from the requirements, will become havens for cybercriminals, including child pornography offenders, who know that the networks cannot be intercepted by law enforcement officials.

Perhaps recognizing that placing significant financial impediments upon the Canadian telecommunications industry might not be beneficial, Parliament also provided that in cases where the Minister of Public Safety and Emergency Preparedness issued an order to a telecommunications service provider to comply with requirements to maintain intercept capability, the Minister would have been required to reasonably compensate the carrier for the costs of compliance.[92] This provision of the Act appears to provide a mechanism for the government to compel all ISPs to comply with the intercept capability requirements, as well as to ensure that at least some of the costs of implementing this regime would be born by taxpayers, in a manner similar to CALEA in the United States.

We do not yet know what the financial and other business-related costs of implementing a lawful access regime will be for ISPs. We do know that other states in other jurisdictions, including the United States and the United Kingdom, have implemented legislation requiring their telecommunications service providers to update their networks to enable the interception and preservation of data. This suggests that the financial costs are not so significant that they make the implementation of this regime impossible. The lawful access regimes implemented in other jurisdictions can also serve as useful models for determining the best approach to take in Canada on these issues.

Requirement to Provide Subscriber Information

Bill C-74 would also have allowed police to obtain subscriber information from ISPs upon request, without judicial authorization.[93] There are good reasons why police may require subscriber information without a warrant in online child pornography cases. They may need it urgently in order to prevent a crime from occurring, such as a luring offence that could lead to the kidnapping or rape of a child. In these rare cases, law enforcement officials may not have time to obtain a warrant before the crime is committed. Access might also be needed when police cannot get a warrant, given the little information available to them. This is particularly critical with respect to online offences where extraordinary measures might be required to reveal the true identity of a suspect who is hiding behind an anonymous or fake online persona.

In the case of the disclosure of basic subscriber information, such as an individual's name, address, telephone number and IP address, without a warrant, the Supreme Court of Canada has stated that as the information collected by the

---

[91] *Ibid*, s. 14.
[92] *Ibid*, s. 15.
[93] *Ibid*, s. 17.

state nears a certain type of "core" personal and "biographical" information about the individual, the privacy interest becomes more important and the need for the government to establish the necessity of collecting this information, and the requirement for judicial authorization, increases.[94] In *R. v. Plant*, the Supreme Court found that information collected by a public utility company about its customers without a warrant, in the form of computerized records, could be freely shared with police without an infringement of s. 8 of the *Charter*. The Court distinguished the evidence disclosed on the basis that it did not fall within the protected "biographical core of personal information" over which individuals in a free and democratic society would justifiably want to maintain and control. The records about electricity consumption did not disclose "intimate details of lifestyle and personal choices of the individual" and revealed little about "the personal lifestyle or private decisions of the occupants."[95]

An important concern is whether subscriber information has a significant privacy element that goes to the core of personal information that the individual would not wish to disclose. In *Plant*, the Court was only asked to consider computerized records about electricity consumption, not information about an individual's address and phone number, which might be said to relate more directly to the "lifestyle and personal choices" of the individual.[96] Conversely, subscriber information only includes basic personal information about an individual, such as that which is published in a telephone book. These important issues would need to be considered, in addition to the threshold.

The issue of whether an individual has a reasonable expectation of privacy in customer name and address information held by an ISP appears to have been resolved by the courts. The determining factor in these cases is the presence of a subscriber agreement or acceptable use policy. For example, in *R. v. Ward*,[97] the court found that given the contractual agreement entered into between the ISP and the user, as well as the information being sought, the customer's name and address did not fall within the protected "biographical core of personal information" discussed by the Supreme Court of Canada in *Tessling* and *Plant*.[98] A similar decision was reached in *R. v. Vasic*[99] and *R. v. Wilson*.[100] In both of those cases, the court held that an individual does not have a reasonable expectation of privacy in his or her name and address when this information is disclosed without a warrant in accordance with the terms of the subscriber agreement.

---

[94] *R. v. Plant* (1993), [1993] S.C.J. No. 97, EYB 1993-66899, 1993 CarswellAlta 94 (S.C.C.).

[95] *Ibid* at para. 20.

[96] Parliament briefly referred to this decision at 12 of its *Lawful Access Consultation Document*, *supra*, note 52, maintaining that basic customer information "such as name, billing address, phone number and name of service provider," would not attract a "reasonable expectation of privacy" because it does not reveal intimate details of the individual's lifestyle and personal choices.

[97] 2008 ONCJ 355 (Ont. C.J.).

[98] *Ibid*. See also *R. v. Tessling*, *supra*, note 4; *R. v. Plant*, *supra*, note 94.

[99] (2009), 2009 CarswellOnt 846 (Ont. S.C.J.).

[100] (2009), 2009 CarswellOnt 2064, (Ont. S.C.J.). See also *R. v. Friers* , 2008 CarswellOnt 6124 (Ont. C.J.).

Orders for the Preservation of Data

Not all ISPs are in the habit of collecting and storing data that passes through their networks. This means that information that could be valuable to the investigation of a suspect for a computer-related crime, such as online child pornography, can easily be destroyed or modified before it can be obtained and used for law enforcement purposes. Section 164 of the *Code* provides that a judge can issue a warrant to law enforcement officials to seize child pornography stored on a computer system, including from an ISP. However, this order will be rendered ineffective if the ISP does not retain the information being sought.

For these reasons, Parliament needs to enact legislation allowing for preservation orders to be made. This valuable procedural instrument is provided for in the Convention on Cybercrime but it does not currently exist in Canadian law.[101] It was also proposed by Parliament in its *Lawful Access Consultation Document* but not included in Bill C-74. Preservation orders can be used to permit the immediate and temporary safeguarding of volatile evidence that is specific to a particular Internet transaction or subscriber. The order is temporary, only requiring an ISP to not delete or destroy the existing data of an individual who is the subject of an investigation until law enforcement officials can obtain a judicial warrant to seize it.[102]

Preservation orders can be short term, requiring an ISP to retain information in cases of urgency until judicial authorization can be obtained. Safeguards can be put in place to require a law enforcement officer to give written notice to the service provider demonstrating that the information is necessary for an ongoing investigation and linking the request to a specific individual, service account, IP address or other defined criteria. Preservation orders can also be made for a longer term, with an increased requirement for judicial authorization and a process for the service provider to challenge the request.

The United States recently adopted a data preservation scheme to minimize the risk of the deletion of information that may be necessary for the investigation of a crime.[103] Under that regime, a law enforcement agent issues a written request to the ISP to preserve identified records or communications related to a particular person. The ISP then preserves the information for up to 90 days, until the law enforcement official obtains the lawful authority to gain access to the communications. Using this framework as a model, Parliament could enact similar provisions into Canadian law, ensuring that digital information necessary to the investigation of a serious crime, such as child pornography, is not unnecessarily lost. This would also enable us to fulfill our commitments to work with other states according to the terms of the Convention on Cybercrime, whereby states can request that information held by an ISP in another state be preserved until it can be lawfully obtained.

---

[101] As mentioned above, Parliament must enact these measures into law, along with those relating to the production of data, before it can ratify the Convention on Cybercrime. See the *Lawful Access Consultation Document, supra,* note 52 at 13.

[102] *Ibid* at 13.

[103] Title 18 U.S.C., s. 2703(f).

It is also noteworthy that the term **data preservation** refers only to orders for the retention of data about a particular individual who is the subject of an investigation. This is different from the term "data retention" which has been used to mean general retention by ISPs of data on all customers, not just those under suspicion of criminal conduct.[104] The European Union recently approved a data retention directive that will apply to its member states and requires that providers of electronic communications, or telecommunications networks, retain data related to mobile and fixed telephony for a period of 1 year, and Internet communication data, for 6 months. Only **traffic** and **location data** is to be retained, which can identify the sender or the time and duration of the communication, for use in investigating and prosecuting serious crimes.[105] The directive is not concerned with the content of the communication, such as the text of an email.

The type of information to be retained by Canadian ISPs, when served with a preservation order, can also be limited to traffic data, which would reduce the risk of sensitive information, such as the content of an email, from being disclosed.[106] Traffic data" generally includes information concerning website visits, email destinations and other general information relating to the routing of the communication's origin, destination, route, time, date, size, duration or type of underlying service.[107] This includes information about an email (including those that are located in a "draft" box, an "inbox" or are in transit), the sender, recipient, size, subject line, as well as the URLs visited, time spent online and requests to search engines for specific information and downloads. This information can be useful in linking a child pornography suspect to a child pornography website, or a child pornography ring; to an online request for child pornography images; or to the downloading of child pornography onto a computer, particularly in cases where the images have been deleted or otherwise erased.

In contrast with the Canadian data preservation proposals contained in the Lawful Access Consultation Document, the scope of the European Union directive is very broad. ISPs in the European Union member states will be required to retain data pertaining to all of their users, regardless of whether they are under suspicion for illegal conduct or not. However, the data retained will only be made available to national authorities in specific cases and in accordance with national law and member states also have to take necessary measures to ensure that any intentional access to, or transfer of, data retained is punishable by administrative or criminal penalties.[108] The data preservation initiatives proposed here are far less intrusive, and likely to be significantly less costly, as they only permit law enforcement officials to request ISPs to preserve records relating to a particular

---

[104] See Lawful Access Consultation Document, *supra*, note 52 at 14.

[105] See Directive of the European Parliament and of the Council on the retention of data, Brussels, February 3, 2006, 2005/0182 (COD), available online at: http://www.ispai.ie/drfinal.pdf.

[106] This was what the government proposed in its Lawful Access Consultation Document.

[107] See Council of Europe's Convention on Cybercrime, *supra*, note 52.

[108] See "Data Retention Receives Rubber Stamp," *The Register*, February 24, 2006, available online at: http://www.theregister.co.uk/2006/02/24/data_retention_directive_ratified/.

individual, for a specified time period, until they can obtain a judicial order to seize it.[109]

Orders for the Production of Data

On June 23, 2003, Bill C-46[110] was introduced by Parliament and the *Code* was subsequently amended to give law enforcement agents the authority to issue a production order to compel third parties to produce documents or data to be used in criminal investigations. The relevant provisions governing the use of production orders requiring **data production** are set out in ss. 487.012 through 487.017 of the *Code*. A production order is a type of judicial order that is similar to a search warrant. There are a number of circumstances in which law enforcement officials obtain judicial search warrants against third parties but do not actually conduct the searches. In order to give law enforcement agents better procedural powers to deal with emerging technologies, Parliament could further amend the *Code* to include language specifying which data an ISP can be required to make available to investigators within a specified time period.[111] More specific definitions would lessen the risk of capturing personal information, such as Personal Identification Numbers (PINs) and passwords, or health and financial information.

The *Personal Information Protection and Electronic Documents Act* (PIPEDA)[112]

When establishing a lawful access regime, Parliament must also keep in mind the requirements set out in PIPEDA. This federal legislation establishes rules for the collection, use and disclosure of personal information by private organizations involved in commercial activities. It applies to federal works and undertakings, which include ISPs. PIPEDA is important because the distinction between the public and private sectors has become progressively more blurred. Private sector entities now have more resources and opportunities to collect information about individuals and public sector organizations often require that

---

[109] Valiquet, *supra*, note 33 at 10. The Office of the Privacy Commissioner of Canada reported, in May 2005, that Canadians send more than 2.7 million text messages per day. This figure demonstrates that ISPs would need to retain an extremely large volume of data if they were to implement the broad-based data retention initiatives implemented in the European Union. Given the cost and technical difficulties associated with collecting and storing such a large volume of data, this measure is not recommended.

[110] *An Act to amend the Criminal Code (capital markets fraud and evidence-gathering)*, S.C. 2005, c. 3, in force September 15, 2004 (SI/2004-119).

[111] Two new specific production orders have been proposed by the Canadian government, which include: tracking data (i.e., "information that would assist in determining the location of a person or thing at a particular time" such as cell phone or Internet usage); and transmission data (i.e., "data relating to telecommunications functions of dialing, routing, addressing or signaling that identifies or purports to identify the origin, type, direction, date, time, duration, size, destination or termination of a telecommunication... ."). Jennifer Stoddart, "Response to the Government of Canada's 'Lawful Access' Consultations," Submission of the Office of the Privacy Commissioner of Canada to the Minister of Justice and Attorney General of Canada, May 5, 2005, Ottawa, available online at: http://www.privcom.gc.ca.

[112] S.C. 2000, c. 5, see ss. 2(1) and 4(1).

data to fulfill their obligations. By drafting privacy legislation targetted specifically at the private sector, Parliament was able to facilitate the exchange of valuable information with private organizations and ensure that the privacy rights of Canadians are protected in both the public and private spheres.[113]

The purpose of PIPEDA is to establish rules for the collection, use and disclosure of personal information in a manner that recognizes the privacy interests of individuals.[114] Personal information is defined in s. 2(1) as "information about an identifiable individual but does not include name, title, business address or telephone number of an employee of an organization." The definition of personal information is very broad and does not refer to the concept of the biographical core of information that arises from the *Charter* jurisprudence.

PIPEDA seeks to establish fair information collection and management practices in the private sector by ensuring that data is responsibly collected from individuals and, then, appropriately held, used or disclosed to a third party. One of the central principles behind PIPEDA is that consent must be obtained before information can be collected from an individual, and then used or disclosed. The standard of the "reasonable person" is used, in that PIPEDA requires private organizations to collect, use and disclose personal information "for purposes that a reasonable person would consider appropriate in the circumstances," in compliance with ten broad privacy obligations specified in Schedule 1 of the Act.[115]

However, PIPEDA also permits the collection and disclosure of personal information without the knowledge and consent of an individual in certain circumstances. An organization can *collect* personal information without the knowledge and consent of an individual under s. 7(1)(e)(ii) if the collection is made for the purpose of making a disclosure that is required by law. An organization can *disclose* personal information, without the knowledge and consent of the individual only if, pursuant to s. 7(3)(c.1), the disclosure is made to a government institution, and pursuant to s. 7(1)(e)(iii), the disclosure will be made "for the purpose of administering any law of Canada or a province." In this respect, PIPEDA is designed to both protect individual privacy and facilitate the sharing of information between third parties and government organizations, particularly for law enforcement purposes.

---

[113] The passage of PIPEDA marked a significant milestone in the development of Canadian privacy law because previous laws only regulated the public sector.

[114] *Supra*, note 112, s. 3.

[115] These include the following: collection limitation (the parties should limit how information is collected; collection must be with consent and knowledge that the information is being collected); data quality (the data must be accurate and relevant); purpose specification (the party must specify the purpose for which the information will be collected); use limitation (once information is collected for one purpose it cannot be used for another purpose unless the individual consents or this is authorized by law); security safeguards (the information must be secured from risk, e.g., from attacks by hackers); openness (transparency, i.e., the individual should know what is being done with her information); individual participation (the individual should have access to her information and be able to look at it and correct inaccuracies); and accountability (there must be an oversight mechanism).

In terms of the collection and disclosure of basic subscriber information, Parliament needs to draft legislation requiring ISPs to collect this information and verify its accuracy. In order to collect and ascertain the reliability of the information, ISPs will need to notify their customers that they are collecting the information up front, perhaps as a condition of service, which means that s. 7(1)(e)(ii) would not apply. Law enforcement officials can then request disclosure of the information, in compliance with s. 7(3)(c.1), with respect to a particular individual, when that information is required for law enforcement purposes only. In terms of orders for the preservation of data, s. 7(1) of PIPEDA would authorize ISPs to collect and retain information from their networks, in response to a lawful request, with a judicial order, without the knowledge or consent of the individual to whom the information pertains. Once a search warrant is obtained, law enforcement officials could then compel disclosure of the data for law enforcement purposes, pursuant to s. 7(3)(c.1).

Section 7(1)(e)(ii) of PIPEDA appears to authorize an ISP to collect personal information, without knowledge and consent of the individual, *only* if the collection is made for the purpose of making a disclosure required by law. In other words, if the request for disclosure has not already been made by law enforcement officials, with the lawful authority, the information cannot be collected. This appears to prevent the enactment of data retention legislation requiring ISPs to retain all of the data passing through their networks, pertaining to all subscribers, as discussed earlier in this chapter. It is important to keep in mind that the lawful access measures proposed here do not include data retention policies, of the sort being implemented in the European Union, but merely data preservation, which would only apply to ISPs in a very limited number of cases, following the issuance of a judicial order. This would also avoid the risk of capturing more personal information than necessary, which might include information about financial transactions, health information, PINs, private correspondence, and other sensitive information, and ensure that the information only relates to a particular suspect who has been identified by law enforcement officials.

CONCLUSION

Due to the unique structural makeup of cyberspace, ISPs have an essential role to play in combatting cybercrime. Parliament has been considering how it can enact legislation to require telecommunications service providers to retain data that moves across their networks, or make data in their possession available to law enforcement agencies on legally authorized requests. Lawful access is a complex and delicate issue because it involves issues of financial costs and competitiveness, privacy, technical capability and the need to enable law enforcement agencies to target criminals who use communications technologies to perpetrate serious criminal offences on a global scale. Canadian ISPs currently have different practices for how long they retain data flowing through their networks, if they even retain it at all. Most ISPs are members of voluntary associations that establish codes of conduct for their members. While these are helpful, they are insufficient to combat online child pornography in any significant way.

In August 2002, Canada tabled its Lawful Access Consultation Document that set out Parliament's argument in favour of modifying Canadian law to ensure that law enforcement agencies are able to engage in the lawful access of modern communications technologies, such as the Internet. This initiative, which is essential to prevent, investigate and prosecute serious offences, including child pornography and terrorism, was fuelled by our international obligations in the struggle against global crime. This includes the Convention on Cybercrime, which Canada signed but cannot ratify until important changes are made to the *Criminal Code*, including provisions for orders to be made for the production and preservation of computer data.

The Convention on Cybercrime is an important response to the realization that while computer networks and digital information are often used for lawful purposes, they are also used to facilitate criminal activities. Due to the increased flow of data over trans-border networks, a harmonized approach to fighting cybercrime is required. We need to enact a comprehensive legislative scheme for dealing with Internet cases and establish requirements for facilitating cooperation between law enforcement agencies within Canada and abroad. The challenge is to implement new measures that respond to technological change and globalization while ensuring that the existing rights and freedoms guaranteed by the *Charter* are protected.

The *Code* already contains well-established procedures for the lawful interception of communications, including telephone networks. However, law enforcement officials are prevented from accessing Internet technology because many ISPs do not have the capability to enable interception built into their networks. A lawful access proposal would require ISPs to update their networks to facilitate lawful interception by law enforcement. Data preservation and production are also important to the implementation of a successful lawful access regime. The *Code* must be updated to enable law enforcement officials to obtain a judicial order to compel ISPs to maintain, or not delete, records about a particular suspect for a specific time period and then provide them to police for use in law enforcement investigations.

QUESTIONS FOR FURTHER THINKING AND DISCUSSION

1. How has our reasonable expectation of privacy shifted as a result of the digital age?
2. What is lawful access and how is it relevant to cybercrime investigations?
3. What can Canadian legislators do to better assist law enforcement officials abroad in the area of computer-related crime?
4. Do you agree with the Supreme Court of Canada's finding in *Tessling*? How does it compare with other electronic surveillance cases decided by the

Court? *Tessling* also stands in direct contrast to the case of *Kyllo v. U.S.* Which result do you think is more reasonable?

5. What is PIPEDA? Who does it apply to and what does it do?
6. What can law enforcement officials in Canada do to enhance their investigative capabilities when it comes to cybercrime?

11

Emerging Trends and Future Concerns

The term cyberspace has been used throughout this text as a synonym for the Internet; however, as we saw in Chapters 1 and 2, its meaning is actually far broader. The term cyberspace was first developed by William Gibson, who conceived of a global computer network in his novel *Neuromancer*. Later, cyber-theorists, such as John Perry Barlow, used this term to describe the new social spaces that had become accessible through the Internet. It soon became clear that this new space was prone to all the same hazards, risks and annoyances found in real space. However, the lack of jurisdictional boundaries and physical constraints in cyberspace, as well as the feature of anonymity, present new challenges for those seeking to control harmful behaviour in this new social sphere.

Cyberspace contains all of the same problems that plague real space, as well as some important new ones. Some businesses and individuals steal intellectual property, in addition to other goods and services on the Internet. Others disseminate malware and deface websites, or destroy data files. There are also those who produce and disseminate child pornography, as well as lure unsuspecting children into sexual encounters, and those who use the Internet to perpetrate fraud, theft and extortion. Bullies and stalkers may also use it as a target or outlet for the expression of their negative opinions or as a tool to coerce, harass or intimidate individuals.

These criminals are able to defy the conventional jurisdictional constraints that characterize real space and loop or weave their attacks through multiple jurisdictions. This is relatively easy because the constraints that govern our interactions in the real, physical world do not apply in cyberspace. Unlike in real space, cyberspace does not require any physical proximity between the victim and the perpetrator and cybercrimes can be committed very quickly against multiple targets. Moreover, given the wide range of moral, legal and ethical constraints that apply throughout the world, the conduct at issue might be considered illegal in one country but perfectly acceptable in another. Cyberspace also provides near-perfect anonymity in that it enables participants to conceal or disguise their identities in ways that are simply not possible in the real, physical world.

Cyber-attacks have affected mainstream computing devices such as laptop and desktop computers. These platforms will continue to serve as ready targets for attackers, due to their prevalence and popularity. However, we can expect cybercriminals to turn their attention toward non-mainstream platforms in the future, particularly if these targets provide a lucrative reward.

As email security improves, attackers will increasingly turn to more sophisticated platforms, such as peer-to-peer networks or Web browsers. Data hiding, through the use of **steganography** (i.e., when information is embedded within other, seemingly harmless, data such as pictures) and **encryption** (i.e., the translation of data into secret code), will also become increasingly useful to cybercriminals. **Cloud computing**, whereby information is stored and delivered through data centres and built-on servers that are exclusively owned and maintained by a third party, is also likely to present challenges in the future. The complexity of security increases with remote storage (i.e., when data is distributed over wider areas and devices). Cybercriminals might also increasingly turn their attention toward virtual assets found in online worlds such as Second Life, if they have real-world value and can be sold in online auction sites for real-world money. In addition, we can expect to see virtual currency, such as the Linden dollars used in Second Life, exploited to facilitate money laundering operations.

Malware is also becoming an increasingly serious threat to our communications infrastructure. It used to be that the authors of malicious code were primarily motivated by fame and notoriety. However, cyber-attackers have now realized that they can make significant money from their exploits. Furthermore, we are relying on networked technologies in a growing number of ways. We are also becoming more networked and, given the increased reliance on communications technologies, malware no longer poses a threat to only Internet commerce, it presents a challenge for everyone.

With more and more people conducting business and social transactions online, malicious code has moved away from simply being harmful toward seeking a significant financial benefit. This trend makes sense when we consider the rapid growth of e-commerce and virtual currency, as well as the robust underground economy that has emerged on the Internet. Well established terror organizations and rogue governments are also capable of inflicting serious damage to our communications infrastructure. However, there are a number of important measures that can be implemented across all sectors of society that will protect us from risk and mitigate the harms suffered when attacks do occur.

The Internet has become an extremely important element in today's society. Communications technologies are now accessible to millions of people from around the world, which illustrates the importance of cyberspace to the global community for politics, information, recreation and commerce. However, Canada is far behind other leading industrialized nations when it comes to confronting computer crime through the implementation of legislation. In fact, it is only in the past couple of years that the Canadian government even proposed the enactment of new laws aimed at combatting spam, identity theft and phishing.

On the other hand, it is also clear that legislative mechanisms are only part of the solution. User education and accountability are also critical. We need to encourage individual users to be more responsible and proactive. As well, public awareness should be facilitated at all levels of the community. This includes educating young children about the perils of communicating with strangers online, as well as the risks of online commerce. We also need to increase public awareness of our existing cyber-reporting mechanisms. As I discussed previously, both Cybertip.ca and PhoneBusters have important roles to play in consumer education and assistance, as well as in facilitating international cooperation and in generating reports and statistics about cybercrime that are especially useful for legislators and policy-makers.

On that note, Canada also needs to facilitate inter-jurisdictional and inter-agency cooperation in the fight against cybercrime. This includes providing the necessary resources to train law enforcement officials and increasing the number of multi-jurisdictional task forces and central reporting stations. Technological assistance to national, provincial and municipal police is also helpful, as is the importance of facilitating relationships between investigative agencies and the private sector. Since many attacks are motivated by profit, a mechanism that limits or reduces the attacker's ability to profit from his or her attack is likely to be a workable solution to combat cyber-threats.

However, given that many cybercrimes are perpetrated internationally, it is also important for us to further international cooperation and partnerships with other nations. This goal would be greatly served by ratification of the Council of Europe's Convention on Cybercrime and the implementation of lawful access legislation in Canada. Lawful access legislation is the critical next step in meeting our international obligations, pursuant to the Convention on Cybercrime, and achieving the means to truly combat computer crime at its source. Without lawful access legislation, there is simply no way for Canada to intercept the online communications of cybercrime suspects, request and receive valuable information about those who perpetrate crime on the Internet and gather the physical evidence linking the suspect to the crime. By implementing these measures, Canada would achieve much greater success in the fight against cybercriminals and become one of the global leaders in the worldwide effort to combat crime on the Net.

QUESTIONS FOR FURTHER THINKING AND DISCUSSION

1. Consider the growth and complexity of the computing environment and ask yourself what is the future of cybercrime?
2. What can Parliament do to respond to developments in computer-related crime?

3. What are some of the most problematic issues and what can be done to lessen their impact?
4. Is the Canadian legal framework capable of dealing with the security threats discussed in this book? Why or why not?

Glossary

Advanced Research Projects Agency Network (ARPANet) A networking project initiated by the United States Advanced Research Projects Agency in the 1960s, which evolved into the modern-day Internet.

American Standard Code for Information Interchange (ASCII) A character-encoding scheme based on the ordering of the English alphabet.

Anonymizer A site that hides the origins of connections. It functions as a proxy server (i.e., it operates on behalf of another entity) and passes data between the origin and destination. The destination believes it is communicating with the anonymizer, rather than the true origin, because all traffic has the anonymizer's address in it. In other words, when you do your Web browsing through an anonymizer, your IP address is not shown on your data packets so there's no way for any site to trace your activity back to your computer or ISP.

Anonymous Remailer A server that purges all the identifying information from a communication before sending it to its destination so that it allows users to send emails or post messages to a discussion group while remaining anonymous. This is accomplished by removing all identifying information from the message and forwarding it to its destination so that it appears to come from an anonymous user at the anonymous remailer's domain.

Anti-Spam Action Plan for Canada Announced in 2004 by the Electronic Commerce Branch of Industry Canada as a proactive measure to prevent and combat spam across Canada. It consists of a six-point initiative targetted at government, business and consumers.

Anti-virus Software Ant-ivirus software is used to prevent, detect and remove malware. These programs may also prevent and remove spyware and forms of malware other than viruses, Trojans and worms.

Application Layer Consists of all the high-level protocols that support the applications and utilities that make the Internet useful to end-users. For example, a Web server uses HTTP to serve up HTML Web pages. Also includes the DNS, File Transfer Protocol (FTP), the Secure Sockets Layer Protocol (SSLP), and more.

ARPANet See Advanced Research Projects Agency Network.

ASCII See American Standard Code for Information Interchange.

Attack Kits Do-it-yourself toolkits that are widely available through the Internet's underground economy. Often used by novices, or script-kiddies, who are unable to write their own programs and often don't understand the programs they execute.

Bandwidth The measure of a channel's data carrying capacity, or the amount of data that can be delivered in a particular time period (i.e., bits per second (bps), thousands of bits per second (kbps), or millions of bits per second (mps)).

Bit Short for "binary digit," it is the smallest unit of information. In binary mathematics, bits are represented by the numerals "0" and "1."

Bit-Stream Copy Is the technical term for the end-product of a forensics acquisition of a computer's hard drive. The bit-stream copy is much more thorough than a standard back-up or mirror image of a hard drive. It consists of all data on a hard drive, including the unallocated file space from which "deleted" files are frequently recovered.

Black Hat Hackers A term applied to the malicious and destructive hackers on the Internet. These individuals are also known as crackers.

Blacklist A list of email addresses of known spammers or a list of websites that are considered dangerous.

Boot Sector The first sector on a disk, from which information is read to start up the computer.

Bot An end-user machine containing software that allows it to be remotely controlled through a command and control (C&C) network, often through a central C&C server. Bots are also referred to a zombies or slaves.

Botnet See Bot Network.

Bot Network (Botnet) Botnets are made up of large numbers of compromised computers, which have been infected with malware, which can be remotely controlled through a command and control network and used to send out spam, launch denial-of-service attacks, or to host phishing attacks.

Bulletin Board The Internet provides access to thousands of bulletin board services that contain ongoing discussions about particular topics and allow users to post messages that others can read.

Bus A systematic collection of wires that transfers data between computer components inside a computer or between computers.

Byte A small unit of storage measurement in computers. Inside the computer, each character (such as the letter A, the letter g, or a question mark) is usually represented by a byte. One byte contains eight bits.

Cash Out The process of converting stolen goods into real currency, either through money transfers or online currency exchange within the underground economy. Often associated with identity theft.

CETS See Child Exploitation Tracking System.

Child Exploitation Tracking System (CETS) A software program that assists law enforcement officials with managing and linking cases related to child protection.

Child Pornography Defined by Parliament in s. 163.1(1) of the *Criminal Code* to include a wide range of material determined harmful to children. It includes representations that involve real children in its production, including pictures, video and audio images, as well as products of the imagination, such as drawings and written materials, including fantasy stories.

Client/Server Model Involves one or more shared computers, called servers, which are connected by a network to the individual users' workstations, called clients.

Clock A unit within the main circuit board of a computer's motherboard that sends information, in electronic pulses, between the processor and other components including memory and ports.

Cloud Computing Refers to on-demand network access to a shared pool of computing resources (e.g., networks, storage, services, applications, and so on). The services are made available in a pay-as-you-go manner to the public.

Clusters Allocation units. Unit of disk space allocation for files and directories.

Codec See Coder/Decoder.

Coder/Decoder (Codec) Software that decodes a binary file and reconstitutes a version of the original audio or video.

Cognitive Distortions Thought distortions that enable a child pornography offender to "cognitively adapt" in order to rationalize, justify and excuse his or her offending. This can include denial of responsibility or injury to the victim.

Computer Forensics A branch of digital forensic science pertaining to evidence found in computers and other forms of digital storage media.

Contact Sexual Offences Hands-on offences involving real victims. In the context of child pornography, some viewers of child pornography claim to view these materials as a means of release and maintain that they do this instead of committing a contact offence against real children.

Content Layer The data available by means of the Internet and transactions enabled by the Internet.

Council of Europe Convention on Cybercrime An international treaty signed by the members of the Council of Europe, as well as several non-member states, whose aim is to "pursue, as a matter of priority, a common criminal policy aimed at the protection of society against cybercrime … by adopting appropriate legislation and fostering international co-operation."

Cyber-bullying A new form of harassment occurring among school-aged children. Wilful and repeated harm inflicted through the medium of electronic text.

Cyberspace A term coined by science fiction writer William Gibson in his 1984 novel *Neuromancer*. It is commonly used to describe the conceptual space made accessible through the Internet.

Cyber-stalking Use of the Internet or other electronic means to stalk or harass someone.

Cybertip.ca Canada's national cyber-tipline for reporting the online sexual exploitation of children.

Data Interception The interception of digital communications for law enforcement purposes.

Data Preservation The preservation of traffic and/or content data by an ISP upon the lawful request of law enforcement officials.

Data Production The lawful production of traffic and/or content data by an ISP for use by law enforcement officials.

DDoS Attack See Distributed Denial-of-Service Attack.

Defamation Written or spoken injury to a person or organization's reputation.

Denial-of-Service Attack (DoS Attack) An attack on a computer system or network that causes a loss of service to legitimate users.

Distributed Denial-of-Service Attack (DDoS Attack) An attack that uses an army of remotely controlled computers (i.e., bots, slaves or zombies) to generate more requests of a device than it can reasonably handle.

DoS Attack See Denial-of-Service Attack.

Drive-by Pharming An attack in which the attacker changes the DNS server designated in the victim's router or access point settings to a DNS server that the attacker has set up. The goal is to direct the victim's Internet traffic and point the victim to the attacker's own websites, which are made to look like common websites (e.g., by mimicking the victim's bank). This way, the attacker can steal confidential information from the victim.

Dual Criminality Occurs when two countries both have statutes prohibiting the same criminal behaviour.

EFF See Electronic Frontier Foundation.

Electronic Frontier Foundation (EFF) An organization dedicated to promoting freedom of speech, privacy, innovation and consumer rights on the Internet.

Encryption Scrambling and encoding data. Used to convert plain text into ciphertext in order to prevent anyone but the intended recipient from reading it.

End-to-End Principle One of the central design principles of the Internet. Intelligence in the networks is located at the ends, not in the network itself.

Federal Trade Commission (FTC) An independent agency of the United States government that promotes consumer protection and the prevention/elimination of anti-competitive business practices.

File Allocation Table To keep track of data within a drive, the operating system makes use of an index. The space physically occupied by the file (i.e., each cluster on the drive) is recorded in the file allocation table.

Filtering Internet filtering software is software that is designed to enable organizations or individuals to restrict access to specific types of Internet content, which may be deemed dangerous or inappropriate for a user or group of users.

Firewall A system to enforce a boundary between two or more networks, with the ability to permit or deny the passage of data according to predefined security criteria.

Flaming A form of netiquette (i.e., hostile and insulting interaction between Internet users).

Fraud Traditional non-computer crime that involves the use of tools and techniques to defraud people out of their money or property, as well as the fraudulent use of personal information.

FTC See Federal Trade Commission.

Grey Hat Hackers Fall between white and black hat hackers. A skilled hacker who sometimes acts illegally, but with good intentions. Usually grey hats do not hack for personal gain or have malicious intentions, but are prepared to commit crimes in order to achieve better security.

Hacker Ethic The values and philosophy that are standard in the hacker community. The term "hacker ethic" is attributed to journalist Steven Levy as described in his book titled *Hackers: Heroes of the Computer Revolution*, written in 1984. The central principles within this ethic are open access to computers, freedom of information and mistrust of authority.

Hacker/Cracker Someone attempting or gaining unauthorized access to a computer system.

Hacking Unauthorized attempts to bypass the security mechanisms of an information system or network.

Hactivist A person who engages in hacktivism, or the hacking for politically or socially motivated purposes.

Hash Value A mathematical algorithm that creates a small digital "fingerprint" from any kind of data.

Hate Propaganda The public promotion or incitement of hatred against an identifiable group.

Honeypot A fake system or network that is designed to lure intruders with fake data in order to detect security breaches. When it is attacked it records all the details of the attack while containing it and preventing it from damaging any other systems.

HTTP See Hypertext Transfer Protocol.

Hypertext Transfer Protocol (HTTP) The protocol or rules used for transferring data on the Internet.

ICANN See Internet Corporation for Assigned Names and Numbers.

ICITAP See International Criminal Investigative Training Assitance Program.

Identity Theft The illegal use or transfer of a third party's personal information with unlawful intent.

IMP See Interface Message Processor.

Injunction A court order that directs a party to do, or to refrain from doing, certain acts.

Innocent Images International Task Force A component of the FBI's Cyber Division at FBI headquarters in Washington, DC, it undertakes multi-agency investigative operations to combat the proliferation of online child exploitation and child pornography. It coordinates with state, local and international governments, as well as FBI field offices and Legal Attachés.

Intercept-Capable Networks Communications networks that are capable of lawful interception by law enforcement officials.

Interface Message Processor (IMP) The packet-switching node used to interconnect participant networks to the ARPANet.

International Criminal Investigative Training Assitance Program (ICITAP) Part of the United States Department of Justice, it works with foreign governments to develop professional and transparent law enforcement institutions that protect human rights, combat corruption and reduce the threat of transnational crime and terrorism.

International Criminal Police Organization (Interpol) An organization facilitating worldwide police cooperation, headquartered in Lyon, France.

Internet A worldwide network of computer networks.

Internet Cache Cache is a high-speed access area that can be a reserved section of main memory or a storage device. Another type of cache is "Internet browser cache" also known as "Temporary Internet Files" in Internet Explorer. Internet cache is used to help improve how quickly data is accessed while browsing the Internet. In most cases, each time a Web page is opened, it is sent to your browser's temporary cache on your hard disk drive. If that page is accessed again and has not been modified, the browser will open the page from your cache instead of downloading the page again.

Internet Corporation for Assigned Names and Numbers (ICANN) A non-profit corporation in California that manages Internet Protocol (IP) addresses and domain names.

Internet Protocol (IP) The protocol used to send data from one computer to another over the Internet.

Internet Relay Chat (IRC) A real-time Internet chat system that allows potentially thousands of people to congregate into "channels" to discuss various topics.

Internet Service Provider (ISP) An organization that customers can connect to in order to obtain Internet access.

Interpol See International Criminal Police Organization.

Interrupt Message A signal to the central processor to stop what it is doing and do something else.

IP See Internet Protocol.

IP Address A unique numeric address that is used to identify a specific machine on the Internet (e.g., 193.342.16.92).

IRC See Internet Relay Chat.

ISP See Internet Service Provider.

Keystroke-loggers Also referred to as key-loggers or key logging software. Programs that monitor and record data being input into a machine and then transmitting it to a remote server.

Lawful Access The interception of communications and search and seizure of information pursuant to lawful authority.

Mailbombing A form of netiquette (i.e., sending a large number of junk email messages to a person).

Malware A collective term for a variety of malicious software programs, including viruses, worms, Trojan horses and spyware.

Morphed Images Child pornography created by electronic or mechanical means, such as innocent images of children modified or "morphed" into sexually exploitative images through the use of computer technology.

Motherboard The principal circuit board in a computer that contains the computer's basic circuitry and components.

MUD See Multi-User Domain.

Multi-User Domain (MUD) Also referred to as Multi-User Dimension or Multi-User Dungeon. One of the first virtual environments in which people could interact online.

Netiquette Rules developed by individuals in Internet communities to govern their online interactions.

Network Architecture Refers to the overall structure of the network system. A computer network is a distributed system of computers in which each computer can exchange packets of data with any other computer in the system. The mechanisms that enable these exchanges, and how they are managed, define the network architecture.

Oakes Test In *R. v. Oakes,* the Supreme Court of Canada set out the analytical framework for determining whether the violation of a *Charter* right can be justified under s. 1. The analysis, which is commonly referred to as the "Oakes test," provides that a constitutional guarantee can be limited if certain conditions are met.

Operation PIN Initiated by the Virtual Global Taskforce in 2003. A website that purports to offer illegal child pornography images. Anyone who attempts to download images is confronted with a message saying that their personal information may have been captured and sent to the local authorities. Functions as a crime-reduction initiative in terms of its ability to catch child pornography consumers and as a deterrent.

Operational Layer Consists of standards and protocols, as well as ISP functions essential to the operation of the Internet. These layers are controlled by private entities, including telecommunications carriers, who carefully manage and oversee the delivery of Internet data.

P2P See Peer to Peer.

Packet Sniffer A program or a device that records the data sent by a computer when communicating over a network.

Packet-switching Occurs when the communication is broken up into small fixed-length packets, which are sent independently across the network to their destination. Packets can arrive out of sequence and be reassembled by the recipient computer into a complete communication.

Password Cracking A means of computer trespass that involves figuring out passwords to access computers or computer systems.

Payload The actions that a virus carries out (other than replication) on an infected system.

Peer to Peer (P2P) A unique way for user machines across the Internet to connect to each other and form networks. The most popular use of P2P networks is for the sharing and distribution of files.

Pharming A type of attack often used by phishers that interferes with the Domain Name System (DNS) on the Internet that translates URLs (www.companyname.ca) to the IP address used by computers to network with each other. A pharming attack causes a connection to the wrong network computer, usually to divert traffic and steal confidential information.

Phishing Assuming the identity of a legitimate organization using forged email or fraudulent websites to steal the credentials of the victim.

Phreaking The act of gaining unauthorised access to a telephone system or network (i.e., making illegal phone calls).

Physical Layer of the Internet The computer equipment and telecommunications networks over which the Internet operates.

Port A circuit on the motherboard that is used to connect external devices to the computer.

Port Scanning Using a network connection to determine what types of services a computer has running at any given time.

Red Box A phreaking device that generates tones to simulate inserting coins in pay phones, thus fooling the system into completing free calls.

Rogue Security Software Also known as scareware. Software that pretends to be legitimate security software. These rogue applications provide little or no value and may even install malicious code or reduce the overall security of the computer.

Rootkit A hacker tool that provides a backdoor into a system and hides the fact that it has been compromised.

Router Hardware or software devices that route data over the network. If a particular path is unavailable, the router determines which is the next best path to route the information.

Script Kiddie Unskilled novices who use scripts or programs written by others to attack computer systems and networks.

Second Life A virtual world developed by Linden Lab that allows users to interact with each other through their avatars.

ShadowCrew Emerged from CounterfeitLibrary. An international crime message board that enabled hackers to trade, buy and sell stolen information.

Shunning A form of netiquette (i.e., refusing to accept messages from a person).

Slack Space The unused space in a disk cluster.

Social Contract An agreement among the members of an organized society or between the governed and the government defining and limiting the rights and duties of each.

Social Engineering The art of conning someone into doing something they wouldn't ordinarily do, such as giving out passwords or other sensitive and confidential information.

Spam The term used to describe unwanted email. It can be harmless (such as an advertisement) or malicious (such as that which comes with viruses or Trojan horses attached).

Spamming A form of netiquette (i.e., flooding the internet with many copies of the same message).

Spoofing A popular method of hacking, which involves modifying the header of a network packet to make it appear to come from a different source. By spoofing the IP address, the destination host can be fooled into thinking that it comes from a trusted source.

Spyware A general term used to describe software that tracks user activity and reports on it, typically without the user's knowledge or consent.

SQL Injection A code injection technique that exploits a security vulnerability occurring in the database layer of an application.

Steganography An information hiding technique that embeds messages within other, seemingly harmless, messages or files.

TCP/IP See Transmission Control Protocol/Internet Protocol.

Traffic Data Any computer data relating to a communication, indicating the communication's origin, destination, route, time, date, size, duration or type of underlying service. This includes information about an email (including those that are located in a "draft" box, an "inbox," or are in transit), the sender, recipient, size, subject line, as well as the URLs visited, time spent online, requests to search engines for specific information and downloads.

Transmission Control Protocol/Internet Protocol (TCP/IP) A suite of protocols, or a collection of standards, that provides a common language for data transmission over the Internet.

Trespass to Chattels Occurs when one party intentionally dispossesses another person of the chattel, or uses or intermeddles with the chattel in the rightful possession of another person.

Trojan Horse Programs that appear to perform a useful or harmless function, but also contain hidden functionality, which causes unwanted and damaging effects for the user.

Underground Economy A well organized and vigorous global marketplace in which stolen goods and fraud-related services are bought and sold, and where the value of goods offered is measured in millions of dollars.

Universal Serial Bus (USB) A port used to connect electronic devices.

USB See Universal Serial Bus.

USENET Newsgroups The linear descendants of the electronic bulletin boards that were popular in the 1980s. Although they are often described as part of the Internet, they can be seen as separate from (and, indeed, a precursor to) the Internet. The newsgroups are open, allowing anyone to submit a comment or opinion.

VGT See Virtual Global Taskforce.

Virtual Global Taskforce (VGT) An international alliance of law enforcement agencies that includes the National Crime Squad in the United Kingdom, the High Tech Crime Centre in Australia, the Royal Canadian Mounted Police, the United States Department of Homeland Security in the United States and Interpol. VGT members have met in Australia, Ireland, the United Kingdom and Canada to discuss how to combat Internet child exploitation and share information and ideas.

Virus A replicating program that enters a computer system concealed in infected materials, such as disks, files or documents. The virus carries a payload, which activates at some point following infection, causing unwanted and often harmful or damaging consequences.

War Dialling A war dialler is a program that automatically dials a range of telephone numbers looking for connections and logging details for later inspection.

War Driving A technique used to search for Wi-Fi wireless networks using a Wi-Fi-equipped computer in a moving vehicle.

Web Browser Hijacking During this type of attack, a user is taken to a different site than the one he or she requested. For example, the attacker can gain access to DNS records stored on the server and modify them (e.g., so that requests for a genuine Web page will be directed elsewhere, such as to a fake page created by the attacker).

White Hat Hackers A term given to ethical hackers whose activities are regarded as being for the benefit of security.

Wiretapping Electronic or mechanical eavesdropping carried out by law enforcement officials with judicial authorization.

World Wide Web (WWW) The multimedia branch of the Internet. Also the collective term for a global network of information, which is accessible through the Internet.

Worm A replicating program that can spread between systems on its own, without the need to infect a carrier in the same way that a virus does.

WWW See World Wide Web.

Zombie Also known as a *slave*. A computer that carries out actions (often malicious) under the remote control of a hacker by means of a virus or other malicious software. A collection of zombie computers is also called a zombie army, or a botnet.

INDEX